Intensifiers in English and German

Intensifiers play a profoundly important role in many areas of grammar, notably reflexivity. This volume represents the first book-length study of this greatly neglected area. It explores the syntax and semantics of intensifiers and offers a contrastive analysis of the properties of these expressions in English and German.

Such little work has been done on intensifiers that not even their basic categorical status is agreed on. Previous studies have subsumed them under classes as heterogeneous as personal pronouns, reflexives and adverbs, with all of these labels highlighting relevant aspects of their distribution and semantic contribution. By contrast, the position taken in this study is that intensifiers belong to the class of focus particles.

Due to its contrastive approach, the book will be of interest to linguists of various persuasions. Theoreticians will find challenging material highly relevant to current syntactic and semantic controversies, while specialists of English and German, as well as linguists working in language typology, can expect new and interesting analyses to complement their current understanding of language.

Peter Siemund is assistant professor (wissenschaftlicher Assistent) at the Free University of Berlin. He studied English, Spanish and computer science at the universities of Leipzig, Leeds and Berlin (Free University). He received his Master's degree in 1995, and his PhD in 1997.

Routledge Studies in Germanic Linguistics
Series editors: Ekkehard König and Johan van der Auwera

Intensifiers in English and German

A comparison

Peter Siemund

R Routledge
Taylor & Francis Group

LONDON AND NEW YORK

First published 2000 by Routledge

2 Park Square, Milton Park, Abingdon, Oxon OX14 4RN
711 Third Avenue, New York, NY 10017, USA

Routledge is an imprint of the Taylor & Francis Group, an informa business

First issued in paperback 2016

Transferred to Digital Printing 2010

Copyright © 2000 Peter Siemund

Typeset in Garamond by Helen Skelton, London

British Library Cataloguing in Publication Data
A catalogue record for this book is available from
the British Library
Library of Congress Cataloging in Publication Data
Siemund, Peter, 1965–
    Intensifiers in English and German: a
    comparison / Peter Siemund.
      p. cm.
    Includes bibliographical references and index
    1. English language – Intensification. 2. English language –
Grammar, Comparative – German. 3. German language –
Grammar, Comparative – English. 4. German language –
Intensification. 5. English language – Particles. 6. German
language – Particles.
PE1321.S54   2000
425 – DC21   99-31508
                                       CIP

ISBN 978-0-415-21713-2 (hbk)
ISBN 978-1-138-97291-9 (pbk)

Publisher's Note
The publisher has gone to great lengths to ensure the quality of this reprint
but points out that some imperfections in the original may be apparent.

Contents

List of illustrations

Abbreviations

Intensifiers

SELF	intensifiers (cover term for English x-*self* and German *selbst*)
ANS	adnominal SELF (the adnominal intensifier)
AVS	adverbal SELF (the adverbal intensifier)
x-*self*	*myself, yourself, himself, ...*

Languages

E.	English	G.	German

Special symbols

?	marked	*	ungrammatical
??	inadequate	//	new tone group
???	unacceptable	caps	stressed syllable

Glosses

ACC	accusative	P	person
GEN	genitive	POSS	possessive
FUT	future	SG	singular
NEG	negation		

Acknowledgements

The present work emerged within the research project 'Typological Investigations into Emphatic Reflexives, Reflexivity and Focus Particles' (KO 497/5-1/2) as part of a six-year nationwide research initiative on language typology sponsored by the Deutsche Forschungsgemeinschaft which started in 1995. It could not have been completed without the financial shelter offered by the programme. I would also like to express my gratitude towards the Freie Universität Berlin for providing office space and adequate computer equipment.

This dissertation could not have been written in the time available without the extremely close and frictionless cooperation of my supervisor Ekkehard König, to whom I would like to acknowledge my utmost indebtedness. Frequent personal discussions ensured that blind alleys could be recognised before they were entered. Embedding the dissertation in a larger research project accelerated its completion noticeably.

There is a considerable amount of authentic material contained in the subsequent text. An extensive body of attested examples is a prerequisite for the elucidation of subtle semantic problems and for the analysis of areas where language does not draw clear-cut distinctions, but is better captured in terms of gradience. I would like to thank Dieter Mindt for granting unlimited access to his stock of computer corpora.

I would also wish to acknowledge my debt for substantial advice to the following former or present members of our research group: Martin Haspelmath, Daniel Hole, Claudia Lange, Juliane Möck, Münevver Özkurt, Renate Raffelsiefen, Sabine Reiter, Birgit Sievert.

The study has further benefited from helpful comments on the parts of Hans-Bernhard Drubig, Dietrich Lange, Ferdinand von Mengden as well as the audiences of the universities of Berlin, Göttingen and Tübingen. David Greeves and Jacob Jacobson have done much to increase the authenticity of the English example sentences.

A special word of gratitude goes to David Greeves, Daniel Hole and Katrin Rösler for their patient revision of the final manuscript.

Peter Siemund
Freie Universität Berlin

1 Introduction

The present study deals with intensifiers or emphatic reflexives as exemplified by the *self*-forms (*myself, yourself, himself,* ...) in the data below:

(1.1) Nevertheless it was the King's ministers, the argument ran, who should be held accountable for the misdeeds of the Crown, not the King himself. [BNC]

(1.2) Thirty years ago Rutherford said, 'it is my personal conviction that if we knew more about the nucleus, we should find it much simpler than we suppose. I am always a believer in simplicity being a simple fellow myself.' [LOB]

(1.3) When those arrested threatened the lord mayor that they would inform the King how they were dealt with, he defiantly replied that he would save them the trouble and do it himself. [BNC]

It will not discuss *self*-forms which function as reflexive anaphors, i.e. as referentially dependent expressions or expressions marking coreference in a local domain. Examples of the following kind will not be treated:

(1.4) He laughingly nicknames himself the 'potato king of the world'. [BNC]

(1.5) For the first time he told himself that he was fully at home in his work. [BNC]

Nevertheless, this study will concern itself with occurrences of x-*self* for which it is not straightforward to decide whether they are anaphors or intensifiers, cf.:

(1.6) Prince is now demanding listeners as mixed up and variegated inside as himself, and is finding that there aren't that many around. [BNC]

(1.7)   In 1944, we had a new house built just outside the village for my husband and myself. [BNC]

This is a contrastive analysis of intensifiers in English and German, and hence it also includes a wide selection of German data, cf. the examples below. It does not, however, aim to be a typological investigation, in spite of the fact that it contains a few remarks concerning intensifiers in languages other than English and German.

(1.8)   Sie selbst kann es nicht entscheiden. [FC]
        'She herself cannot take that decision.'

(1.9)   Ich habe das selbst einmal erlebt bei einem Kollegen. [FC]
        'I have experienced that myself with a colleague.'

Although the terms 'intensifier' and 'emphatic reflexive' are often used with similar extensions, the former will be given preference over the latter because it also covers languages in which intensifiers and reflexives are formally distinguished. SELF will throughout be used as an abbreviation for the intensifier.

1.1 Background

No consensus has been reached on what intensifiers exactly are, nor on what their precise contribution to the meaning of a sentence is. On the one hand, intensifiers have been analysed as pronouns and, applying the following terms in their most general sense, as appositions, adverbs or adverbials on the other. When considered pronouns, intensifiers are subsumed under either personal or reflexive pronouns, depending on their form, cf. (1.10).

(1.10) anaphor   Bickerton (1987)
        complex anaphor   Keenan (1988)
        emphatic compound
        personal pronoun   Poutsma (1916)
        emphatic/intensive reflexive   Leskosky (1972), Quirk *et al.*
                                         (1985), Kuno (1987)
        (intensive) pronoun   Cantrall (1973b), Moravcsik
                                         (1972)
        locally free reflexive   Baker (1995)
        nominative reflexive   Abraham (1997)
        reenforcing pronoun   Penning (1875)

The pronoun analysis can be motivated by the fact that intensifiers are always in association with an NP (Noun Phrase) and may hence be regarded as a copy thereof. In addition, intensifiers can sometimes be used as pronouns (Latin *ipse*). The reason for viewing them as reflexives can be found in their formal identity to reflexive anaphors in many languages (English x-*self*, Mandarin *ziji*). Moreover, they often appear to interact with the binding properties of referentially dependent expressions. Intensifiers are assumed to restrict the binding domain of such expressions, cf. the examples from Icelandic below:

> (1.11) Icelandic
> Jón$_i$ segir að María$_j$ elski sig$_{i/j}$.
> 'John says that Mary loves him/herself.'

> (1.12) Icelandic
> Jón$_i$ segir að María$_j$ elski sjálfa sig$_{*i/j}$.
> 'John says that Mary loves herself.'

Analysing intensifiers as appositions, adverbs or adverbials, by contrast, stresses their modifying function. Intensifiers nearly always modify an NP. There are also good reasons to believe that they interact with the focus structure of a sentence. Then they are analysed as focusing devices, i.e. as belonging to a particular class of adverbs. Several attempts have been made to capture their pronominal and adverbial characteristics within one label, cf.:

> (1.13) adverbial reflexive   Browning (1993)
> emphasizer   Dirven (1973)
> focus marker/particle   König (1991), Ferro (1993), Sánchez (1994)
> intensifier   Edmondson and Plank (1978)
> intensive   Farr (1905)
> scalar adverb   Primus (1992)

Apart from those studies analysing intensifiers as anaphors or at least as interacting with the binding properties of referentially dependent expressions, the contribution of these expressions to the meaning of an utterance is usually explicated in terms of emphasis or intensification. Although it is certainly not wrong to use the labels 'emphatic' or 'intensifier' for the expressions in question, such terminology is much too imprecise to allow a proper description of the contribution intensifiers make. Nevertheless, the term 'intensifier' is the most general term available and the one that is least misleading and will therefore also be used here. More promising results yield analyses of intensifiers within the focus structure of a sentence, i.e. as focus particles. Here, they have mainly been regarded as scalar particles (Primus 1992 and to a certain extent also Edmondson and Plank 1978), and as centralising particles (König 1991), although the latter approach is restricted to a subset of intensifiers. Nevertheless, it appears to allow for a generalisation to all occurrences of intensifiers.

1.2 Three uses of intensifiers

In the following, a distinction will be drawn between three uses of intensifiers, an adnominal use on the one hand and two adverbal uses on the other. The former will be abbreviated by ANS (which stands for 'adnominal SELF'), the latter by AVS ('adverbal SELF'). As these labels suggest, adnominal intensifiers can be analysed as part of an NP, adverbal intensifiers as part of the VP (Verb Phrase). Nevertheless, AVS, just as ANS, is always in association with an NP. Intensifiers invariably evoke alternatives to the referent of that NP. (1.14) gives an example of ANS, (1.15) of AVS:

(1.14)   Finally, the conductor himself went on the stage. (ANS)

(1.15)   The conductor had to turn over the pages himself. (AVS)

As far as adverbal intensifiers are concerned, it is possible to differentiate between a type of AVS which is, semantically speaking, roughly equivalent to *also* and a type which is related to expressions like *alone* and *on one's own*. The major difference between these two uses consists in the fact that in the former, the referent of the NP the intensifier interacts with, as well as the alternatives evoked, are characterised as equally participating in the situation denoted by the predication, whereas the alternatives do not partake in it in the case of the latter, cf. the contrast between (1.16) and (1.17). In other words, one type of AVS can include these alternatives, the other can exclude them, and hence it appears reasonable to label them 'inclusive AVS' and 'exclusive AVS' respectively. In the course of this study it will become apparent that this differentiation is accompanied by a number of more subtle differences, both syntactic and semantic.

(1.16)   I know what it means to be poor because I have been poor myself. (inclusive AVS)

(1.17)   I have written this article myself. (exclusive AVS)

Classifying intensifiers into three types of usage is, of course, not the only possible approach to the subject. Previous studies on intensifiers usually differentiate only between what are here called ANS and AVS. A systematic analysis of adverbal intensifiers is a more recent development and represents one of the main objectives of the present enquiry.

Assuming three uses of intensifiers, however, does not mean that there is no common denominator. Although adnominal intensifiers as well as the two types of adverbal intensifiers differ substantially in the contribution they make to the meaning of a sentence and the implicatures they evoke, it is none the less possible to regard all of them as devices to structure sets of entities, individuals or simply things. One could call them 'set structuring operators'. The structure intensifiers impose upon sets is always of binary character and can be described in terms of centre versus periphery in the sense of König (1991: 87ff.), important versus unimportant, good versus bad, etc. In a way, they can be used to separate the wheat from the chaff. Considering the significance of this pursuit to the human species, it can come as no surprise that natural languages should offer devices for precisely that task.

1.3 Outline and objectives

The organisation of the present study is as follows. There are broadly two parts. Chapters 2 to 4 form the first part and deal with the syntax of inten-sifiers. The second part comprises Chapters 5 to 8 which explore intensifiers from a semantic perspective. Each part commences with an overview of the relevant area followed by an in-depth analysis of the separate types of usage intensifiers are presumed to divide into. Note, though, that the syntax of adverbal inclusive and adverbal exclusive intensifiers is discussed in the same chapter. As far as meaning is concerned, separate chapters are devoted to each type of usage.

Chapter 2 – the introduction to the syntax of intensifiers – also takes up some issues which are of great concern, but, nevertheless, do not justify inde-pendent chapters. Section 2.2 defends the basic contention of this study, namely that intensifiers should be analysed as focus particles. The discussion there is kept extremely concise because this issue is repeatedly taken up throughout the study. Section 2.3 draws attention to the fact that English x-*self* and German *selbst* are only the core members of a much larger group of intensifying expressions. Their proper treatment, in fact, would yield substance for a separate study. Another area which offers more open ques-tions than answers is the historical development of intensifiers. Section 2.5 devotes a few pages to this problem, but cannot do more than list the most controversial points and their proposed solutions. Here too, an individual study would be urgently required.

The nature of this study is both descriptive and analytic. Among the most important problems it seeks to address are the following.

1   There is no agreement on the number of use types that have to be distin-guished with intensifiers. Whereas previous studies mainly acknowledge one and maximally two uses of intensifiers, the stance taken here is that there are three. This approach requires convincing motivation.

2   There is no conclusive categorisation of intensifiers. The multiplicity of labels proposed for intensifiers, cf. (1.10) and (1.13), demonstrates that there is general disagreement about where to place them. The question is whether they can be subsumed under some existing class of expres-sions or whether they must be analysed as expressions *sui generis*.

3   The syntactic analysis of intensifiers must largely be considered an open

question. There simply is no study available dealing with the syntax of intensifiers in a detailed way. The working hypothesis adopted in this study is that adnominal intensifiers are endocentric expansions of NPs whereas adverbal intensifiers are endocentric expansions of the VP. This is reflected in the labels chosen.

4   Most of the syntactic properties of adnominal intensifiers still wait to be explored. A brief glance at the data available suggests that there are well-defined constraints on the behaviour of adnominal intensifiers with respect to dislocation (topicalisation) as well as their interaction with pronouns.

5   Similarly poor is our current knowledge of the syntactic properties of adverbal intensifiers. However, this type of intensifier shows quite surprising behaviour under topicalisation and passivisation and in the context of scope bearing elements, particularly from an English–German contrastive point of view. Most of these properties have never been described before.

6   Certain occurrences of English x-*self* pose serious problems for standard accounts of the distribution of anaphora. These long-distance bound, locally free or untriggered reflexives have long been a prominent topic of investigation in the field of anaphora, but have evaded a convincing classification so far. The analysis of intensifiers can bring some clarification on this point.

7   Edmondson and Plank (1978) suggest that there is a special type of intensifier whose particular function consists in indicating the role reversal of a referent relative to the preceding context. Its operational conditions are assumed to require that the referent of the NP it modifies undergoes a change in terms of its thematic role, cf. *Lucrezia poisoned Lorenzo, and was herself poisoned by Cesare.* It is the aim of this study to subsume this use type under adnominal intensifiers.

Apart from these general questions and syntactic problems, there are also a number of complications concerning the semantic analysis of intensifiers.

1   It has frequently been proposed in the literature that intensifiers are scalar expressions, cf. Edmondson and Plank (1978), Primus (1992), etc. According to these accounts, they are supposed to characterise the referent of the NP they interact with as the least likely/expected or most remarkable participant in a situation. Such an analysis of intensifiers, however, is at variance with a great amount of data.

2   Previous studies on the subject give the impression that the range of possible NPs intensifiers can modify is confined to those denoting human referents of elevated position. Although such NPs appear to represent the lion's share of the data, a glance at authentic examples suggests that this is a gross oversimplification. It is the aim of the present study to paint a more balanced picture. In addition, various semantic

constraints on these NPs have been proposed. However, these seem either too restrictive or do not cover all cases.

3   Although it is possible to subsume those intensifiers occurring in role reversal structures under the adnominal variety, cf. *Lucrezia poisoned Lorenzo, and was herself poisoned by Cesare*, the specific properties and effects of these structures call for an explanation. In particular, it is necessary to delimit the semantic contribution of the intensifier in these cases as opposed to the semantic load of its environment. Moreover, an explanation for the role reversal observed has to be given.

4   The analysis of adverbal intensifiers has so far received little attention. Most of the relevant phenomena and properties have not even been described. Before an appropriate analysis of these intensifiers becomes possible, a careful survey of the data is necessary. The differentiation between two types of adverbal intensifiers offers a fresh starting point and ensures reasonably fine-grained results.

5   There are a few studies which seem aware that certain occurrences of intensifiers can receive an interpretation similar to the additive focus particle *also*, cf. Plank (1979a), Browning (1993), etc. However, the scope of these investigations is restricted to detecting components of the intensifier which allow for a drift towards such an interpretation. According to the view defended here, there is an intensifier which shares its core meaning with *also*, but which makes a well-defined additional contribution. Before linking this contribution to the central meaning all intensifiers have in common, it is necessary to elucidate the differences and similarities between inclusive intensifiers and *also*.

6   There simply is no semantic analysis of adverbal inclusive intensifiers on the market. The contention held in this study is that inclusive intensifiers deserve a semantic analysis of their own. It is one of the major objectives pursued here to make a convincing proposal for how to tackle this problem.

7   Analyses dealing with the semantics of adverbal intensifiers are usually developed on the basis of the exclusive variety. It is common practice to apply the results obtained to examples which are, within the current framework, singled out as inclusive intensifiers. Since the present study develops an individual analysis for inclusive intensifiers, the remaining amount of data not covered by the analysis is drastically reduced. As a consequence, a major rethinking of the basic contentions becomes possible. Although existing treatments provide valuable insights and results, it is argued here that the basic semantic contribution of adverbal exclusive intensifiers is not adequately captured and has to be specified in a different way.

2   The syntax of intensifiers – overview

English intensifiers or emphatic reflexives illustrate all the formal characteristics of ordinary reflexive pronouns. Merely judged by appearance, it is
impossible to tell one from the other. There are basically eight forms which
can be divided into two groups of four:

> (2.1)   a myself, yourself, ourselves, yourselves
>   b himself, herself, itself, themselves

All eight expressions are the result of a fusion process taking place in Old and
Middle English in the course of which the original intensifier *self* came to be
attached to the still visible pronominal forms. According to the pronoun
involved, a distinction may be drawn between a series of nominal (2.1a) and
adjectival forms (2.1b), cf. Faiß (1989: 170).

The members of the former group are composed of a pronoun in the genitive plus *self* and cover first and second person singular and plural. Those of
the latter, by contrast, make use of pronouns in objective or dative case,
historically speaking. They cover third person singular and plural. Notice
that there could be some argument about the status of *herself* and *itself*.
Intensifiers inflect for person and number, but also for gender as *himself,
herself* and *itself* make clear.

The generic or rather indefinite emphatic reflexive *oneself* is a little peculiar since it is, in contrast to the eight forms discussed so far, somewhat more
restricted both in the positions it is available in and the range of its possible
meanings. Originating in Early Modern English, it is also much younger by
comparison. There is one more form to be found in English, namely *ourself*.
This is the reflexive form of the so-called royal *we* which, although a little
old-fashioned, can also be found as an emphatic.

Given that there are no formal features distinguishing emphatic reflexives
from reflexive anaphors in English, let us briefly examine which devices there
are to separate one from the other. Consider the following prototypical
examples:

> (2.2)   a She made herself a cup of coffee.

b The chieftain himself told me about the tribe's history.

First, in the great majority of cases, reflexive pronouns and their antecedents are co-arguments of one and the same predicator, i.e. reflexives are arguments, cf. (2.2a). Emphatic reflexives as in (2.2b) rather look like appositions or adverbials – they are adjuncts. In other words, reflexive anaphors can never be removed from a sentence without risking grammaticality. Taking away emphatic reflexives will influence the meaning of a sentence, but not its grammaticality. Their presence or absence, however, may be vital for well-formed discourse.

Second, reflexives function as true replacements for NPs. They are in paradigmatic contrast to additional anaphoric expressions as e.g. reciprocals and personal pronouns ('pronominals') as well as referential expressions. Emphatic reflexives never replace NPs. Thus, it is justified to call reflexives 'pronouns', but such a terminology does not easily carry over to emphatics, although it is often done, particularly in grammar books, cf. Quirk *et al.* (1985), Givón (1993), etc. In view of their formal make-up it is easy to see how such terminology is motivated in English. Moreover, emphatics are always in association with an NP with which they show agreement; they are in the majority of cases a co-constituent of that NP and they may therefore be analysed as pronominal copies thereof. This is why the same categorisation is also proposed for G. *selbst* in the relevant handbooks even in the absence of overt agreement features. In this study, an adverb analysis (in the most general sense) of intensifiers will be argued for.

Third, reflexives (in their referential usage) are always co-referential with some antecedent and their main task is to indicate co-reference. Put differently, reflexives are devices to map two argument positions of e.g. a two-place predicator on to one and the same referent. Their antecedent is nearly always a subject. The co-constituents of emphatics are less restricted. NPs in object position are feasible as well as those embedded in adverbials. On their own, intensifiers cannot be regarded as markers of co-reference. No mapping of argument positions occurs. This is why we will abstain from using the highly biased term 'antecedent' for the NP they interact with. What they achieve semantically is to modify that NP in a certain way. For the time being, the best general term available for describing their semantic contribution is probably 'emphasis' or 'intensification', although these terms are rather vague. Still, they are the least harmful of those alternatively proposed.

Note that the situation in English, i.e. to map intensifier and reflexive on to the same form, is by no means unique, but can be found in many languages around the globe, for example in Persian, Turkish, Arabic, Mandarin, Hungarian, etc.

(2.3)   Persian [Moyne 1971: 155]
    a hušang   xodaš   āmad
      Hushang   self.3P   came
      'Hushang himself came.'

b hušang   xodaš-rā   did
   Hushang   self.3P-ACC   saw
   'Hushang saw himself.'

Whereas we find eight, nine or even ten forms for the intensifier in English, there are only two in German – *selbst* and *selber*, the latter, according to a common assumption, mainly being a stylistic variant of the former. They show no inflection and are well separated from the third person reflexive pronoun *sich*. There is no situation in which *selbst* could possibly replace *sich*. *Selbst* does not bear agreement features, but there can be no doubt about it being in association with some NP. It should be apparent that a categorisation of *selbst* as an emphatic reflexive would be misleading if not totally beside the point. As far as German is concerned, the label 'intensifier' seems to be much more justified. Reflexive pronoun and intensifier can occur together as the sequence *sich selbst*, which has some unique and peculiar properties of its own.

To sum up, English has up to ten forms in an area where German has maximally two. Moreover, English emphatics show inflection whereas German intensifiers remain uninflected and English reflexives are formally indistinguishable from intensifiers whereas German separates them neatly. English disambiguates them mainly by position.

As for inflection, English intensifiers agree with some other constituent in person, number and gender (the so-called ϕ-features). This agreement pattern is paralleled by the one found in the pronominal system, which can hardly come as a surprise in view of the aforementioned fusion process. Intensifiers in both languages interact with another constituent in the same manner:

(2.4)   a Paul himself, Mary herself, we ourselves, the house itself
        b Paul selbst, Maria selbst, wir selbst, das Haus selbst

That intensifiers show agreement with a nominal constituent, however, is a widespread phenomenon in natural languages so that with respect to this property, G. *selbst* turns out to be the exception rather than the rule. The intensifiers of Romance languages usually agree with an NP in gender and number, those of Slavic languages in gender, number and case and in the Scandinavian languages, which are, genetically speaking, closely related to German, we often find agreement in gender and number, cf. (2.5). There, intensifiers look very much like adjectives.

(2.5)   Swedish
        a Hon är godheten själv (utrum, singular).
           'She is kindness itself.'
        b Barnet självt (neutrum, singular) sa ingenting.
           'The child himself said nothing.'

c Barnen själva (plural) bestämde.
   'The children themselves decided.'

Intensifiers are not restricted to interacting with full NPs, and interesting differences between English and German come to light when one looks at certain combinations of pronoun and intensifier in German and their respective English renderings. When translating such examples into English, it is usually not necessary or even ungrammatical to convert the sequence [pronoun intensifier] on a one-to-one basis. Rather, it is sufficient to use x-*self* on its own, cf. (2.6). For some reason or another, English appears to disfavour the pronoun in the sequence.

(2.6) a Irgend jemand ist immer schlechter dran als [du selbst].
       b There is always someone worse off than [*you yourself/yourself].

What is puzzling about these cases is that the English intensifier seems to be able to suddenly occur without a proper co-constituent. Given the proposed categorisation of intensifiers as adjuncts, such behaviour should clearly be ruled out. Even more striking, the analyst is faced with the question whether these occurrences of x-*self* should be regarded as intensifiers or, alternatively, as reflexive pronouns. Judged by their form, both options are viable. The latter view, however, poses some serious difficulties for standard assumptions on the distribution of reflexive pronouns (anaphors) in English. A third view could hold that they are something completely different.

A related problem concerns English examples in which reflexives can be freely exchanged with ordinary pronouns. Both pronoun and reflexive in (2.7) are co-referential with the NP *John*, i.e. the pronoun functions as a marker of reflexivity in that case.

(2.7) John pushed the brandy away from him/himself. [Levinson 1991: 120]

The two forms, however, do not convey exactly the same meaning. Using *himself* instead of *him* makes a difference and adds some extra meaning – only a nuance though – which can also be captured by the notion 'emphasis' and has often been discussed under the heading 'logophoricity' or 'perspective', cf. Cantrall (1973a, 1974), Kuno (1987), Zribi-Hertz (1989). Note in passing that sentences like (2.7) also pose severe problems to common structural accounts of the distribution of reflexive anaphors and pronominals in English.

2.1 The three uses of intensifiers

Recall from section 1.2 that the present study distinguishes three uses of intensifiers, adnominal SELF (ANS), adverbal inclusive SELF (inclusive

AVS) and adverbal exclusive SELF (exclusive AVS). That these three interpretations represent a clear case of polysemy can be proved as follows. First,
AVS cannot replace ANS and vice versa:

(2.8)   a Bill has a good job, a beautiful wife and a fortune. I myself
             have nothing at all (?myself).
         b Bill has just told me that he has lost everything. But I
             (?myself) have nothing at all myself.

Second, and this already concerns the differentiation between inclusive
and exclusive AVS, there are contexts in which adverbal intensifiers are
ambiguous between these two interpretations. The following example (2.9)
may receive an interpretation according to either (2.10a) or (2.10b).

(2.9)   I have read this book myself.

(2.10)   a I know what it is about, so you don't have to tell me.
             (inclusive)
         b Nobody else has read it to me or told me about its contents.
             (exclusive)

Third, there are contexts which clearly disambiguate the two possible
interpretations of adverbal intensifiers, cf. (2.11). The a-sentence cannot
mean that there was only one driver for the car model in question and the b-
sentence excludes an interpretation according to which somebody apart from
God created the earth.

(2.11)   a I know what it means to drive a Buick because I used to
             drive such a car myself$_{inclusive}$/*myself$_{exclusive}$.
         b God created the earth himself$_{exclusive}$/*himself$_{inclusive}$.

And finally, all three uses of the intensifier can co-occur in one and the
same sentence while being in association with the same NP, cf. (2.12). This
convincingly shows that they make different contributions to the meaning of
a sentence. (2.12) means that Bill, in contrast to somebody else, had to be
told the answer and that he was not the only one for whom that was necessary. Note, however, that such constellations will hardly ever turn up in
reality. (2.12) is a true laboratory sentence.

(2.12)   Bill himself has himself not found the answer himself.

Concerning the distribution of the three uses of SELF, it has already been
indicated that one of them is a nominal modifier whereas the remaining two
are verbal modifiers. Consequently, adnominal SELF (ANS) is usually found
next to an NP whereas adverbal SELF (AVS) rather occurs somewhere in the
VP. (2.13a) shows ANS modifying the subject NP, (2.13b) an object NP.

Under certain conditions to be made precise, ANS can be separated from the NP it interacts with.

(2.13)   a Freud himself lamented his inability to understand women. [LLC]
         b And if you want to meet the man himself, well on Sunday it's the nineteen ninety three pooh sticks championships, and he'll be there. [BNC]

Dominant positions of AVS are first behind a modal or auxiliary, second behind the main verb and third in sentence-final position, i.e. after the arguments of the verb and possibly additional adjuncts. Inclusive as well as exclusive AVS are possible in each of these positions although the latter tends to prefer the sentence-final position. (2.14) displays the relevant examples.

(2.14)   a She had herself travelled with groups like this. [BNC]
         b Moreover, he had himself violent pains in the head. [LLC]
         c She has cooked this hand lotion herself. [LLC]

As far as German is concerned, ANS and AVS show a similar distribution. The translations of (2.13) and (2.14) can be found in (2.15) and (2.16). A noteworthy difference is that due to the verb second constraint in German, AVS can end up adjacent to the NP it interacts with, cf. (2.16b). Moreover, German complex VPs open up the so-called '*Satzklammer*' (sentence brace) made up of e.g. finite verb and main verb, which encloses a region referred to as the '*Mittelfeld*' (middle field). The *Mittelfeld* is the area where arguments, adjuncts, etc. are to be found so that AVS as part of complex VPs must be sought there, cf. (2.16c).

(2.15)   a Freud selbst beklagte sich über seine Unfähigkeit, Frauen zu verstehen.
         b Und wenn sie ihn selbst treffen wollen, ja, am Sonntag findet das 'pooh sticks championships' 93 statt, und er wird dabei sein.

(2.16)   a Sie war selbst mit solchen Gruppen gereist.
         b Außerdem hatte er selbst furchtbare Kopfschmerzen.
         c Sie hat diese Handlotion selbst zubereitet.

2.2 Intensifiers as focus particles

Section 1.1 has shown that there is great terminological confusion in the area of intensifiers. Depending on the perspective taken, intensifiers can be subsumed under various classes of expressions. Given that there are factors pointing in different directions, the choice appears to be between opening up a separate class for intensifiers, i.e. to regard them as expressions *sui generis*, or accepting a certain amount of incongruity. By subsuming intensifiers under the class of focus particles (following König 1991) and hence regarding them as a special kind of adverb, the latter approach is taken here. Nevertheless, the pros of such an analysis clearly outweigh the cons.

As far as the cons are concerned, English intensifiers deviate from the bulk of the class in that they show agreement with a nominal constituent. Focus particles are called particles precisely because they do not inflect. German *selbst*, by contrast, passes this test. A further problem for an analysis of intensifiers as focus particles is that they are restricted to nominal foci. This holds for both English and German and is also a parameter that is cross-linguistically stable. Core members of the group of focus particles, however, usually do interact with verbs, adjectives, prepositions, etc.:

(2.17)   a   She even SMILED.
         b   He has also bought the GREEN car.
         c   She only lives NEAR Berlin.

A third point that may be advanced against such an analysis is that intensifiers occur, disregarding a few special cases, in a position behind their focus. This position is often supposed to be untypical of focus particles, cf. Altmann (1976: 297, 1978: 35), Primus (1992: 61), etc. The view that focus particles c-command their focus (Jackendoff 1972: 251, Jacobs 1986: 116ff.; König 1991: 23, Primus 1992: 59) correlates with this topological restriction to a certain extent and, with regard to this criterion too, intensifiers often behave differently from most members of the class. Another problem, in a way related to the pre/postfocal position, is that the focus of a particle (or a part thereof) is usually intonationally prominent whereas the particle itself is not. It is the intensifier, however, that always carries nuclear stress. These differences are exemplified in (2.18) and (2.19) below.

(2.18)   a   Hong Kong itSELF is a fascinating place: incredibly crowded, vital, energetic, noisy. (adnominal) [BNC; my emphasis]
         b   He has experimented successfully himSELF with low price hardbacks, but stresses that price cannot be looked at in isolation. (inclusive) [BNC; my emphasis]
         c   Bill refitted the bathroom himSELF. (exclusive) [BNC; my emphasis]

(2.19)   a   Of the senses, only TOUCH brings presence to the body. [LOB; my emphasis]
         b   The problems confuse even the EXperts. [BROWN; my emphasis]

There is no alternative stress pattern available for intensifiers:

(2.20)   a The baronet himSELF told him about the family.
         b *The BARonet himself told him about the family.

Nevertheless, position, c-command and intonation are parameters which can differ even among well-established members of the group of focus particles, cf. (2.21), so that the third point does not really argue against subsuming intensifiers under that class.

(2.21)   a Size and longevity aLONE can be indicators. [LLC; my emphasis]
         b Uncle Donald Murkland found himself nodding agreement TOO. [BNC; my emphasis]

This naturally leads over to a discussion of the pros. A major point in favour of analysing intensifiers as focus particles is that they interact with the focus structure of a sentence. All sentences containing intensifiers divide into a focused or highlighted part and a backgrounded part, i.e. intensifiers structure propositions. Moreover, intensifiers always evoke alternatives to the focused constituent (F = focus):

(2.22)   a [F The director] himself came to welcome us.
         b I came to talk to [F the director] himself.

Another property that intensifiers have in common with established focus particles is their positional variability, cf. (2.18) and (2.22) above. The position of the intensifier depends on its type (ANS or AVS) as well as on the constituent that is in focus. Also, similarly to uncontroversial particles like e.g. *alone*, intensifiers can occur more than once in a sentence:

(2.23)   Paul alone/himself can solve this task alone/himself.

Finally, many languages possess expressions which are clearly related to the relevant intensifier – often they are even homophonous – and whose status as a focus particle has never been disputed. These particles usually precede their focus and make a contribution equivalent to E. *even*, cf. (2.24). In French (as in German) this particle cannot be distinguished from the intensifier, both share the form *même* (*selbst*), whereas there is a slight difference between them in Dutch (*zelfs* versus *zelf*). Note, however, that the two particles are not related in English (*even* versus *x-self*).

(2.24)   Selbst den Kindern hat das Konzert gefallen.
         'Even the children enjoyed the concert.'

German prefocal *selbst* is a scalar additive particle and characterises the value of its focus as unlikely with regard to the remaining open sentence or background. Prefocal *selbst* thus structures propositions into a focused and a backgrounded part. A possible representation is depicted in (2.25).

(2.25)   selbst [λx (x hat das Konzert gefallen), den Kindern]

The difference in meaning between prefocal and postfocal *selbst* is considerable, as we will see, and it turns out to be a rather nice coincidence that German possesses the secondary form *selber* besides *selbst* because it cannot occur in prefocal position in the meaning of 'even':

(2.26)   *Selber den Kindern hat das Konzert gefallen.

As a consequence, written *selbst* in a position between two potential foci, which could be interpreted as prefocal or postfocal respectively, can be disambiguated with the help of *selber*. Of course, oral communication can make the difference plain even with only one form.

(2.27)   Paul hat selbst/selber Aristoteles gelesen.
         'Paul has even/himself read Aristotle.'

In view of the points discussed above, analysing intensifiers as focus particles appears to be a reasonable move, but it is certainly not beyond criticism. It is mainly the restriction to nominal foci which makes intensifiers somewhat particular. Moreover, that English intensifiers show agreement with an NP is reminiscent of adjectives. Note, however, that adjectives like *mere* and *very* (cf. König 1991: 12) do interact with the focus structure of a sentence.

2.3 Related expressions

English x-*self* as well as German *selbst* are not singular phenomena, but the core members of a relatively substantial group of expressions for which the label 'intensifier' is equally justified. (2.28) shows the relevant English group, (2.29) the German one. The common property of these related expressions is that they are, in one way or another, more specialised than *selbst* or x-*self*.

(2.28)   personally, in person, own, in itself, by x-self, etc.
(2.29)   persönlich, höchstpersönlich, höchstselbst, in Person, eigen, an
         sich, in sich, von sich aus, leibhaftig, etc.

The expressions most closely related to the core members are G. *eigen* and E. *own*. They can be regarded as the adjectival counterparts to the appositive intensifiers. Some languages even prefer the adjectival expression over SELF in certain contexts, cf. the translation of the German example in (2.30a) into

Norwegian (2.30b). Note that English avoids x-*self* in this context too, cf. (2.30c).

(2.30)   a Ich habe selbst ein Auto.
          b Norwegian

Jag	har	egen	bil.
I	have	own	car

          c I've got a car of my own/?myself.

Some languages do not even distinguish between appositive and adjectival intensifiers, cf. Turkish, Persian, Mandarin, Welsh, etc.:

(2.31)   Turkish
          a müdür-ün   kendi-si
             director-GEN   self-POSS.3P.SG
             'the director himself'
          b kendi   oda-m
             own   room-1P
             'my own room'

Own is also available in the meaning of 'even' for which G. *selbst* can be used too, recall (2.24). The prerequisite is that the stress falls on the focused NP.

(2.32)   He does not recognise his own DAUGHter.

Other members of the group of intensifiers are restricted to particular nominal constituents or to specific interpretations. *Personally*, for instance, can only interact with human NPs and does not allow the inclusive interpretation, cf. (2.33). For G. *höchstpersönlich*, the referent of that NP must be of high rank. German *höchstselbst* is a little archaic and requires the referent to have a high status too.

(2.33)   a ??My dog came personally to welcome me.
          b I would like to give this speech personally. (only exclusive)

Very rarely does it happen that SELF and one of the related expressions intensify the same constituent:

(2.34)   I myself personally thought it went in like a ... well, never mind. [LLC]

2.4 Previous analyses

The differentiation between adnominal and adverbal intensifiers is, as indicated above, not new, although it used to be wrapped in alternative terminology. Moravcsik (1972) tries to capture the difference by the pair 'head-bound' versus 'sentence-final'; Dirven (1973) labels them 'discourse emphasizer' and 'predicate emphasizer'; Edmondson and Plank (1978) propose 'head-bound' versus 'non-head-bound', but they decide in favour of using the shortcuts *himself*$_1$ and *himself*$_2$; Verheijen (1986) offers 'head-bound' (HB) versus 'after-aux' (AA) and 'end' (E); and König (1991) takes up Edmondson and Plank's 'head-bound' versus 'non-head-bound'.

On the one hand, the above terminological proposals want to draw attention to the fact that intensifiers are always in association with another constituent, their head as it were, and that they show a certain positional mobility on the other. This is particularly obvious in the pair 'head-bound' versus 'non-head-bound'. Labels pertaining purely to position, as e.g. 'sentence-final', suppress the former aspect in favour of the latter. None of these proposals, however, makes a syntactic commitment in the sense that it would specify the kind of phrase an intensifier modifies or belongs to. The advantage of the categorisation of intensifiers into adnominal and adverbal, as is done here, lies in precisely that point. There are good reasons to believe that all intensifiers can either be analysed as endocentric expansions of NPs or of VPs. What is lost in this classification is the fact that all intensifiers interact with an NP, but precisely for that reason it can be neglected.

Another point that argues against positional labels is that they are often not precise enough. Although intensifiers do frequently occur in sentence-final position, other positions are possible apart from the position adjacent to an NP, recall (2.14). Moreover, in German sentences containing complex VPs, a very common position of the intensifier is before the main verb and not behind it, cf. (2.35) taken from Edmondson and Plank (1978: 375).

(2.35)   Der Premierminister hat die Königin selbst beleidigt.
'The Prime Minister has insulted the queen himself.'

The only author to acknowledge an additional position is Verheijen (1986) who differentiates between 'after-aux' and 'end' intensifiers. This, however, can be no more than a convenient taxonomic aid because these positions do not necessarily correlate with a difference in meaning.

According to Dirven's (1973) classification of intensifiers into 'discourse' and 'predicate emphasizers' (ANS and AVS respectively), the important property of the former type lies in the fact that the contribution it makes is relevant beyond the boundaries of the actual sentence, whereas in the case of the latter, the main effect is to somehow highlight the predicate. Besides being non-syntactic labels, this classification gives the impression that only ANS is necessary for the coherence of discourse. However, all intensifiers make a semantic contribution which has clear repercussions on the discourse level. Moreover, the semantic analysis of AVS to be given in this study will show that it does not emphasise the predicate, but that it rather characterises a referent before the background of the VP-denotation.

What the above brief remarks show is that, abstracting away from the actual terminology used, there is general consensus concerning the differentiation of intensifiers into two major types of usage. We will favour the classification into adnominal and adverbal intensifiers here because these two types of intensifiers belong to NP and VP respectively and have clear correlates on the semantic level.

When we here take the stance that a clear distinction should be drawn in English between reflexive x-*self* on the one hand and intensive x-*self* on the other, it should also be borne in mind that, as an alternative approach, it would be possible to argue that, in spite of all their functional differences, intensive and reflexive x-*self* are in fact the same expression because they share the same form. Hence, it might be proposed to capture both types of expressions with the same explanatory machinery. The only studies where such an analysis is spelt out in detail appear to be Jayaseelan (1988) and Browning (1993), however, it is at least hinted at in Moyne (1971), Leskosky (1972), Moravcsik (1972) and Cantrall (1973b, 1974).

Jayaseelan regards all occurrences of E. x-*self* as intensifiers, 'emphatic adjuncts' in his terminology. The major problem he has to solve in this approach is how to license occurrences of reflexive x-*self* which become adjuncts in argument positions. This is done by assuming empty pronominal heads. Emphasising a pronoun is supposed to result in its co-referential interpretation. Browning, by contrast, sees the common denominator of English reflexives and intensifiers in their argument structure. Following a proposal in Reinhart and Reuland (1991), she assigns to the basic expression *self* an argument structure containing two open positions, of which one is saturated by the incorporated pronoun that English intensifiers and reflexives always possess. Two mechanisms (θ-saturation and θ-identification) are sufficient to handle the integration of x-*self* into a syntactic tree.

Alternative analyses could depart from the assumption that reflexive x-*self* is generated by a rule which converts an NP co-referential with another NP within a certain syntactic domain into reflexive x-*self*, i.e. reflexives as such are never base-generated, cf. e.g. the Reflexive Rule in Lees and Klima (1969: 152). This was how reflexivity was viewed in the early days of Transformational Grammar (cf. Jackendoff 1972: 108ff. for an alternative approach which base-generates reflexives). Thus, a reflexive sentence would typically be derived as follows:

(2.36)   a Max sees Max. $\Rightarrow$
         b Max sees himself.

Since intensive x-*self*, or rather the NP supposed to be underlying it, is an adjunct and not an argument, it is not required by a verb's θ-grid and hence needs a separate rule to be generated. Here, one could assume with Moyne (1971: 151) and Moravcsik (1972) a rule which duplicates NPs for emphasis. This assumption gains some plausibility from the observation that intensifiers often derive from nominal expressions somehow related to the

NP they intensify. When the output of this rule is processed by the Reflexive Rule mentioned above, or a derivative thereof, the desired result is produced, cf. (2.37).

(2.37)   a   Max came. ⇒
         b   Max Max came. ⇒
         c   Max himself came.

   This transformation based approach to language analysis, of course, went out of fashion many years ago. The corresponding question to ask today would be how to subsume intensifiers under the Binding Theory. Nevertheless, although our observations can so far be called no more than cursory, it will have already become clear that emphatic reflexives or intensifiers will not easily subsume under the principles of the Binding Theory as developed within the framework of Government & Binding. The Binding Conditions for nominal expressions as they are formulated in Chomsky (1981: 188, 1986b: 166) make use of a threefold differentiation of nominals into 'overt anaphors', 'pronominals' and 'R(eferential)-expressions'.

   Anaphors include reflexives such as E. x-*self* and G. *sich* as well as reciprocals like E. *each other*, *one another* or G. *einander*, i.e. they are expressions which lack potential for 'inherent reference'. The subclass of pronominals relevant here are personal pronouns. Finally, R-expressions are nominals which are not referentially dependent, but have reference of their own. The Binding Theory assumes that anaphors and pronominals are in complementary distribution. Referentially dependent expressions are supposed to occur within well-defined domains.

   Trying to subsume emphatic reflexives under the Binding Conditions encounters the problem that the binding mentioned there refers to 'A-binding', i.e. is meant to cover anaphors in 'A(rgument) positions'. However, emphatic reflexives do not occur in argument positions and can hence hardly be called arguments. It is generally held that an argument bears a θ-role and occurs in the θ-position of a head, cf. Chomsky (1981: 101). Recalling the adnominal examples given in (2.13) above, it is unconvincing to argue that these occurrences of x-*self* bear a θ-role since proper nouns do not assign θ-roles. Such an assumption is even more unconvincing for the adverbial intensifiers in (2.14). Another point against subsuming emphatic reflexives under the Binding Theory is that they are never in paradigmatic contrast with nominal expressions. The Binding Theory, however, has explicitly been developed to account for the distribution of nominal expressions. As will become clear in Chapters 3 and 4, intensifiers invariably are adjuncts.

   Nevertheless, examples like (2.6b) and (2.7) have shown that the English form x-*self* also inhabits a certain grey area in which it becomes difficult to tell whether x-*self* belongs to the group of anaphors or intensifiers. What is worse, reflexives and pronouns are often interchangeable without there being any obvious difference in meaning. (2.38) gives some more examples. Preferred positions are after spatial prepositions, prepositions that introduce some sort of comparison and in coordinations. Section 3.2 deals with these occurrences of x-*self* in some detail.

(2.38) a John put a blanket under him/himself.
        b She never felt quite at ease with people who were richer than her/herself.
        c They have never invited Margaret and me/myself to dinner.

Not surprisingly, there have been various attempts to interpret examples like (2.38), particularly (2.38a,b), in such a way as to make an analysis on the basis of the Binding Conditions possible, however, with varying success. It has turned out that the cases most difficult to come to grips with are those in which the 'antecedent' of x-*self* not only crosses a clause boundary, but must be recovered in the surrounding discourse as in (2.39), or is even missing completely, cf. (2.38c). These examples are extremely hard to explain with purely structural devices, which is why solutions involving semantic and pragmatic factors become more and more fashionable.

(2.39) He [Zapp] sat down at the desk and opened the drawers. In the top right-hand one was an envelope addressed to himself. [Zribi-Hertz 1989: 716]

On the whole, the literature dealing with reflexives in this grey area between intensification and reflexivity is abundant in comparison with studies discussing emphatic reflexives or intensifiers themselves, cf. Zribi-Hertz (1989), Reinhart and Reuland (1993), etc. As far as the terminology used is concerned, proposals range from the aforementioned 'untriggered reflexives' via 'unbounded', 'locally free', 'non-local' or 'long-distance bound' reflexives/anaphors (Chomsky 1981, 1986b; Kang 1988; Parker *et al.* 1990; Pica 1991; Ferro 1993; Baker 1995, etc.) to 'complex anaphors' (Keenan 1988). By adopting labels such as 'locally free' or 'long-distance bound' for E. x-*self,* it is grouped on a par with anaphoric expressions of languages which readily allow long-distance binding (Swedish *sig,* Icelandic *sig,* etc.). It is doubtful whether such a comparison is also permitted on semantic grounds. Locally free x-*self,* just as those occurrences of locally bound x-*self* which are in free alternation with pronominals, always contributes something beyond the mere expression of co-reference.

To conclude, it is explicitly not the aim of the present study to treat reflexive and intensive x-*self* in the same manner, although it would be an extremely enticing question to ask why these two functions can collapse in one and the same form, even more so because this is a fairly widespread phenomenon in the languages of the world. To investigate the common ground of reflexivity and intensification, however, affords sufficient material for a separate study. The contrastive function these expressions have would probably be a good starting point.

2.5 Historical development

English *self* as well as German *selbst* are both assumed to derive from Proto-Germanic **selba-*, **selban-*. A cognate of this form can be found in almost all modern Germanic languages: Afrikaans *self*, Danish *selv*, Dutch *zelf*, Faroese *sjálvur*, Frisian *self*, Icelandic *sjálfur*, Norwegian *sjølv* (Nynorsk) and *selv* (Bokmål), Swedish *själv*. It has also survived in some Germanic-based Creoles such as Berbice Dutch *selfu*. A notable exception is Yiddish, which has lost SELF and uses *aleyn* (cf. E. *alone*) as the intensifier.

No matter which language we take, SELF can easily be traced back for many centuries right into the past millennium. Among others we find Old English *self*, *seolf* and *sylf*, Middle High German *selp*, Middle Low German *sulf*, *self*, *silf*, *solf*, Old High German *selp*, Gothic *silba*, Old Frisian *self* as well as Old Norse *sjálfr*. Germanic languages commonly differentiate between a strong and a weak declension in which SELF, particularly in the old languages, also participated. Thus, we find e.g. *self/selfa* in Old English, *self/selva* in Old Frisian and *selp/selbo* in Old High German. Old Norse *sjálfr* manifests only strong inflection whereas Gothic *silba* shows only weak inflection.

It is not easy to find a convincing explanation for the origin of SELF. According to the relevant dictionaries and grammars, as e.g. Grimm (1905, 1967), Skeat (1910), Klein (1967), Heyse (1968), Holthausen (1974), Barnhart (1988), Duden (1989), Kluge (1989) as well as the OED (1989), its etymology is either not entirely safe or totally obscure. Still, there have been various attempts at shedding light onto that area. Explanations for the etymology of SELF can be divided into two groups. On the one hand, SELF is considered a proper stem in itself. On the other hand, SELF is regarded as a compound of essentially two forms. The second approach aims at reconstructing the meaning of the whole as the combined meaning of its parts.

Regarding the first approach, it has been proposed to relate SELF to Old Irish *selb* which means 'possession', cf. Grimm (1905), Kluge (1995). Old Irish *selb* is cognate with Gothic *saljan* 'offer', 'hand over' and Indo-European **sel-* 'seize', 'grasp', 'grip' (cf. Modern English *sell*). This analysis is based on formal similarity as well as on contrastive evidence from Lithuanian where the intensifier is assumed to have a similar origin. The Lithuanian intensifier *pats* can also mean 'master', 'husband', 'landlord' or 'owner'. Considering the conceptual vicinity of 'possession' and 'owner', Old Irish *selb* may also have denoted the latter concept. This etymology is considered unlikely in Grimm (1905), but endorsed in Kluge (1995). Another proposal, to be found in Grimm (1905, 1967), postulates a link between SELF and Old Prussian *subs/suba*, but this is considered unconvincing. Further research will have to make clear whether this approach can be maintained at all.

As far as the second approach is concerned, it is unanimously agreed upon that the Indo-European reflexive base *se-* is involved in one way or another (cf. e.g. Kluge 1957). From that stem, reflexive anaphors such as Gothic *sik*, German *sich* and Swedish *sig* derive. A related form can be found in the Romance languages, cf. Latin *se*, Italian and Spanish *sé/se*, and in the group of Slavic languages, there is also a cognate form, cf. the Russian enclitic *-sja*. Many Germanic languages used to have separate forms for genitive, dative as well as accusative reflexives, cf. Gothic *seina*, *sis*, *sik* and Old Norse *sîn*, *ser*, *sik*. In most modern languages, maximally two forms have survived, usually a possessive and an accusative/objective form, cf. German *sein*, *sich* and Swedish *sin*, *sig*. A notable exception is Icelandic which has preserved the original paradigm: *sín*, *sér*, *sig*.

The origin of the other component of SELF, i.e. the one headed by the consonant *l*, is much more disputed. Klein (1967) sees it in the Indo-European pronominal base *lo-*. On that account, SELF is thought to originate in *se-lo-* which comes to mean something similar to Modern English *itself*. Given the fusion of pronouns and *self* in the history of English, the motivation for this analysis is not far to seek. Still, conclusive evidence for such a line of argumentation is not easy to come by. Since it is entirely unclear why pronouns in Old English and Early Middle English fused with *self* to form a compound intensifier, how much harder it must be to find a motivation for a similar process in Indo-European. Even worse, this analysis is incompatible with our present knowledge about the semantics of intensifiers. Intensifiers do make a fairly precise contribution, however, two semantically almost empty stems are unlikely to acquire it.

Grimm (1905, 1967), by contrast, relates the problematic element to a stem with a substantive semantic contribution. The second part of SELF is assumed to derive from the Proto-Germanic stem *lib-* (Indo-European *lip-*) which is the source of Modern German *Leib*, *Leben*, *leben*, etc. and Modern English *life*, *live*, etc. The stem *lib-* could also produce a verb which used to mean 'remain', 'persevere' or 'continue'. According to Grimm, SELF may originate in the composite form *si-liba*, the meaning of which can be paraphrased by 'that which rests in itself'. What appears to argue against this analysis is the loss of the root vowel in the second part of *si-liba*. This, it is said, is unlikely to happen in stems. However, a point in favour of this analysis consists in the fact that in all Germanic languages, the non-reflexive component of SELF and the relevant word for *life* underwent the same sound changes. Thus we find *zelf* and *lijf* in Dutch, *selv* and *liv* in Norwegian and Danish and *själv* and *liv* in Swedish.

Another interpretation of *si-liba* becomes possible if *liba* is analysed as a nominal rather than a verb. In this case, the most likely paraphrase becomes E. 'his body' or G. 'sein Leib'. The German gloss in particular shows a strong affinity to the original compound. Modern English *body* comes from a different source, so that the parallel cannot be drawn here. However, such an interpretation is plausible for several reasons.

First, some Germanic languages still possess an appositive intensifier in which the root *lib-* can be recognised beyond all doubt, cf. G. *leibhaftig* and Swedish *livslevande*. These intensifiers mirror adnominal SELF in meaning, but have a more restricted set of possible foci. G. *leibhaftig* e.g. is mainly restricted to the devil:

(2.40)   Sie sieht aus, als hätte sie den Teufel leibhaftig erblickt.
         'She looks as if she has seen the devil incarnate.'

Second, such an analysis is compatible with the semantic contribution intensifiers make today. As will be discussed in detail later on, intensifiers make a referent central and oppose it to peripheral alternatives. One's body, however, is a central object indeed. And third, there is also a typological argument. It is certainly no coincidence that in most languages in which the original meaning of the intensifier is still visible, it is derived from an expression denoting either the body itself or a central part of it such as 'head' (Hausa), 'heart' (Swahili), 'eye' (Arabic), 'bone' (Hebrew) and 'body' (Japanese), cf. Moravcsik (1972), Schladt (1995). *I myself* e.g. translates into Hausa as *ni dakaina* which literally means 'I with my head'. On that account, Proto-Germanic *lib-* would be exactly on a par with Japanese and many more languages in the world. To be sure, expressions denoting the body (or a part thereof) are the most widespread source of intensifiers in the languages of the world, and against that background, viewing SELF as being derived from *si-liba* no longer seems all that implausible.

A minor question that may also be dealt with in these preliminaries concerns the origin of the suffixes -*st* and -*er* in G. *selb-st* and *selb-er* respectively. Here, we mainly find two competing views. On the one hand, *selber* and *selbst* may be viewed as comparative and superlative of the base form *selb*, hence the paradigm *selb – selber – selbst*, cf. Grimm (1905). Support for such an argument mainly comes from Latin and related Romance languages where we do find superlative forms, but probably no comparative forms (because this is an elative), cf. Latin *ipsissimus*, Italian *stessisimo* and Spanish *mismísimo*. Given that Latin used to be the touchstone of each and every language, such an analysis can hardly come as a surprise. This view is probably wrong. On the other hand, there have been proposals to regard these suffixes as frozen case endings. On that account, -*er* is analysed as a fossilised strong nominative singular masculine (2.41) whereas -*st* is viewed as a strong genitive. *Selbst* is assumed to have developed from *selbes* through attachment of an unorganic *t*, cf. (2.42). A similar development is assumed for *einst* 'once', *sonst* 'else', *Obst* 'fruit' and *Papst* 'Pope'. The *e* simply dropped out, but there is evidence for the co-existence of *selbest* and *selbst*.

(2.41)   Middle High German
sich, nû hab ich dich gelêret
des ich selber leider nie gepflac. [W. v. d. Vogelweide 92.4,
Grimm 1905: 430]
'I have taught you what I myself never used to do.'

(2.42)   a   Middle High German
daჳ Jhêsus Crist sîn selbes blût
vor uns wolde gieჳen. [Livländ. Reimchron. 858, Grimm
1905: 420]
'that Jesus Christ wanted to give his own blood for us.'
b   Dies ist der Wille des Königs selbst.
'This is the will of the king himself.'

That *selbst* is a fossilised genitive whereas *selber* is an old nominative form has repercussions even today. It cannot be due to chance that *selbst* is better suited for modifying genitive NPs than *selber*:

(2.43)   a   Dies ist der Wille des Königs selbst/?selber.
'This is the will of the king himself.'
b   Er schrieb das Buch ohne Schonung seiner selbst/?selber
nieder.
'He wrote down the book without paying heed to his
health.'
c   um der Sache selbst/?selber willen
'for the sake of the matter itself'

Although, meanwhile, a not inconsiderable amount of effort has been directed at understanding the historical development of the English compound x-*self,* cf. Penning (1875), Farr (1905), Visser (1970), Mitchell (1985), Ogura (1989a), Keenan (1996), there nevertheless can be no denying the fact that major pieces of the puzzle are still missing. This particularly concerns x-*self* in its usage as an intensifier. What is reasonably well understood, though, is why English developed a compound reflexive anaphor.

Old English did not possess a separate reflexive anaphor and had to resort to personal pronouns (dative and accusative) in order to indicate referential dependence in a local domain. These pronouns, however, were in many (though not in all) contexts ambiguous between two interpretations. They could mark co-reference as well as disjoint reference. This is demonstrated in (2.44). Note that this ambiguity occurs in the third person only.

(2.44)   Old English
a   hine he bewerað mid wæpnum [ÆGram 96.11]
'he defended himself with weapons'

b ða behydde Adam hine & his wif eac swa dyde [Gen 3.9]
'and Adam hid himself and his wife did the same'

When confronted with ambiguities in important areas, languages tend to develop means to resolve them. Old English is no exception in this respect. In order to mark co-reference in a local domain unambiguously, the intensifier *self* could be added to the relevant pronouns, cf. (2.45) and (2.46). Exactly why the intensifier disambiguates these cases is discussed in König and Siemund (1996c).

(2.45)   Old English
  a   se Hælende sealde hine sylfne for us [ÆLet 4 1129]
   'The Saviour gave himself for us.'
  b   He [Moses] sceawode hine selfne, & pinsode, ða ða him ðuhte ðæt he hit doon ne meahte, ... [CP 7.51.14, translation provided]
   'He contemplated himself, and thought that he could not do it, ...'

(2.46)   Old English
  a   he ... selð Gode his æhta, & hine selfne diobule [CP 44.327.23, translation provided]
   'He gives his possessions to God and himself to the devil.'
  b   Hannibal ... hine selfne mid atre acwealde [Or 4 11.110.2]
   'Hannibal killed himself with poison.'

Old English is not singular in employing the intensifier to facilitate a co-referential interpretation of otherwise unspecified pronouns. A comparable situation can be found today in Frisian and in Afrikaans. Moreover, a related phenomenon is observable in the Scandinavian languages, where long-distance bindable anaphors can thus be restricted to a local domain. Note, however, that the intensifier does no more than to strongly suggest the co-referential interpretation. Intensified object pronouns need not be locally bound in all contexts, as (2.47) demonstrates. This fact obstructs a purely syntactic explanation.

(2.47)   Old English
  Be ðam cwæð se æðela lareow sanctus Paulus: Ic wille ðæt ge sien wise to gode & bilwite to yfele. Ond eft be ðæm cwæð Dryhten ðurh hine selfne to his gecorenum: Beo ge swa ware sua sua nædran & sua bilwite sua culfran. [CP 35.237.18, translation provided]
  'Therefore the noble teacher St. Paul said: "I wish ye to be wise for good and simple for evil." And again, the Lord spoke about the same through himself to his elect: "Be cunning as adders and simple as pigeons."'

Given that the intensifier could disambiguate otherwise ambiguous object pronouns, it is certainly not surprising to see these expressions fuse in the further development of English. However, three important questions remain to which so far no convincing answer has been given. First of all, it is not easy to comprehend why the fusion of pronoun and *self* was not confined to the third person, but was extended to the first and second persons. This is remarkable in so far as no ambiguity arises in these cases. Second, it is intuitively not plausible that the newly developed compound form came also to be used as an intensifier, although, as demonstrated by (2.3), this is by no means an uncommon situation in the languages of the world. Third, and this is the most bizarre of these questions, why did English abandon its original intensifier *self*? Old English *self* was used in much the same way as its modern equivalent and there seems to have been no obvious reason to replace it with a new intensifier.

(2.48) Old English
a se cyning sylfa [GD 14.131.3]
   'the king himself'
b Swa swa Crist sylf cwæð [ÆLet 3 173]
   'as Christ himself said'

A common answer to the first question is to say that the extension of *self*-marking to the first and second persons happened by analogy, cf. Penning (1875: 13) who writes that 'from the third person this usage was naturally transferred to the first and second persons'. Such statements, however, can hardly count as functional motivations, so this must still be regarded an open question.

As for the second point, more substantial explanations have been offered. Penning, again, hypothesises that the abundance of dysfunctional reflexive dative pronouns in Old English, the so-called pleonastic pronouns, is the reason why the compound intensifier developed. The essence of his idea can be found on page 22 where he writes that 'as this dative on account of its pleonastic nature forms no integral part of any other part of the sentence, it is quite natural that it gradually lost its original signification and became closely connected with „seolf".'

As the following examples show, these pronouns nearly always occur before *self*, and Penning somehow appears to regard the intensifier as a magnet attracting dysfunctional elements of language. Mitchell (1985: 188ff.) takes up a similar position.

(2.49) Old English
a He næs na ofslagen, ac he him sylf gewat, ... [ÆLet 4 661]
   'He was not slain, but he departed (died) on his own ...'
b 7 he sende of his mannan to þissum lande. 7 wolde cuman
   him sylf æfter [Chron 1087.60]

'and he sent his men to that country and wanted to follow
later on himself'.

Farr (1905), by contrast, holds case syncretism responsible for the emer-
gence of the compound intensifier. He observes that the intensifier in Old
English could occur in distant (non-juxtaposed) position from the NP it
interacts with and that the gradual loss of case endings began to blur which
NP *self* was in association with. As a consequence, the relation came to be
specified by a pronominal copy of the NP or, in his words (1905: 42): ' the
non-juxtaposed *self* of the Nom. lost its power of standing alone. [...] It
became necessary then to repeat the subject as a reinforcement to *self*'.
(2.50) shows some examples.

(2.50)   Old English
   a   forðæm ic hit no self nauht ne ondræde [Bo 20.47.5]
       'I do not fear it myself.'
   b   ac he ægðer fleah ge þa dæd ge þa sægene 7 eac self sæde
       þæt seo dæd his nære [Or 3 5.59.23]
       'but he rejected both the deed [sacrifice] and the statement
       and moreover said himself that this deed [peace] was not
       his.'

A third view is expressed in Ogura (1989a), who argues that it was the
relative abundance of sequences like *he him self* and *7 him self* in comparison
to *he self* and *he him selfum* in Old and Middle English which finally led to
a fusion of pronoun and intensifier. The levelling of inflectional endings is
also supposed to have a stake in this process. To put it in Ogura's terms
(1989a: 68), Modern English '*I myself* and *he himself* may be explained as a
contamination of *self* in an emphatic use'.
   The contaminating item is meant to be the non-nominative pronoun in
these sequences, cf.:

(2.51)   Old English
   a   þæt he him sylf hæfde sume lisse his sawle [ÆHom 13.66]
       'that he himself had his soul in peace'
   b   ... mid broðor blode 7 mid sweora 7 mid Romuluses
       eame[s] Numetores, þone he eac ofslog, ða he cyning wæs, 7
       him self siþþan to ðæm rice feng! [Or 2 2.39.17]
       '... with the blood of a brother, and that of fathers-in-law,
       and with that of Romulus' uncle Numitor, who he also slew,
       when he was king, and afterwards took the kingdom to
       himself.'

Although the above survey cannot claim to be exhaustive, the three analyses
discussed are nevertheless a representative sample of what is available. They

all are open to serious objections. As for Penning and Mitchell, it is simply not true that the reflexive dative in Old English was dysfunctional and that it therefore could be affixed to *self*. On closer scrutiny, it turns out that these pleonastic pronouns could be used as markers of derived intransitivity in much the same way as e.g. German *sich* can be today, cf. (2.52) and (2.53).

(2.52)   Old English
    a and stod him under þam treowe [Gen 18.8]
       'he placed himself under the tree'
    b þa bewende Nero hine to Paulum and cwæð [ÆCHom 1
       378.8]
       'then Nero turned to Paul and said'
    c he ... astrehte hine to eorþan [Gen 18.2]
       'He bowed down to the ground.'

(2.53)   Old English
    a se wisa Catulus hine gebealg [Bo 27.61.17]
       'The wise Catulus was angry.'
    b Wineleas, wonsælig mon genimeð him wulfas to geferan,
       felafæcne deor. [Max I 146]
       'The friendless unfortunate man takes wolves as compan-
       ions, very crafty animals.'

Moreover, Old English possesses verbs taking obligatory pronouns which resemble obligatory reflexives in Modern German:

(2.54)   Old English
    a ... ðæt ðu ðin scamige, Sidon. [CP 52.409.33]
       '... that you be ashamed, Sidon.'
    b hit is cyn ðæt we ure scomigen [CP 52.407.15]
       'It is appropriate that we be ashamed.'
    c he gereste hine on ðone seofoþan dæg [Gen 2.2]
       'He rested on the seventh day.'

Note that in Modern German precisely these reflexives cannot be intensified:

(2.55)   a *Nero wandte [sich selbst] an Paul.
       'Nero turned to Paul.'
    b *Er schämt [sich selbst].
       'He was ashamed.'

A more relevant question to be asked in this context is why pronouns in these usages were abandoned and, once they were lost, why English did not start anew to develop pronouns with these functions.

Farr's thesis is questionable mainly from a typological perspective. In many languages (Dutch, German, Swedish, etc.), the intensifier is perfectly able to occur in a distant or non-juxtaposed position to the NP it interacts with even without case marking or similar means to indicate this relation. Subsequently, one would be under pressure to explain why English should be exceptional in this respect.

Finally, since Ogura's argument is mainly based on frequency of occurrence, it fails to give a convincing functional explanation. Moreover, that the modern English intensifier should be a contaminated expression can hardly be regarded as a serious analysis. In sum, then, the development of the English compound intensifier can still be considered an undecided question.

A similarly negative statement must be made in connection with the third question, i.e. why English discarded its original intensifier *self*. To my knowledge, no explanation has been offered on that question.

3 Adnominal intensifiers

In the following, a distinction will be drawn between those occurrences of adnominal intensifiers that are in association with an overt head NP and those that seem to lack one. This distinction is only relevant for English. German intensifiers always interact with an overt head. As long as there is a visible head, ANS can straightforwardly be analysed as an adjunction to it and may therefore be regarded as an apposition in the widest sense of the word. There are hardly any problems concerning the syntactic analysis of this variety of ANS. However, as mentioned in section 2.4, certain occurrences of E. x-*self* resemble intensifiers although there is no overt head NP present in these cases. Here, a number of options arise. First, the existence of headless ANS may be denied altogether and the relevant occurrences of x-*self* may simply be viewed as (long-distance bound) reflexive anaphors. This approach has been extensively investigated and has yielded many interesting results (cf. Zribi-Hertz 1989 for a good summary).

Second, certain occurrences of E. x-*self* may be regarded not as simplex forms, but as duplex forms consisting of head NP plus intensifier, cf. Ferro (1993) and Baker (1995) for such a view or hints pointing towards such a direction. On that account, there would be three types of E. x-*self*: (i) an anaphor, (ii) an intensifier and (iii) a compound intensified pronoun. As usual, the intensifier would be analysed as an adjunct, however, the duplex form would have to be regarded as a full NP. It is by no means implausible to assume such a tripartite distribution of x-*self*.

Third, it may be argued that the head NP is deleted in certain positions. This will mainly be the stance taken here, but this view requires an explanation and some sort of specification where and under what condition deletion of the head is possible or even necessary.

Evidence for a differentiation between overt and covert head NPs mainly comes from two sources. On the one hand, in certain positions headless x-*self* makes a contribution to the meaning of a sentence comparable to that of ANS with an overt head. On the other hand, there is contrastive evidence from e.g. German, but also many other languages, where the intensifier cannot be headless. English headless intensifiers typically translate into German as a sequence of pronoun plus intensifier, cf.:

> (3.1)   a John noticed that Mary was taller than himself.
> b John bemerkte, daß Maria größer als er selbst ist.

Sentence pairs such as (3.1) are by no means idiosyncratic or rare, rather the opposite is the case. The relevant contexts and positions are important domains of intensifiers. That covert heads can only be found within a fixed domain is shown by the following examples. Here, English translates into German on a one-to-one basis.

> (3.2)   a He himself opened the bottle.
> b Er selbst öffnete die Flasche.

3.1 Adnominal SELF – overt heads

Apart from the fact that adnominal intensifiers must be generated to the right of their head NPs, there are very few syntactic restrictions. As for their head NP proper, even fewer restrictions apply so that it becomes possible to adjoin them to nominals in virtually any position irrespective of their class and grammatical function. It is probably no exaggeration to say that almost anything goes.

But let us look at the distribution of adnominal intensifiers in a more systematic way. ANS is not sensitive to grammatical function. It readily combines with NPs in subject position, with direct and indirect object NPs and can also modify those NPs which are the complement of a preposition, cf. (3.3). What the examples in (3.3) also reveal is that the differentiation of NPs within a sentence into arguments and adjuncts is unimportant for ANS. In (3.3a–c) it interacts with an argument of the relevant verb whereas in (3.3d,e) it modifies NPs contained within adverbials.

> (3.3)   a Harold Macmillan himself has had a difficult time.
> b I once spoke to the Pope himself.
> c She put the ashtray onto the table itself.
> d She tried to push the cart onto the road itself.
> e Within the town itself, the report produced a sensation.

Interaction of ANS is not restricted to simple NPs. On the contrary, it can be adjoined to even highly complex NPs and bounds to their complexity seem to be imposed by general processing limitations rather than by ANS. As (3.4) shows, we do not only find complex NPs (3.4a), but also gerunds (3.4b) and infinitival clauses in subject position (3.4c) as well as NPs taking a complement clause with possibly infinite *that*-recursion, cf. (3.4d).

(3.4)   a The construction of the houses itself is cumbersome.
             b Constructing the houses itself is cumbersome.
             c To construct the houses itself is cumbersome.
             d The suggestion that Paul thought that Ann was in love with him itself surprised nobody.

To be sure, at first reading these examples appear a little odd and are certainly not as acceptable as those given in (3.3). However, ANS makes a semantic contribution which is relevant beyond the boundaries of the sentence in which it is contained, so that making the examples in (3.4) more acceptable simply boils down to embedding them into suitable context. They are far from being ungrammatical, cf.:

(3.5)   The designing of new houses can be a very stimulating task. The actual construction of the houses itself often turns out to be rather cumbersome.

(3.6)   The spread of English as the first universal language itself has helped give modern English-speakers a taste for foreign writers. [*Economist*, 18 May 1996]

What has been said so far applies to both English and German and it is impossible to make out differences between the two languages on that level. Independently of whether we take (3.3) or (3.4), the relevant translations into German would yield comparable structures with similar degrees of acceptability.

As far as the NP itself is concerned, it turns out that common nouns, proper nouns and pronouns are all valid NPs for ANS to interact with, cf. (3.7). However, the pronominal system is an area where some syntactic restrictions as well as some variation between English and German can be discovered. Given the tight interaction between pronominal system and intensifiers in the development of English, a certain amount of variation is to be expected.

(3.7)   a You will find the answer to the question in the text itself.
             b Henry VIII himself had six wives.
             c She herself noticed the error.

In the following paragraphs, we will be pursuing a number of goals. First, we will seek evidence for the claim that there is a type of intensifier which can justly be called 'adnominal'. This involves verifying the implicit assumption that ANS can be analysed as an integral part of the NP it interacts with. That ANS is in association with an NP, however, will mainly be taken for granted, but this is an issue which can easily be settled for English since intensifiers always show agreement with an NP. As for German, it is not possible to provide visible evidence, but it is relatively unproblematic to semantically motivate a relation between *selbst* and some NP. Note that intensifiers are always in association with some NP, but not all intensifiers also belong to that NP, i.e. are a co-constituent of it. This is a particular property of adnominal intensifiers and it is necessary to keep these two issues apart.

Second, once the matter of co-constituency has been resolved, it seems reasonable to ask what kind of relation there is between ANS and its co-constituent or head, i.e. we will mainly investigate whether ANS is an adjunct or an argument of it. This point is not particularly difficult to decide and it will turn out relatively quickly that a categorisation as adjunct should be the analysis of choice.

Third, we will pursue the question of whether ANS is adjoined to a lexical item or rather to a phrase, which is equivalent to asking whether it is a sister of a minimal or a non-minimal projection. ANS always expands maximal projections so that the above observations culminate in the statement that ANS is an endocentric expansion of the NP it interacts with.

A fourth question concerns some particular properties of the head NP. Here, it will mainly turn out that ANS interacts with definite NPs, but appears to reject indefinite ones. Although the underlying constraint is semantic in nature, it can have syntactic consequences

Section 3.1.2 deals with syntactic restrictions observable with ANS. On the one hand, it is possible, under certain conditions, to dislocate ANS from its head NP either to its left or to its right. Left-dislocation or topicalisation of adnominal intensifiers is particularly interesting from an English-German perspective. On the other hand, English, in contrast to German, shows asymmetries in the intensification of pronouns. Only pronouns in subject position can be intensified. ANS cannot modify object pronouns.

3.1.1 ANS – the NP-adjunct

Whether ANS belongs to another constituent – more precisely, whether it is a syntactic sister of some constituent – can be tested using various means. Of course, some tests are better than others in that they yield more convincing evidence. Let us start with the weak tests first.

One such test would be the following. We take a verb participating in the so-called object alternation (cf. Levin 1993), i.e. one of those verbs that can be used with and without a direct object, and intensify the object NP with ANS. In a subsequent step we delete the object NP and observe whether ANS follows suit or not. If it does, it belongs to the deleted constituent, if not, it does not. English should be the preferred language for this test since we can make sure via agreement that ANS is in association with the object NP and not with the subject. As we would expect, it is not possible to delete the object NP while retaining the intensifier, cf. (3.8) and (3.9).

(3.8)   a Mike ate the cake itself.
            b Mike ate (*itself).

(3.9)   a I used to teach the president himself.
            b I used to teach (*himself).

A similar test consists in observing the behaviour of ANS when used within an adverbial phrase. Since adverbials are nearly always optional, we are free to add them or to take them away. If ANS belongs to a constituent inside the adverbial, we should not be allowed to remove the adverbial while keeping ANS. This prediction is borne out in (3.10). Note, however, that an adverbial PP (Prepositional Phrase) as used in (3.10) does not convincingly prove that ANS is part of the NP inside the PP, it could just as well be a sister of the PP itself.

(3.10)   a I saw the thief in the underground itself.
            b I saw the thief (*itself)/(*in itself).

In fact, it would not at all be unconvincing to assume that *itself* in (3.10a) is adjoined to a constituent apart from the NP *the underground* or the PP. This would, of course, render the test ill-suited for our purposes, but given that co-constituency is not a necessary prerequisite for interaction, this option must be taken into consideration. We know that there is a whole class of expressions commonly referred to as focus particles which are, just as intensifiers, in association with another constituent and often make a comparable semantic contribution.

Moreover, it has been argued in Jacobs (1983: 42ff.) that focus particles are not necessarily co-constituents of their focus and that the mere fact that they semantically interact with it is not sufficient reason to believe that they form one constituent. Evidence for such a view can be provided by examples in which particle and focus are separated by another expression or tree node (3.11) and by those which even block adjacency of focus and particle (3.12).[1]

(3.11)   I only like BIG cars.

(3.12)   a *Louise was warned against smoking by even her DOCtor.
            b Louise was warned against smoking even by her DOCtor.

Although we will not accept such data as counter-evidence to our view that intensifiers can be successfully subsumed under the class of focus particles, they nevertheless show that intensifiers are somewhat different from the bulk of the class. As a rule, ANS cannot be separated from its focus, which is no problem for most focus particles. However, it is precisely the fact that ANS behaves differently in this respect which supports the assumption that it is a sister of its focus NP:

(3.13)   a   Louise was warned against smoking by her doctor himself.
         b   *Louise was warned against smoking himself by her doctor.

Let us now proceed to have a look at some hard evidence. With regard to German, as is pointed out by Primus (1992: 67), extremely conclusive evidence can be drawn from embedding ANS into postpositions or even circumpositions. The argument is based on the assumption that German is a language which puts heads into a position in a phrase which is farthest to the right, with arguments and adjuncts branching off to the left of their head.

Now, consider the examples in (3.14). In all three cases we find a PP taking an NP-argument. The question still is where ANS belongs, either to the NP, the PP or potentially the to the VP which, however, is not given in the examples below. Since it occurs between the nominal and the preposition and the nominal is an argument of the preposition, it cannot belong to the VP. Since the prepositions in (3.14) invariably are of arity one with the nominal being their only argument, ANS must be an adjunct (which can be confirmed by independent data, as we will see). Finally, ANS cannot be an adjunct to the head of the PP because it intervenes between the head and the argument thereof. Therefore, it must belong to the NP. It appears as if preposition and corresponding argument work like a trap.

(3.14)   a   des Ästhetischen selbst wegen
         b   das Ästhetische selbst betreffend
         c   um des Ästhetischen selbst willen
             'regarding the aesthetic itself'

Another test for co-constituency can be based on the fact that German is a V2 (verb second) language. As is well-known, in a German root sentence there can be one and only one constituent before the finite verb. Since the string [NP ANS] can occur before the finite verb, it must be a single constituent, cf.:

(3.15)   Den Direktor selbst haben wir getroffen.
         'We met the director himself.'

This line of argumentation, however, is restricted to German. It makes no sense whatsoever to transfer it to English because English is right-branching and no V2 language. For English we will need a different test.

As a matter of fact, there are a number of syntactic operations which rearrange the order of the constituents present in a clause/sentence. If ANS adheres to a constituent affected by such an operation, we can conclude that it belongs to this constituent. Of course, most of the following tests are also applicable to German. We will start with passivisation.

For the time being let us assume, rather conservatively, the following analysis of the passive construction. The passive is a derived structure. It is produced by an operation which is called 'passivisation'. The input for this operation is an English or German sentence containing subject, verb and object which is often labelled 'active'. The output of the operation is a sentence containing at least subject and verb. The output subject constituent is the input object constituent, i.e. the original constituent in subject position is replaced by the one in object position. The verb is formally modified and its argument structure as well as its thematic structure are adjusted. The original subject constituent is optionally made available via the *by*-phrase in English or the parallel *von*-phrase in German. The property of passivisation that is relevant for our analysis of ANS is that it always exchanges entire constituents and never only parts of them. It follows that if passivisation affects the sequence [NP SELF] as a whole, as it does in (3.16), we can be fairly sure that both expressions belong together and form one constituent:

(3.16)   a   Mark himself fetched a bottle of Algerian wine.
         b   A bottle of Algerian wine was fetched by Mark himself.
         c   *A bottle of Algerian wine himself was fetched by Mark.

In fact, the view of passivisation given here is a hybrid. It is a blend of the purely structural operation (passive transformation) proposed in Chomsky (1957) and those passivisation operations that merely affect the argument structure of a verb and trigger the exchange of constituents from there, cf. Williams (1981). However, these technicalities are unimportant as long as it is ensured that the constituents in subject and object position are affected in full.

Note, however, that we cannot fully rely on more modern views (Chomsky 1981; 1986b) which abandon the traditional differentiation and relation between active and passive and regard sentences such as (3.16b) as derived from a base-generated structure with a missing constituent in subject position and a non-subcategorised constituent in object position which then causes a violation of Case Filter as well as θ-criterion and subsequently moves into subject position. This means on the one hand that we no longer have any visible evidence for the displacement of constituents and on the other that if we want to use this analysis of passivisation as a test, we must restrict our attention to the constituent that is in object position in deep structure. But even within these bounds it can be successfully shown that ANS is part of the NP it interacts with:

(3.17)   a   was fetched the bottle itself. $\Rightarrow$
         b   The bottle itself was fetched.
         c   *The bottle was fetched itself.

Passivisation is by far not the only way to reorganise thematically the constituents of a sentence. Another option that is offered by both English and German is clefting, which splits (cleaves) a single sentence up into two units, the effect being that one of the constituents of the source sentence becomes focused. The relevant literature usually distinguishes between (real) clefting and pseudo-clefting, cf. Huddleston (1984: 459ff.). (Real) clefts are often referred to as '*it*-clefts' because they are introduced by *it* plus a form of *be* followed by the focused constituent, cf. (3.18), where the NP *the faulty switch itself* is clefted. What clefting again makes clear is that ANS is part of the NP it modifies since it is not sufficient to simply cleave the sequence *the faulty switch* alone, cf. (3.18c). In other words, we are encouraged to prefer the analysis [NP *the faulty switch* [*itself*]] to [XP [NP *the faulty switch*] [*itself*]], i.e. ANS must be seen as somehow embedded within the NP it modifies.

(3.18)   a   The faulty switch itself caused the trouble.
　　　　　b　It was the faulty switch itself that caused the trouble.
　　　　　c　*It was the faulty switch that itself caused the trouble.

Exactly the same point can be made on the basis of pseudo-clefts, cf. (3.19). These clefts are not genuine in that they bear a striking resemblance to fused relatives of which they are often considered just a special case. They may even be reversed, which is a property they do not share with *it*-clefts, cf. (3.19c). What is again important for our analysis of ANS is that it is equally ruled out to separate ANS from its co-constituent, cf. the ungrammaticality of (3.19d).

(3.19)   a   The faulty switch itself caused the trouble.
　　　　　b　What caused the trouble was the faulty switch itself.
　　　　　c　The faulty switch itself was what caused the trouble.
　　　　　d　*What itself caused the trouble was the faulty switch.

Passivisation and, to a certain extent, also clefting are means to reorganise thematically the structure of a clause, more precisely to adjust the topic-comment structure to the needs of discourse. There are even more ways to achieve similar effects which all share the property of shifting complete constituents from one position within a clause to another. The simplest method by far consists in moving an element to the front of the clause into a position before the subject. A wide variety of expressions can be moved in that fashion, but the ones relevant for our investigation are object NPs supposedly containing the intensifier. That they indeed contain it is shown by the following examples:

(3.20)   a   I have not yet climbed Ben Nevis itself.
　　　　　b　Ben Nevis itself, I have not yet climbed.
　　　　　c　*Ben Nevis, I have not yet climbed itself.

Since the list of possible tests could probably be prolonged endlessly and would invariably yield the same results, we will cut a long story short and only briefly draw attention to a wide variety of syntactic alternations which, generally speaking, are operations modifying the argument structure of a verb. They too result in a reordering of the constituents involved, cf. Levin (1993).

Let us, for the sake of exemplification, focus on two prominent and frequently discussed alternations. (3.21) shows the so-called causative/ inchoative alternation whereas (3.22) is an example of the dative alternation. The former intransitivises a transitive verb (or vice versa) and leads to a reduction of (or increase in) the arguments present by one, the latter can be characterised as a structural change from the syntactic pattern [NP V NP$_1$ PP NP$_2$] to [NP V NP$_2$ NP$_1$] (or the other way round), i.e. again, we are confronted with operations exchanging complete constituents. The results given below speak for themselves.

(3.21) a Janet broke the cup itself.
        b The cup itself broke.
        c *The cup broke itself.

(3.22) a Bill sent Tom the book itself.
        b Bill sent the book itself to Tom.
        c *Bill sent the book to Tom itself.

One final piece of evidence can be procured by replacing the sequence [NP SELF] with interrogative pronouns (Verheijen 1986: 681), *wh*-pronouns, and probably by pronouns in general. Since these always stand for entire NPs, there is no other conclusion possible than that ANS always belongs to the one substituted. The question-answer pairs given in (3.23) are particularly illuminating since the relevant answers only comprise the intensified NPs themselves and no surrounding syntactic context. Similarly in (3.24a) the relativiser replaces [NP SELF] and so does the pronoun co-referential to it in (3.24b).

(3.23) a Who mowed the lawn? John himself.
        b What did he mow? The lawn itself.

(3.24) a The director himself, who ...
        b Paul himself thinks that he ...

Thus it appears safe to conclude that [NP SELF] forms one single constituent and we can now go on to looking more closely at the relationship between the two expressions itself. Here two alternatives must be checked since SELF could be (i) an argument and (ii) an adjunct to the nominal head. However, the available data seem to point unanimously to an adjunct analysis. We will provide some evidence for this in the following paragraphs. We will attempt to prove the case by showing that SELF is not an argument.

Note, for a start, that data on omissability will not do the trick since arguments of nouns are mostly optional anyway, i.e. the fact that ANS is always optional does not tell us for sure that it is an adjunct. However, we know that ANS readily combines with nouns independently of whether they possess an argument structure or not. It is not confined to modifying action nominals (cf. Grimshaw 1992), but occurs, probably even in the majority of cases, adjacent to proper nouns and common nouns, i.e. the entire class of nouns denoting simple objects material or immaterial:

(3.25)   Ken himself, Kate herself, the PM himself, the fish itself, the monitor itself, etc.

We can conclude that since ANS can modify nouns without an argument structure, it cannot be an argument and hence it must be an adjunct. It is possible to arrive at the same conclusion with an argument made on the basis of nominals which do possess an argument structure, i.e. the group of nominals which are supposed to have been derived from verbs (deverbal nouns) in view of evidence such as the following:

(3.26)   a John analyses the figures.
         b John's analysis of the figures.

If all the argument positions of a nominal such as *analysis* are saturated, it should be impossible to add further arguments. This is certainly the case in (3.26b). We can now try to adjoin ANS to this NP and see if it is accepted. As (3.27) makes clear, this is no problem at all, which rules out argument status for ANS – it must be an adjunct.

(3.27)   John's analysis of the figures itself.

Examples like (3.27) clearly indicate that ANS does not combine with the bare nominal as it comes from the lexicon, often referred to as minimal projection or N^0 in frameworks such as Government & Binding, but to a string that has already the status of a (noun) phrase, i.e. a projection other than N^0, as e.g. some N' level or, even more likely, N^{max}. Otherwise we would expect ANS to be an argument, obligatory and immediately right-adjacent to its head when additional elements come into play and not separated from it. However, as we have seen, ANS is an adjunct, always optional and takes up the position farthest to the right in a phrase. Put differently, it is never required for the formation of a phrasal category, it can only modify an existing one.

Note also that sequences of common noun plus ANS are ungrammatical (*[N SELF]), which shows that ANS cannot modify a nominal as such. Determiner plus noun plus ANS, in short [DET N SELF], however, is a valid combination and hence we can conclude that ANS can only connect to

NPs because [DET N] is an NP, cf. (3.28). Proper nouns are less transparent in that respect since they hardly ever take a determiner (although they obviously can), but it is nevertheless reasonable to assume that they too form a proper NP first and then allow modification by ANS. After all, they can replace full NPs and ANS is just as optional with them. In brief, data like (3.28) make clear that sequences of [DET N SELF] should be analysed as [[DET N] SELF] or simply [NP SELF] and not as [DET [N SELF]].

(3.28) a *queen herself, the queen, the queen herself
        b *examination itself, John's examination, John's examination
           itself

On a more particular level, it turns out that within the framework of Government & Binding, it is not entirely clear whether ANS would be adjoined to N' or to N^{max}. According to Haegeman (1991: 88ff.), adjunction is generally supposed to occur at the level of N' so that an NP like *the queen herself* would be analysed as shown in (3.29a) rather than (3.29b).

(3.29) a [NP the [N' [N queen] herself]]
        b [NP [N' the [N queen]] herself]

To discuss the reasons for such an analysis of adjunction is absolutely beyond the scope of the present investigation, but notice that within the X-bar framework too, ANS would not combine with N^0, but with some N-bar level, which is the level reserved for adjunctions, and that ANS and its head are co-constituents. I would like to stress that the two syntactic analyses differ only in degree and not kind and that the relevant insights can be equally well expressed in either structure. These are technical differences.

Although an analysis according to (3.29a) must seem somewhat counter-intuitive, it nevertheless gains some momentum in view of the DP-hypothesis, i.e. the proposal to analyse determiners as heads and structures like *the queen herself* in the spirit of (3.30), i.e. as Determiner Phrases (cf. Abney 1987). Of course, such reasoning only makes sense on the assumption that ANS must be constructed with a nominal and cannot be adjoined to a DP.

(3.30) [DP the [NP [N queen] herself]]

Radford (1988: 175ff.) analyses adjunction to NPs in roughly the same manner by claiming that 'Adjuncts recursively expand N-bar into N-bar' (p. 193). However, he does not rule out that adjunction to maximal phrases could be possible too (cf. p. 255ff.) particularly in view of examples like (3.31). Given that, semantically speaking, a focus particle like *even* has a lot in common with ANS, adjunction of ANS to N^{max} becomes all the more likely.

(3.31)   a   [NP Even [NP the older residents]] were surprised.
         b   [PP Even [PP right at the top]] life is hard.

To sum up briefly, we have seen so far that ANS and the noun it interacts with form one constituent, that ANS should be analysed as an adjunct and that it always connects to non-minimal nominal projections and, in all likelihood, to maximal projections.

It is also illuminating to observe the behaviour of ANS in constituents in which it is not the only element apart from the head, i.e. constituents in which there are additional adjuncts or even arguments. As already hinted at above, ANS is always restricted to the right-most position in an NP, i.e. it is not allowed for ANS to intervene between the head nominal and arguments or further adjunctions to it.

Primus (1992: 68) makes a similar observation for German *selbst*. Since we parse strings from left to right by default, ANS will, semantically speaking, always connect to the most specific NP. In the case of extra arguments this restriction seems to follow from general principles. Consider (3.32) and (3.33) where ANS modifies a noun taking one and two arguments respectively and is barred from assuming a position immediately after the head or between the two arguments.

(3.32)   a   the examination of the results itself
         b   ??the examination itself of the results

(3.33)   a   the feeding of seeds to birds itself
         b   ??the feeding of seeds itself to birds
         c   ??the feeding itself of seeds to birds

This is plausible in view of the fact that adpositions other than ANS behave in exactly the same manner, cf. (3.34), and the relevant generalisation seems to be that the internal make-up of complex NPs, at least in English and German, obeys the order [head – argument(s) – adjunct(s)].

(3.34)   a   the feeding of seeds to birds in winter
         b   ??the feeding of seeds in winter to birds
         c   ??the feeding in winter of seeds to birds

The very same reason, namely that ANS is restricted to occurring at the right periphery of NPs, explains the distribution of ANS in the following genitive NPs.

(3.35)   John's house itself

(3.36)   a   *John's house himself
         b   *John's himself house
         c   *John himself's house

The picture becomes more interesting when additional adjuncts come into play, i.e. when ANS has to cooperate with expressions of its own status. In environments such as these, it becomes difficult to attribute the necessity of ANS to appear in the right-most position to general syntactic principles, cf. (3.37)–(3.38). Here, we would rather be forced to explain the required sequence on semantic or even pragmatic principles.

(3.37)   a   the opera 'La Traviata' itself, *the opera itself 'La Traviata'
           b   the room underneath the kitchen itself, *the room itself underneath the kitchen

(3.38)   a   Henry the Sixth King of England himself
           b   ??Henry the Sixth himself King of England
           c   ??Henry himself the Sixth King of England

Note in passing that multiple adjunctions other than ANS are far from free to occur in any possible order either, cf. (3.39). It is usually pointed out that locative adjuncts precede temporal adjuncts, cf. Quirk *et al.* (1985), and that, as e.g. in (3.39), an NP must be made more specific strictly proceeding top-down in terms of the information relevant for picking its referent. From this follows what was mentioned above, namely that ANS always combines with the most specific NP, and also that it makes the least relevant contribution with respect to figuring out what the referent of the NP is.

(3.39)   a   Henry the Sixth King of England
           b   ??Henry King of England the Sixth

In point of fact, the only environment in which ANS can overrule this constraint appears to be an NP with a non-restrictive (or non-defining) adjunct. That is, if we change the appositions in (3.37) from restrictive to non-restrictive, ANS can occur next to its head noun, cf. (3.40). Given what we have said so far, the reason for this is plain to see. Non-restrictive adjuncts do not contribute information necessary for the identification of the referent, they are more or less an optional afterthought. In other words, the NP in question is already as specific as it possibly can be and subsequently ANS can modify it.

(3.40)   a   the opera itself, 'La Traviata' I mean
           b   the room itself, you know, the one underneath the kitchen

Exactly the same pattern is observable with restrictive versus non-restrictive relative clauses. The restrictive sentence in (3.41) is fully acceptable only with ANS in right-most position. In the non-restrictive context of (3.42), however, ANS is only acceptable adjacent to the noun.

(3.41) a the man (that) you met himself
        b ??the man himself (that) you met

(3.42) The president himself, who was considered the most likely to veto a tax increase, proposed to put up an entirely new tax instead.

In this respect, restrictive relative clauses behave in the same manner as complement clauses, as (3.43) makes clear. Both help to identify a referent more precisely.

(3.43) a the belief that linguistics is easy itself
        b ??the belief itself that linguistics is easy

The final question must necessarily concern the categorial status of the constituent that results out of adjunction of ANS to an NP. Although it must seem fairly obvious that the arising constituent is also an NP and that ANS therefore must be regarded as an endocentric expansion of the NP it modifies, we will nevertheless present and discuss a few arguments to that effect. After all, adjunction can hardly result in an exocentric structure.

First of all, let us assume that there is a principle in grammar which tries to minimise the categories necessary. Then it becomes reasonable to regard the string *Kate herself* in (3.44a) as an NP because otherwise we would be forced to invent a new category, i.e. for reasons of economy it seems a safe choice to replace the question mark in (3.44a) by 'NP'.

(3.44) a [? Kate herself] seemed somewhat nonplussed.
        b [? Kate herself] opened the window.

Also, many verbs assign a unique thematic role to their arguments or, viewed from the opposite perspective, accept only arguments, i.e. ultimately referents, which fulfil specific semantic requirements, e.g. transitive *open* expects an agent in subject position. Since ANS by and large does not interfere with the referential properties of NPs, i.e. they still pick the same referent whether they are modified by ANS or not, it does not seem justified to invent a new category for an expression which essentially does the same as an ordinary NP. *Open* in (3.44b) is perfectly satisfied with the modified NP and hence there is no reason to keep the question mark.[2]

But apart from considerations appealing to common sense and plausibility, there is also some hard evidence in favour of an analysis which classifies NPs modified by ANS as endocentric structures. Notice, for instance, that such NPs readily coordinate with unmodified NPs which, on the assumption that only constituents of the same category may be coordinated, immediately leads to the conclusion that sequences of [NP SELF] are to be analysed as NPs, cf. Jacobs (1983, 1986), Kowalski (1992).

(3.45) a ... the signal itself, and the integral of the signal give
        sufficient control. [LOB]
     b Dr. Watson and even Sherlock Holmes himself thought that
        it was the cry of a hound.
     c B lies between C and A itself.

Moreover, the option to use [NP SELF] as a PP complement would be sufficient in itself to prove that it is an endocentric NP. The relevant assumption
here is that PPs take NPs as their complements. Since we have already shown
that [NP SELF] must be analysed as one constituent, there is no other
conclusion possible.

(3.46) a I'd rather we met in [NP Rio itself].
     b I saw him in front of [NP the station itself].

Let us now consider the semantic restriction mentioned above, namely
that the grammaticality of the sequence [DET N SELF] strongly depends on
the kind of determiner involved, and see whether it can be integrated into
the model of ANS we have built up so far. As a rule, ANS interacts well with
nouns preceded by a definite determiner, i.e. with definite NPs, whereas it is
distinctly odd with indefinite NPs, i.e. those nouns converted to an NP by
an indefinite determiner, cf. (3.47).

(3.47) *A chieftain himself would not lead the onslaught.

Just as there are two sources for definite NPs, namely proper nouns
provided directly by the lexicon and those produced by preposing a definite
determiner (article, demonstrative) to a common noun, we have exactly the
same two options for the production of indefinite NPs. On the one hand, an
indefinite determiner, such as the indefinite article, may be put in front of a
noun, cf. (3.47), or, on the other hand, the lexicon itself already offers a
number of expressions, as e.g. indefinite pronouns, cf. (3.48).

(3.48) *Someone/*anyone/*nobody himself would know the answer.

Although it would now be possible to postulate a syntactic restriction to
the effect that modification of an NP by ANS is ruled out if the NP is
headed by an indefinite determiner, such a rule would be inadequate since
the restriction is most certainly semantic in nature. The advantage of
explaining the distributional facts observed on the basis of a semantic restriction lies in the simple fact that it covers the two types of definite and indefinite NPs at the same time, i.e. it would also account for the contrast
between proper nouns and indefinite pronouns.

It is noteworthy at this point that ANS is equally ungrammatical with
quantified NPs as well as with interrogative pronouns, an explanation of
which has to be postponed for the time being:

(3.49)   *Some/*many/*all presidents themselves were uneasy about the contract.

(3.50)   *Who/*which president himself came?

That the compatibility of ANS with definite but not with indefinite NPs is due to semantic and not syntactic restrictions becomes apparent as soon as we look at some more data involving indefinite NPs. What is striking about them is that, under certain conditions, even they can function as a proper head for ANS, cf. (3.51), which is taken from Edmondson and Plank (1978: 381). In brief, ANS with the indefinite NP *a Cretan* is possible in (3.51) because this NP allows for a specific interpretation. This and related issues will be discussed in detail in section 6.3.

(3.51)   A: All Cretans lie.
         B: Where did you hear that?
         A: A Cretan himself told me.

That ANS, generally speaking, disfavours interaction with indefinite NPs is probably the reason why the indefinite intensifier *oneself* hardly ever finds application as ANS. There is only one possible head imaginable for *oneself* and this is the indefinite pronoun *one* which *grosso modo* has the same status as *someone* or *anyone* in (3.48) and nearly always comes in an unspecific interpretation, cf. (3.52a) in contrast to the well-formed instance of AVS in (3.52b).

(3.52)   a ??One oneself would like to know the answer.
         b One would like to know the answer oneself.

There is only one example of the sequence *one oneself* in the entire British National Corpus (BNC), and in this case, *one* appears to require a specific interpretation, cf. (3.53).

(3.53)   That is to say they constructed a picture of the world, a picture which one oneself no longer believes to be viable. [BNC]

Interestingly enough, what is almost impossible in English turns out to be a valid option in German. Here, the equivalent to E. *one* – *man* – can be intensified, in subject position (3.54) as well as in object position (3.55). However, G. *man* is much more likely to receive a specific interpretation than E. *one*.

(3.54)   Man selbst kann da nur schweigen.
         'All one can do is keep oneself quiet.'

(3.55)   Schließlich könnte der Vorfall problematisch für einen selbst werden.
'Finally, the incident could turn out to be a problem for oneself.'

(3.51) is certainly not the only example showing that adequately tailored context can do a lot to increase the acceptability of certain sentences containing ANS. It is an example of context forcing an exception to the possible rule that ANS is compatible with definite but not with indefinite NPs. The opposite scenario is possible too. Although demonstrative NPs are prototypical definite descriptions, they show some, if not even strong resistance to modification by ANS (3.56a), unless appropriate context is supplied (3.56b).

(3.56)   a   ?I phoned this man himself.
         b   Phone his secretary! There is no point in phoning this man himself.

The lesson to be learnt from the above examples is that grammar ought not to be burdened with a rule which allows strings such as [the NP SELF], but excludes [a NP SELF]. The way to avoid this crude syntactic approach is to attach a semantic feature, say [+DEF], to ANS and to the NP it is going to modify and to make sure that the two features can be checked for compatibility, i.e. that they can match.

Let me briefly summarise the main points. We started out by investigating whether ANS and the NP it modifies form one constituent and found overwhelming evidence for answering this in the affirmative. Next, we asked if ANS could possibly be an argument to that NP, but had to reject that idea and settle for an adjunct analysis. It also turned out that ANS never connects to the nominal as it is supplied by the lexicon. Put in terms of a widely used syntactic theory, this translates as adjunction to a nominal category other than N^0, i.e. to one of the higher projections of the nominal base form.

The subsequent discussion concerned the position of ANS in complex NPs, i.e. NPs containing arguments and/or additional adjuncts. What we have found is that ANS obeys a very simple syntactic rule: it is always the right-most adjunction to an NP. Next, we were interested in the category emerging from the adjunction of ANS to an NP. This question is almost superfluous because adjuncts are by definition prohibited from forming exocentric structures or even projecting their own category, but still, there are tests to show that ANS and its co-constituent form an endocentric NP.

Finally, we explored the incompatibility of ANS with indefinite NPs and decided that it was better to regard it as a semantic restriction which, nevertheless, can and probably should be represented in syntax, namely as the feature [+DEF].

These basic properties apply to both English and German and, in all likelihood, to many other languages. Figure 3.1 reflects these findings.

```
              NP₂
             /  \
            /    \
          NP₁     \
          / \      \
         /   \      \
       the  president  himself
```

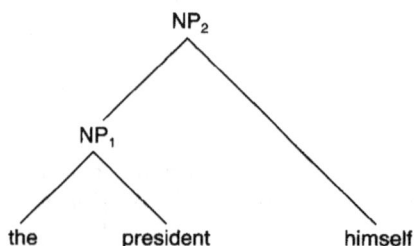

Figure 3.1 Adnominal SELF.

Note that in this syntactic structure ANS c-commands its head so that an analysis as a focus particle is not obstructed on the part of syntax. Focus particles are generally assumed to c-command their focus, cf. e.g. König (1991: 23).

3.1.2 Syntactic restrictions

Let us now come to a discussion of what is, syntactically speaking, possible and impossible in the case of ANS beyond what has been stated so far. This is also the place to review some English-German differences.

Topicalisation (Dislocation)

The first issue to be drawn attention to in this context is that ANS allows for more positional variability than so far admitted, i.e. there are fewer syntactic restrictions than previously assumed. Up to now, we have taken for granted that ANS always occurs right-adjacent to its head or at the right-most periphery of the relevant phrase. However, on closer scrutiny it turns out that it can be dislocated to its left as well as further to its right in a well-defined manner.

As for left-dislocation, ANS may be placed in sentence-initial position, a process which is often referred to as topicalisation. Regarding right-dislocation, the relevant restriction is that ANS may not occur further to the right than behind the finite verb.

(3.57)   a I myself had no clue at all.
         b Myself, I had no clue at all.
         c I had myself no clue at all.

A question that immediately comes to mind, of course, is what makes it possible to regard occurrences of intensifiers which are disconnected from their head as instances of ANS. After all, they could just as well be examples of AVS or something entirely different. The claim is that all the sentences in

(3.57) have the same meaning, i.e. they are freely interchangeable in one and the same context. Take e.g. context like (3.58) and it becomes apparent that a continuation with any sentence of (3.57) is possible.

(3.58) a My brother would have known the answer to such a difficult question.
        b John had already heard that Mary was going to marry.

This claim, however, is linked to a crucial precondition. Dislocation is possible only under double focusing which splits the sentences in question up into two tone groups (the tonality in the sense of Halliday (1966) is increased by one). In (3.59) capitalisation indicates focusing and the double slash marks the beginning of a new tone group.

(3.59) a MySELF // I had no clue at ALL.
        b I had mySELF // no clue at ALL.

If this condition is not satisfied, topicalised, i.e. left-dislocated SELF, becomes ungrammatical, cf. (3.60a), whereas post-finite SELF in (3.60b) must be interpreted as adverbal inclusive.

(3.60) a *MySELF I had no clue at all.
        b I had mySELF no clue at all.

It is important to realise that already the original sentence, from which a version containing topicalised ANS is to be produced, must possess a double focus structure, cf. the contrast between (3.61) and (3.62). Roughly, (3.61a) means that somebody else or even a certain set of people apart from the person referred to by *I* were surprised at the new figures, but (3.62a) stresses that whereas *I* was surprised at the new figures, somebody else was surprised at some other figures, most likely the old ones. Indeed, we are here confronted with two slightly different uses of ANS. Only the latter use allows for topicalisation and dislocation in general.

(3.61) a I mySELF was surprised at the new figures.
        b *MySELF I was surprised at the new figures.

(3.62) a I mySELF was surprised at the NEW figures. ≠ (3.61a)
        b MySELF // I was surprised at the NEW figures.

Examples like (3.59b) and (3.60b) are further evidence in support of the hypothesis expressed in König (1991: 48) that 'the scope of a particle in English is co-extensive with the tone group containing it'. The contrast is repeated in (3.63) below. If two tone groups are present as in (3.63a), the intensifier has narrow scope which results in ANS; in case there is only one as exemplified in (3.63b), it takes wide scope, and this produces inclusive AVS. Put differently, the division of a sentence into tone groups (tonality) serves as an indicator of relative scope. Notice, however, that this analysis is at variance with the observation that ANS within one tone group does not take scope over the entire tone group. Various semantic facts indicate that the scope of ANS is always confined to its head NP.

> (3.63)   a   I had mySELF // no clue at ALL.
>   b   I had mySELF no clue at all.

Interestingly enough, topicalisation of ANS in English seems to be restricted to the first person singular, cf. (3.64). By and large, native speakers tend to reject topicalisations in the context of the remaining person/number combinations.

> (3.64)   a   Myself, I come from Stockholm.
>   b   ?Yourself, you come from Stockholm.
>   c   ?Himself, he comes from Stockholm.

Nevertheless, in the literature on intensifiers, we can every now and again encounter an example of topicalised *himself.* (3.65a) is taken from Edmondson and Plank (1978: 375), (3.65b) from Dirven (1973: 298).

> (3.65)   a   Himself he favours a more step-by-step approach to the theory of understanding.
>   b   Himself he defended brilliantly.

This is certainly a point corpus linguistics can help to clear up because these examples contain relatively straightforward search patterns. A systematic look into these texts confirms the native speakers' intuitions, cf. Table 3.1. Within the BNC, which is the only corpus of reasonable size to settle this question, topicalised *myself* outnumbers the remaining singular forms almost by factor five. The other corpora do not allow for such a comparison because they do not contain topicalised *yourself, himself* or *herself,* apart from one occurrence in the Longman/Lancaster Corpus (LLC). *Myself,* however, is always represented.

(3.66) through (3.68) give the rare topicalisations to be found in the BNC, (3.69) the one occurrence present in LLC; all examples are supplied with some context (two preceding sentences). Neither the Brown Corpus nor the Corpus of English Conversation (CONV) contains examples of topicalisations. Topicalised ANS in the plural does not appear to exist.

> (3.66)   You're actually cleaning the run up. It's clean, it's spotless. Yourself, you've done it all yourself after nagging about five years. [BNC]

Table 3.1 The distribution of topicalised x-*self*

Topicalised x-*self*	LOB	LLC	BNC	TIMES	IDP
Myself	1	2	27	11	4
Yourself	0	0	1	0	0
Himself	0	1	4	0	0
Herself	0	0	1	0	0

(3.67) a Mr Hughes's mother was a suffragette. His wife's grand-father helped found the ILP (Independent Labour Party) in 1893. Himself, he was a railwayman who travelled all over the country, campaigned in more than 20 constituencies and was elected a Labour councillor in three towns. [BNC]

b Gary was as frightened as the horse. Hoomey thought he could easily start frothing at the mouth, the way his colour had drained. Himself, he felt better and better. [BNC]

c It was grey daylight when they crossed the moat of the Château Franc and besides himself only Astorre, Nicholas saw, had tried to keep the iron back and square shoulders of duty. Astorre, because he was content under orders. Himself, because alone of them all, he knew what he was committed to. [BNC]

d Even so, the way they had just accepted their deaths made him feel odd. It wasn't that he felt pity for them; far from it – their passivity revolted him. Himself, he would have died fighting for his life, clawing and scratching his way out of existence. [BNC]

(3.68) It became mingled with the tales of a folk who lived in the east of your world; they called it Adam's Paradise. Jake turned and looked urgently at his son; but Adam's gaze had fallen back to Undry, and Ruth wasn't sure he'd heard. Herself, she felt only the irony; hell was nearer Adam's experience than paradise. [BNC]

(3.69) And the priest came round with the collecting bag taking their centavos, abusing them for their small comforting sins, and sacrificing nothing at all in return – except a little sexual indulgence. And that was easy, the lieutenant thought, easy. Himself he felt no need of women. [LLC]

As far as the remaining five person/number combinations apart from *myself* are concerned, a means for topicalising these occurrences of ANS lies in the application of complex prepositions such as *as for, regarding,*

concerning, as far as x is concerned, etc., cf. (3.70) below. Since these prepositions are often viewed as devices to mark a topic, cf. Molnár (1991: 43ff.), it
becomes a tempting idea to try to analyse part of the functionality of ANS
as a topic marker. This could turn out to be a particularly valid approach for
German since here, topicalisation is restricted neither by person nor by
number (cf. König and Siemund 1999a).

(3.70)   a   Without giving her an opportunity to reply, she went on, 'As
             for yourself, I have the most splendid notion!' [BNC]
         b   As for himself, he was sorry she was upset – and also, if
             he was honest, a little irritated too, because the crisis had
             wrecked his plans for the morning. [BNC]
         c   As for herself – she had enjoyed the feel of his arms about
             her. [BNC]

In German, topicalisation goes hand in hand with an inversion of subject
and finite verb because it is a true V2 language, whereas English is not.
Nevertheless, both languages share the restriction on the double focus:

(3.71)   a   SELBST fand er das Buch NICHT langweilig.
             'Himself, he didn't find the book boring.'
         b   *SELBST fand er das Buch nicht langweilig.

Having seen to which positions ANS can be dislocated (sentence-initial,
post-finite) and what additional constraints are valid for these processes
(double focus, two tone groups), the next appropriate step is to ask whether
dislocation is possible from all positions in a clause or whether there are
restrictions to be found in that area too. Remember that ANS can modify
NPs in subject as well as in object position and that those contained within
PPs, no matter whether the latter are arguments or adjuncts, do not block
modification either. Dislocation, however, is only possible from an NP in
subject position. This restriction is valid for both English and German. Any
attempt to dislocate ANS, say, from object position or from within an adverbial, will not yield the desired interpretation and may even lead to ungrammaticality.

(3.72)   a   Mary would never dare to ask the chancellor himself.
         b   *Himself, Mary would never dare to ask the chancellor.

(3.73)   a   I caught him in the garage itself.
         b   *Itself, I caught him in the garage.

Due to the fact that English intensifiers agree with their head in person,
number and gender, such properties quickly come to light in that language.
German, by contrast, offers no such clear clues. Still, judged by the meaning
of the relevant sentences, it becomes clear that *selbst* in (3.74) is in associa-

tion with the NP inside the adverbial whereas dislocation in (3.75) forces interaction with the subject NP (cf. König and Siemund 1996a: 8).[3]

(3.74)   Am Hochzeitstag SELBST // hatte ich KEINE Zeit.
'On the wedding day itself I was not free.'

(3.75)   a SELBST // hatte ich am Hochzeitstag KEINE Zeit. ≠ (3.74)
         b Am Hochzeitstag hatte ich SELBST // KEINE Zeit. ≠ (3.74)
         'I myself was not free on the wedding day.'

The same pattern can be found when dislocating *selbst* from an object NP, cf.:

(3.76)   Den Parteichef SELBST // habe ich NICHT getroffen.
'I did not meet the party leader himself.'

(3.77)   a SELBST // habe ich den Parteichef NICHT getroffen. ≠
         (3.76)
         b Den Parteichef habe ich SELBST // NICHT getroffen. ≠
         (3.76)
         'I myself did not meet the party leader.'

Whereas English and German intensifiers behave very much alike as far as dislocation is concerned, there are also several areas where the usage of the intensifier differs substantially between the two languages. Among other things, these differences can result from the fact that English intensifiers inflect for person, number and gender whereas German intensifiers do not show agreement with their head. The ϕ-features present on English intensifiers allow, for instance, to disambiguate the NP with which the intensifier is in association in case complex NPs are intensified, i.e. NPs which are built up from two or more simplex NPs. To give an example, in sequences of the form [NP PP NP SELF], ANS can potentially be adjoined to either the entire NP, i.e. [NP PP NP] or only to some part of it, i.e. the second NP (not the first, though, due to the right-periphery constraint). In (3.78a) below, ANS modifies the NP *the king* whereas it is adjoined to *the crown of the king* in (3.78b).

(3.78)   a [the crown [of [the king himself]]]
         b [[the crown of the king] itself]

(3.79) provides an example of a complex NP consisting of three simplex NPs. Even here, English can neatly disambiguate the NP being modified by ANS:

(3.79)   a the duties of the mayor of London itself
         b the duties of the mayor of London himself
         c the duties of the mayor of London themselves

This entails the question of how complex NPs can possibly be in order to allow complete disambiguation of the head NP of ANS. In theory, it should seem possible to successfully disambiguate sequences of up to eight NPs. After all, there are eight different forms at our disposal (three persons + two numbers + three genders). However, in practice such NPs will rarely occur and it turns out to be relatively difficult to even invent such NPs for the sake of the argument. Let us therefore be content with four NPs, but, as (3.80) shows, the additional gender distinction can be easily made clear.

(3.80)   the duties of the wife of the mayor of London herself

Uninflecting G. *selbst*, by comparison, must remain vague with regard to these distinctions. In (3.81), which is the translation of (3.80), it can be in association with any of the four NPs present and there is no way to clear this situation up.

(3.81)   die Pflichten der Frau des Bürgermeisters von London selbst

Another differentiation that can be made in English (mainly British English) on the basis of the ϕ-features present is the following. It is a well-known fact that English possesses a class of singular nouns denoting sets of entities which are ambiguous between a collective, i.e. a singular interpretation and a distributive, i.e. a plural interpretation. Nouns such as *public, audience, family, police*, etc. may either denote the entire set and refer to the group as a whole, i.e. the collective body of people – then they are, semantically speaking, in the singular, or may receive an interpretation which stresses the existence of a set with more than one element – then they are in the plural.

ANS can also modify these nouns. Depending on which interpretation is desired, it will appear either in the singular or plural, cf. the difference between (3.82) and (3.83).[4]

(3.82)   a The public itself consists of you and me.
          b The audience itself is enormous.

(3.83)   a The public themselves are tired of demonstrations.
          b The audience themselves were enjoying every minute of it.

The following example shows an authentic minimal pair:

(3.84)   a Sometimes they are better equipped than the police itself
             and have good connections with the West. [BNC]
          b Operating as a one man police force in fact if not in name,
             he is at once more independent and more dedicated than
             the police themselves. [BROWN]

ANS can also be encountered in identity statements of the form 'X is Y x-*self*'. Here, a minor difference between English and German can be observed. Whereas German needs the definite article in front of the noun ANS interacts with, English can dispense with it. One might wonder whether the pronominal part of English x-*self* supplies the necessary definiteness.

(3.85) a Maria was innocence itself.
        b Maria war die Unschuld selbst.

A further important point in which English and German differ is that the former collapses intensifier and reflexive anaphor in one form whereas the latter separates the two expressions neatly. This not only leads to problems when we translate intensifiers from the one language to the other, it also entails genuine syntactic restrictions in English.

First of all, there is a certain chance to mistake the reflexive for the emphatic in case it is dislocated behind the finite verb. Put differently, in positions in which reflexive and intensifier compete with one another, the reflexive appears to win out. Note, that this remark pertains to relative positions within a string, not to structural positions. Reflexive and intensifier never compete for structural positions. Such a scenario is very likely to occur with optionally transitive/ditransitive verbs, cf. (3.86). Here, it is almost impossible to interpret SELF as modifying the subject NP, even under double focus; the sentence says rather that the subject referent is sender and recipient of the postcard at the same time, i.e. SELF is understood as the reflexive.

(3.86)   She wrote herself // only a postcard

The reflexive interpretation becomes unavoidable with semantically transitive verbs as e.g. *dress, shower* and *shave*, i.e. the verbs of grooming. However heavily *herself* is stressed in (3.87a), it will reject being squeezed into an interpretation equivalent to (3.87b), even if adequate context is provided to bring about the desired reading. Interpreted within the context of (3.88), (3.87a) clearly is an inadequate continuation whereas (3.87b) poses no problems whatsoever.

(3.87)   a She showers herSELF // only in the MORning.
         b She herSELF // showers only in the MORning.

(3.88)   Her DAUGHter showers twice a DAY.

As soon as context is supplied which allows for the reflexive reading, (3.87a) immediately becomes felicitous. Still, the reflexive appears to be intensified, which is a point we will be discussing shortly.

(3.89)   She showers her daughter twice a day. But she showers herself only in the morning.

As for German, no such problems exist. (3.90a) is equivalent to (3.90b) and both are adequate translations of (3.87b). The intensified reflexive reading given in (3.89) must be rendered with *sich selbst*, cf. (3.90c).

(3.90)   a   Sie selbst // badet nur am Vormittag.
          b   Sie badet selbst // nur am Vormittag. = (3.90a)
          c   Sie badet sich selbst // nur am Vormittag.

Having mentioned optionally transitive/ditransitive verbs, verbs of ingestion such as *eat* and *drink* form a subclass of that group which is semantically totally incompatible with reflexives, cf. (3.91). The ungrammaticality of (3.91b) again underlines that ANS cannot be dislocated behind the finite verb when competing with the reflexive.

(3.91)   a   She eats an apple/drinks a coke.
          b   *She eats/drinks herself.

However, filling the only available argument slot with a referential NP while dislocating ANS behind the verb may slightly improve things. It is now possible to understand *herself* in (3.92a) as the intensifier although it needs a lot of effort and native speakers tend not to like it. Again, this is no problem for German as (3.92b) makes clear. The reason, of course, is the availability of the independent form *selbst* which will not be understood in a reflexive sense.

(3.92)   a   She eats herself // only fish.
          b   Sie ißt selbst // nur Fisch.

Interaction with pronouns

Another restriction of the English language that appears to be due to the formal equivalence of reflexive and intensifier concerns the intensification of reflexives. Any such attempt results in blatant ungrammaticality, cf. (3.93).

(3.93)   a   *John has dressed [himself himself].
          b   *He has seen [himself himself] in the mirror.
          c   *Jack has tried to kill [himself himself].

It is also worth pointing out that it is not the occurrence of the same form twice that makes these examples corrupt. The intensifier reading of the second x-*self* is available, however, not as ANS modifying the reflexive. (3.93) can be made grammatical, though not perfectly felicitous, if the latter x-*self* is understood as modifying the VP, i.e. as AVS, cf. (3.94). This seems to point to the conclusion that (3.93) is not barred on phonological grounds.

(3.94)   a ??John has dressed [himself] himself$_{exclusive}$.
            b ??He has seen [himself] himself$_{inclusive}$ in the mirror.
            c ??Jack has tried to kill [himself] himself$_{inclusive/exclusive}$.

The strategy English applies to resolve the restriction on intensifying reflexives is to make do with one occurrence of x-*self* only, but to pronounce it in a slightly different fashion, namely by putting heavy stress on *self*. Normally, reflexive anaphors come unstressed so that the difference between a simple reflexive and an intensified reflexive is visible on the level of phonology. However, the different stress pattern entails a sharp semantic contrast: only the b-sentences in (3.95) to (3.97) evoke a contrast with another referent which is one of the essential contributions of ANS. (3.95a) needs no reflexive because *dress* belongs to the verbs of grooming.

(3.95)   a John has DRESSED.
            b John has dressed himSELF.

(3.96)   a He has seen himself in the MIRror.
            b He has seen himSELF in the mirror.

(3.97)   a Jack has tried to KILL himself.
            b Jack has tried to kill himSELF.

Cantrall (1973b) draws a distinction between what we have so far referred to as ANS and the use of x-*self* depicted in (3.95b) through (3.97b). The former he labels 'intensive pronouns' whereas the latter runs under the name 'emphatic reflexive'. The problem with (3.95b) to (3.97b) is that it is not entirely clear whether x-*self* is a reflexive, an intensifier or something in between. Cantrall decides in favour of the latter option which increases the stock of necessary lexical categories because a hybrid is acknowledged. From my perspective, such a distinction is unnecessary and the coming section will provide some arguments for analysing x-*self* in environments like (3.95b) to (3.97b) as instances of ANS albeit with an invisible or covert head.

The question that remains to be answered is why exactly intensification of reflexives is barred in English. One option seems to be to hinge the restriction to principles of language economy. If there are two formally equivalent expressions which are supposed to occur together, but one of them can take over the workload of both, there is then no need to use two. But why should one of them be sufficient?

What the reflexive does is to indicate co-reference with another NP, its antecedent as it were. One possible way to analyse the reflexive would be to say that the pronominal part of x-*self* traces the antecedent whereas *self* functions as a restrictor on the domain in which the antecedent can be found. Since the intensifier contains both these elements, it can trace the antecedent successfully on its own and hence the reflexive can be dropped. Note that the intensifier could not be dropped in favour of the reflexive because it contains one additional specification: it is stressed.

As for German, no such considerations are necessary. Since reflexives and intensifiers are, with regard to their form, neatly separated, it can never become a problem to establish which is which and, what is more, ANS readily modifies the reflexive. There can be no reason to look for a hybrid in German. (3.98) gives the translations of the intended interpretations of (3.93).

(3.98)   a John hat [sich selbst] angezogen.
          b Er hat [sich selbst] im Spiegel gesehen.
          c Jack hat versucht, [sich selbst] umzubringen.

Note in passing that intensification of the G. reflexive *sich* is only possible in those cases in which it has a truly referential function. When being used as an intransitiviser, modification by ANS is barred and under that reading, the examples given in (3.99) are clearly out. Again, (3.99a,b) can be made sense of if the intensifier is read as AVS, but for (3.99c) even that escape hatch is closed for reasons to be discussed in the chapters on semantics.

(3.99)   a *Paul schämt [sich selbst].
             'Paul is ashamed of himself.'
          b *Elly dreht [sich selbst] im Kreis.
             'Elly is spinning around.'
          c *Das Fenster öffnete [sich selbst].
             'The window opened.'

A third factor leading to differences in the distribution of English and German intensifiers consists in the fact that the former are complex expressions made up of a pronominal part and *self*. Section 2.5 showed that Modern English intensifiers are the product of a fusion process between pronouns on the one hand and the simplex intensifier *self* on the other. German, by contrast, did not replace its original intensifier. The pronominal part of the intensifier appears to account for why there is a tendency in English to avoid sequences of pronoun plus x-*self* in positions other than subject. This applies particularly to those sequences which contain the same substring twice, i.e. *him himself, her herself, it itself* and *them themselves*. ANS modifying these pronouns is often felt as ill-formed and some speakers reject it entirely. Note that it does not matter whether the relevant pronouns are used in a referentially dependent or independent interpretation.

(3.100) a She herself found the task problematic.
       b *I met [her herself] at the party.

(3.101) a He himself doesn't know.
       b *I would like to talk to [him himself].

(3.102) a The bank punished its clients for what [it itself] required of
         them.
       b *Then he opened [it itself].

(3.103) a They sell wine which [they themselves] would never touch.
       b *He bought the new toys for [them themselves].

The relevant questions to be asked in this context are first, which means English provides to remedy this deadlock, i.e. which alternative constructions it offers instead of intensified object pronouns, and second, why precisely it is the case that object pronouns block intensification.

As for the first question, note first of all that it is not possible to copy the strategy we applied to intensified reflexives, i.e. to simply leave out the pronoun. This results in a constellation most native speakers of English reject, cf. (3.104) below.

(3.104) a *I met herself at the party.
       b *I would like to talk to himself.
       c *Then he opened itself.
       d *He bought the new toys for themselves.

This problem can be circumvented by substituting the object pronouns involved with referentially unspecified full NPs as e.g. *man, lady, children, boys, girls, thing,* etc. Since these NPs may be regarded as behaving, semantically speaking, very much like anaphoric expressions in that they need a proper antecedent or a narrow enough universe of discourse in order to resolve their reference, they can be used to replace the pronouns without adding too much further information. (3.105) shows how that would look.

(3.105) a I met the lady herself at the party.
       b I would like to talk to the man himself.
       c Then he opened the thing itself.
       d He bought the new toys for the boys themselves.

The German intensifier, by contrast, has not fused with object pronouns and hence there is no problem in modifying them. (3.106) gives the translations of (3.100b) through (3.103b).

(3.106) a Ich habe [sie selbst] auf der Party getroffen.

    b Ich würde gern mit [ihm selbst] sprechen.
    c Dann öffnete er [es selbst].
    d Er hat die neuen Spielsachen für [sie selbst] gekauft.

However, this difference between English and German is not as clear-cut as it is presented here. Whereas the situation in German is entirely undisputed, native speakers of English do not judge unanimously on this point. On the one hand, McDaniel and Battistella (1986), Bickerton (1987) and Keenan (1993) assert that sequences such as *him himself* in (3.101b) are ungrammatical. McKay (1991), on the other hand, judges them as correct. Moreover, even Bickerton points out in a footnote (2) that in contexts forcing a very strong contrast, *him himself* sounds correct to some speakers, cf. (3.107). It can be shown that there are points in favour of either view, but that the general strategy of English is to avoid such sequences.

    (3.107) A: Did you see Bill's secretary?
             B: No, I saw him himself.

As a matter of fact, the ungrammaticality of intensified object pronouns is only a minor issue in Bickerton's analysis of intensified pronouns in general. The point Bickerton tries to make is that sequences of pronoun plus adnominal intensifier as, e.g. *he himself, him himself,* etc., are a special type of anaphoric expression so far undiscovered. However, these would-be anaphoric expressions possess properties which make them difficult to subsume under either of the established groups, anaphors or pronominals. Let us briefly review his main points.

In the same way as pronominals, *he himself* does not require its antecedent to c-command it (3.108a) and, what is more, it can even take an antecedent outside the sentence it occurs in (3.108b).

    (3.108) a Explaining what John$_i$ really believes is something that [he himself]$_i$ can't always do.
             b A: How will Mary$_i$ do in the exam? – B: I don't know, but [she herself]$_i$ says she'll pass.

As far as anaphors are concerned, Bickerton claims that *he himself* could be analysed as one because if there is a possible c-commanding antecedent in the sentence, *he himself* must be bound by it and cannot find a non-c-commanding antecedent elsewhere, neither in the same sentence nor in the discourse:

    (3.109) a Susan$_i$ told everyone who knew Mary$_j$ that she$_{i/j}$/[she herself]$_{i/*j}$ was pregnant.
             b A: How will Mary$_i$ do in the exam? – B: I don't know, but Susan$_j$ says that she$_{i/j}$/[she herself]$_{*i/j}$ will pass.

What sets *he himself* apart from pronominals on the one hand and anaphors on the other is that its occurrence is restricted to positions in which it is nominatively case-marked. This would be the explanation for why examples (3.100b) to (3.103b) are ill-formed. Bickerton makes this point with the following constructions:

(3.110) a *John believes he himself to be in danger.
    b *John believes him himself to be in danger.
    c John believes that he himself is in danger.

McKay (1991) strongly opposes Bickerton's view that *he himself* must be analysed as an anaphoric expression in its own right. He can see no convincing evidence for doubting our natural understanding of *he himself* as a pronoun modified by an apposition. In particular, he shows that Bickerton is wrong in assuming that if there is a c-commanding antecedent for *he himself*, it also must be bound by it. In the following example, *she herself* may be co-referential with either Ann or Joan, i.e. with regard to the Binding Theory, it rather behaves like a pronominal and not like an anaphor. This, however, should be expected as long as sequences like *she herself* are analysed as instances of pronominal modification by ANS.

(3.111) Ann$_i$ wants to interview the winner. Joan$_j$ believes that [she herself]$_{i/j}$ will win.

Also, McKay manages to show that Bickerton makes too strong a claim for his own examples. As for (3.109), it is by no means adequate to say that *she herself* cannot find an antecedent other than the one c-commanding it. A little more context helps to clear this point up, cf. (3.112).

(3.112) a Mary$_k$ always lectured at the pregnant girls. Susan$_i$ did something to get even. Susan$_i$ told everyone who knew Mary$_k$ that [she herself]$_k$ was pregnant.
    b A: Mary$_i$ has been concerned about her friends. Susan$_k$ said that several were going to fail the course, and Susan$_k$ might be right. But Mary$_i$ should think more about her$_i$ own work. How will Mary$_i$ do on the exam? – B: I don't know, but Susan$_k$ says that she$_i$ (she$_k$) (she herself$_i$) (she herself$_k$) will pass.

However, assuming such an analysis leaves McKay with the same problem we started out from and are still confronted with, namely to explain why sequences such as *him himself* and *her herself* are felt to be ill-formed. Here, two things have to be borne in mind. First, these sequences are not entirely ruled out. Bickerton cites a possible exception (3.107) and McKay even goes a step further claiming that the grammaticality of *him himself* is simply a matter of adequate context. In particular, he proposes that wherever *him* as well as *himself* are grammatical so will be *him himself*:

(3.113) a John thinks that Mary is taller than him.
          b John thinks that Mary is taller than himself.
          c John thinks that Mary is taller than him himself.

He concedes that not everybody will find such examples acceptable at first sight, but has the impression that they increase the more the context is extended. And indeed, (3.114b) seems easier to make sense of in the context of (3.114a).

(3.114) a Rupert was concerned about his students, and so wanted Peter to think well of them.
          b But Rupert was not unduly worried about Peter's opinion of him himself.[5]

Second, it is not only *him himself* and *her herself* that pose problems. As was shown above, similar restrictions hold for *it itself* and *them themselves*, but also the remaining object pronouns are not straightforwardly intensified by ANS, cf. (3.115). Notice that native speakers judge the second persons slightly better than the rest.

(3.115) a ???Why didn't you phone me myself?
          b ??I sent the letter to you yourself.
          c ???He insulted us ourselves.
          d ??I would like to invite you yourselves too.

What makes the situation complicated is that native speakers of English have extreme difficulty assessing the acceptability of these sentences. As a rule, examples like (3.100b)–(3.103b) and also (3.115) are rejected when given to informants as such, but it is also true that well-tailored context can improve things a lot, i.e. McKay seems to be making a valid point.

However, trying to reduce the problem to a matter of context does not seem satisfactory either. After all, even within adequate context, most of the above examples are not fully acceptable to many speakers. Let us therefore have a look at the distribution of intensified subject pronouns versus intensified object pronouns in the corpora available. Table 3.2 provides a brief overview.

It is clear that intensified object pronouns are a species which is hard to find indeed. There are no occurrences whatsoever in either BROWN or LOB. Hence there seems to be a problem. Clearly, if the data pool is selected large enough, it is possible to find them; nevertheless, intensified subject pronouns outrank those in object position at least by factor fifty. On average, the figure will be much higher. There are merely two occurrences to be found

Table 3.2 The distribution of intensified pronouns (x-*self*)

x-self	BROWN	LOB	LLC	BNC
Subject	12	22	112	805
Object	0	0	2	3

in LLC and only three within the entire BNC. Let us have a look at these examples before trying to find an explanation for why they are so rare.

(3.116) a Given to us in the eating and drinking of the body and blood, the Spirit makes of us ourselves a spiritual offering, so that we are worthy to render praise and thanksgiving to the Father as a true and acceptable worship. [LLC]

b The first house is concerned with you yourself as a physical entity, your appearance, and your health. [LLC]

(3.117) a And he besought his mother that she would love her even as she loved him himself, and that she would do good to her and show her great honour, for which he should ever serve her with the better good will. [BNC]

b How much better it is when any facts or pieces of information come from you yourself. [BNC]

c Any evidence, whether actual or a product of your subconscious, comes from you yourself and is not simply given to you by another person who might or might not know what he is talking about. [BNC]

In (3.116) and (3.117), we find the following distribution of object pronouns: three in second person singular, one in third person singular and one in first person plural. The distribution found is not particularly illuminating although there might be a point in checking whether there is something to the relative abundance of the second person singular. This could only be done on larger amounts of data which, to my knowledge, do not exist. But even if the second person singular were slightly over-represented, the fairly arbitrary distribution of object pronouns in the examples above seems to indicate that there are no restrictions on which pronouns can potentially be intensified. With the right amount of data at hand, we would probably find the entire paradigm.

Apart from using full NPs instead of pronouns in order to allow for intensification, recall (3.105), a further option is provided by the existence of alternative expressions for the intensifier itself, cf. section 2.3. One way to intensify object pronouns in English is to fall back on the related expression *personally*.

Table 3.3 The distribution of intensified pronouns (personally)

personally	BROWN	LOB	LLC	BNC
Subject	6	9	26	365
Object	5	5	8	173

(3.118) a 'Language', Marx says, 'is as old as consciousness, language is practical consciousness that exists also for other men, and for that reason alone it really exists for me personally as well.' [LLC]

b It was very desirable to take Buonaparte alive, and with as little violence, and even inconvenience to him personally, as possible, but that he was to be taken. [*Economist,* 19 July 1997]

c Mr. Rifkind did not reply to my letter although I addressed it to him personally at the House of Commons. [BNC]

Moreover, intensification of object pronouns by *personally* is no rare phenomenon at all. A comparative search in the corpora available reveals that *personally* is approximately two times as frequent with subject pronouns than with object pronouns.[6] Recall that the relevant factor is well above fifty in the case of x-*self.* Table 3.3 gives the relevant figures.

The following explanation appears feasible for why x-*self* adjoined to object pronouns is so rare. Remember that we tried to motivate the impossibility to intensify English reflexive pronouns on grounds of language economy. We argued that ANS cannot intensify reflexives because the intensifier is able to express co-reference with an antecedent as well as intensification at the same time. Since the specifications of the reflexive (ϕ-features + *self*) are a subset of the specifications of the intensifier (ϕ-features + *self* + stress), the reflexive can be dropped although it seems reasonable to assume that it is merely deleted and that the intensifier is still in association with it.

Similarly, we may argue that English intensifiers can take over the role ordinary pronouns play. After all, their specifications are also properly included within the specifications of the intensifier. In fact, pronouns possess even fewer specifications than reflexives, namely for ϕ-features only, so that it should be even less of a problem for the intensifier to take over their duties. In other words, we will argue that the examples given in (3.100b) to (3.103b) and also those in (3.115) are felt as inadequate because the object pronouns are superfluous. Language economy wants them to be suppressed. This is captured in the following principle Π.

Π If two expressions E_1 and E_2 form a complex expression E_c, and if the semantic features of E_1 are a subset of those of E_2, then E_1 is superfluous and can be dispensed with.[7]

At first sight, such an approach might seem unreasonable because if these pronouns are superfluous, it should be possible to leave them out, and the relevant examples should thereby become grammatical. Although such a strategy worked in the case of reflexives, it is not really applicable here, cf. (3.104) repeated in (3.119) below. Leaving out the pronouns only makes the relevant examples worse and results in clear ungrammaticality. (3.120) illustrates the same point for the remaining person-number combinations.

(3.119) a *I met herself at the party.
b *I would like to talk to himself.
c *Then he opened itself.
d *He bought the new toys for themselves.

(3.120) a *Why didn't you phone myself?
b *I sent the letter to yourself.
c *He insulted ourselves.
d *I would like to invite yourselves too.

The difference between reflexives and object pronouns is that the former indicate co-reference whereas the latter indicate disjoint reference in a local domain. This rule applies with particular force when reflexive and antecedent are co-arguments of one and the same predicator, cf. Reinhart and Reuland (1993: 661). In this position, pronoun and reflexive are not interchangeable. Under intensification this situation is unlikely to change, and when language economy forces the intensified pronouns to be dropped, we are required to interpret the remaining x-*self* as the reflexive and not as the intensifier. However, the reflexive interpretation is barred because there is no valid antecedent available in its domain. Consequently, these examples cannot even change their interpretation and become ungrammatical. If intensification is indispensable, then a full NP or an alternative intensifier must be used as done in (3.105) and (3.118) above.

Note that this behaviour is similar to what we observed with optionally transitive verbs. As far as (internal) argument positions of the matrix verb are concerned, the reflexive reading is the default interpretation for the form x-*self.*

Let me briefly summarise the main points. We have argued that sequences like *him himself, her herself,* etc. are ungrammatical in English because they violate the simple principle of economy that the same information should not be specified twice. Both pronoun and intensifier supply information as to which antecedent to pick and in that respect one of them is superfluous. However, since the goal of combining them in the first place is to intensify the pronoun, it seems reasonable for the latter to be discarded. In addition to that, we have seen that deletion of the pronoun is obstructed in argument positions of the predicator. This is due to the fact that the form x-*self* as an argument of the predicator is interpreted as a reflexive by default.

Another possible line of argumentation could suggest that these sequences are ruled out on phonological grounds. Since the pronoun is fully contained in the intensifier and the two pronouns occur in adjacent position, so the argument could go, the resulting sequence is blocked for reasons of *horror equi*. It should seem imaginable to assume that two equivalent consecutive expressions are reduced due to haplology. However, such an argument can be refuted for at least two reasons. First, it is not always the case that the pronoun is entirely embodied within the intensifier, but strings in object position like *me myself, you yourself, us ourselves* and *you yourselves* are just as rare. And second, it is not the case that the sequences in question could not be encountered. Rather the opposite is the case, cf. (3.121). However, they can, apart from a few exceptions, never be understood as ANS modifying the pronoun. Nearly all of them must be interpreted as instances of adverbal intensifiers.

(3.121) a Ladies and gentlemen, let me myself hazard a guess as to the answer, for such a gentleman capable of the levels of deceit he has displayed over these past days should not be relied upon to provide a truthful reply. (inclusive) [BNC]

b She wanted somehow to have her mother for herself, but only so that she could reject her herself. (inclusive, exclusive) [BNC]

c He advised me not to do so, as, he said, the Captain was a difficult man, and he had no intention of telling him himself. (exclusive) [BNC]

d On top of this, add 1,000 consultants, hired to do the work which the bank is – let us pretend – too understaffed or overworked to do for it itself. (exclusive) [BNC]

e More senior men had perhaps less freedom to diversify, although in the south they all kept gardens and sometimes worked them themselves. (exclusive) [BNC]

f Owners and vets rarely like to consider the possibility of psychosomatic problems with horses, in much the same way as people do not like to admit to suffering from them themselves. (inclusive) [BNC]

Note that there is another potential source from which the disputed sequences discussed above can emerge. It can happen in ditransitive verbs that the two internal argument positions are saturated with a pronoun on the one hand and with a so-called untriggered reflexive, a phenomenon to be dealt with in the next section, on the other, as shown in (3.122) below. Again, phonology does not prohibit such sequences.

(3.122) Peggy flushes, backs off, looks stony, as if an unexpected mirror has shown her herself too harshly. [LLC]

It remains to be added that there is no need for a similar discussion in the case of German. There, it is no problem to intensify object pronouns either in the dative or accusative. The reason, of course, is that the G. intensifier on its own is unable to trace an antecedent and hence the issue of economy and subsequent deletion of the pronoun does not arise in the first place. (3.123) repeats the German translations of (3.100b) through (3.103b) and (3.124) gives those of (3.115).

(3.123)   a   Ich habe [sie selbst] auf der Party getroffen.
          b   Ich würde gern mit [ihm selbst] sprechen.
          c   Dann öffnete er [es selbst].
          d   Er hat die neuen Spielsachen für [sie selbst] gekauft.

(3.124)   a   Warum hast du nicht [mich selbst] angerufen?
          b   Ich habe den Brief an [dich selbst] geschickt.
          c   Er hat [uns selbst] beleidigt.
          d   Ich möchte [euch selbst] auch einladen.

The final question must necessarily concern the problem of why intensification of object pronouns should be prohibited for reasons of language economy when intensification of those in subject position is no problem at all and is an option which is frequently made use of, cf. Table 3.2. After all, why should the intensifier in subject position be unable to trace the antecedent of the pronoun or pick a referent on its own? Functionally speaking, this should be no problem since it possesses all the relevant features. This is indeed an interesting point, however it is relatively easy to settle. The reason simply lies in the fact that the case specifications of adnominal intensifiers and subject pronouns do not match. Hence, the economy principle Π cannot operate.

Notice, however, that some dialects of English, predominantly Irish and Scottish English, provide the option to use x-*self* even in subject position, i.e. in a way as fully fledged pronouns. These occurrences of x-*self* can establish a reference of their own. However, there is an additional condition that these dialects impose on this usage of x-*self*. If x-*self* is to be used in subject position, the corresponding referent has to be important in one way or another. He could, for instance, occupy a high social rank. This will turn out to be the prototypical contextual condition of intensifiers. In e.g. (3.125a) below, it is essential to know that *himself* refers to the chief of a Scottish clan. Similarly, the context of (3.125b) provides the necessary clues to infer that *himself* refers to Jack's master.

(3.125)   a   Clan Campbell prospered, but himself was still not satisfied. [Hintikka and Kulas 1985: 145]
          b   Himself and his man Jack went riding to some place and they went for shelter into a public house. [LLC]

There are some further examples in (3.126). I know of no theory that would try to cope with these phenomena in the first place and some authors, as e.g. Jackendoff (1972: 114ff.) in his 'interpretive theory' of reflexives and pronouns, explicitly disallows such occurrences of x-*self* stating that if there is a reflexive form in some sentence, then another NP co-referential with it must be in the sentence too.

(3.126)   a   How is yourself today?
          b   Himself is not well today.
          c   It's herself is coming.

Whatever dialect is chosen in German, *selbst* in subject position is absolutely prohibited:

(3.127)   *Selbst   eröffnete   das   Parlament.
           self   opened   the   parliament

Some languages, however, offer this use of the intensifier as a standard option. Still, it is necessary for the relevant referent to occupy an elevated social position, cf. the example from Turkish below.

(3.128)   Turkish
          Kendi(-si)   bizim-le   konuş-acak.
          self(-POSS.3P.SG)   with-us   speak-FUT.3P.SG
          'He/She him/herself will talk to us.'

Note, finally, that the usage of x-*self* in subject position, i.e. in the function of a pronoun, used to be a widespread property of Middle and Early Modern English, cf. (3.129). König and Siemund (1996c) show that this pronominal usage of x-*self* can be attributed to the compounding of pronouns with the original intensifier *self* in the history of English. This led to a considerable confusion within the pronominal system from which English began to recover only after about 1700, cf. Keenan (1996).

(3.129)   a   Middle English
              Hymself drank water of the wel,
              As dide the knyght sire Percyvell [Chau, *Tale of Sir Thopas*, 915]
          b   Early Modern English
              For it engenders choler, planteth anger,
              And better 'twere that both of us did fast
              Since of ourselves ourselves are choleric,
              Than feed it with such overroasted flesh. [Shakespeare, *The Taming of the Shrew*, 4.1]

3.2 Adnominal SELF – covert heads

This section provides a survey of a phenomenon which is commonly referred to by the labels 'untriggered reflexives', 'unbounded reflexives' or 'long-distance bound' reflexives, the incentive for these labels being the observation that English reflexives may occur in locations in which they are prohibited according to the Binding Conditions (Chomsky 1981), i.e. where they are bound by an antecedent outside their governing category, are consequently condition A violations, and where a pronoun should be expected instead. To look at the data to be discussed from the point of view of long-distance binding only, however, is somewhat misleading since the underlying problem turns out to be of a much more general nature. The empirical problem for the Binding Theory is that there are a number of contexts where anaphors and pronominals are not in complementary distribution, i.e. where both of them are grammatical in one and the same position under an interpretation in which they are co-referential with the same antecedent. The assumption of a complementary distribution between anaphors and pronominals is one of the cornerstones of the Binding Theory. Depending on where complementarity breaks down, we are confronted with either condition A or condition B violations, meaning that either a reflexive or a pronoun is the unpredicted expression in the relevant position. Viewed from a slightly different angle, we could also say that there are contexts where reflexives occur, predicted by the Binding Conditions or not, but where a pronoun, in fact, would be sufficient – in the sense that E. reflexives are more complex than E. pronouns – and here, the label 'untriggered reflexives' will be used precisely to cover these cases.

In the following, we will try to analyse these reflexive forms not as anaphors, but as intensified expressions. This is an idea which goes back at least to Ross (1970) and was most recently taken up in Baker (1995). However, whereas Ross and Baker regard these occurrences of x-*self* as intensified pronouns, we will try to analyse them as intensifiers, i.e. adjuncts, with covert heads. The relevant type of intensifier underlying untriggered reflexives will turn out to be ANS.

We will proceed in three steps. First, we will investigate the environments where untriggered reflexives occur. Second, we will briefly review the proposals that have been put forward to explain their distribution. I will mainly draw on Kuno (1987), Zribi-Hertz (1989) and Baker (1995) in order to flesh these two points out. And finally, we will supply arguments for the intensifier hypothesis.

As for the locations in which untriggered reflexives occur, at least eight dominant areas can be singled out, cf. Ross (1970), Cantrall (1973a, 1974), Chomsky (1981, 1986b), Kuno (1987), Keenan (1988), Reinhart and Reuland (1993), Zribi-Hertz (1989, 1995), etc. Perhaps, the most widely discussed environment in the literature are the so-called picture NPs, or description NPs in general. (3.130) and (3.131) provide some examples, first a set including the classic one in the post office, then some further evidence from the corpora. Recall, however, once again that the distinctive feature of untriggered reflexives, according to the view taken here, is that they can be interchanged with pronouns.

(3.130)   a   John noticed a picture of him/himself in the post office.
            b   Max hates jokes about him/himself.
            c   Bill likes stories about him/himself.

(3.131)   a   The person is different from my picture of him. [BNC]
            b   Notice that if God really were like our picture of him, then the doubt would be valid. [BNC]

Another area in which pronouns and reflexives alternate in violation of the Binding Conditions is after spatial prepositions. The relevant PP can simply be an adjunct as in (3.132) or even an argument of the verb as (3.133) demonstrates. Again, we first provide some examples from the literature, which include the famous 'snake sentences', followed by some attested evidence.[8]

(3.132)   a   Max noticed a snake near him/himself.
            b   She grabbed the book to the right of her/herself.

(3.133)   a   She put the book behind her/herself.
            b   She pulled the blanket over her/herself.

(3.134)   a   She went quickly along the landing to her room and shut the door behind her. [LOB]
            b   He took her to the cabin and went back to the ante-room himself to wait for her. In the little sleeping cabin she looked about her curiously. [LLC]

(3.135)   a   Now he supported his half of Lazzaro with one hand while he closed the door behind himself with the other. [LLC]
            b   Quiss sat down heavily on his small chair, wrapping some more furs around himself to keep warm. [LLC]

There is another set of prepositions allowing untriggered reflexives as their argument which we will discuss as group three. These mainly introduce an (exclusively) disjunctive contrast between two sets of entities, meaning that what holds for the one set does not hold for the other. Prominent members of that group are *but (for)*, *except (for)*, *besides*, *apart from*, etc.

(3.136)   a   John believes that letter was sent to everyone but him/himself.

    b John asked Mary whether anyone besides her/herself got an A.

    c Lucie wondered why everybody apart from her/herself knew the guy who loved her.

(3.137) a As a free-lance investigator, the fictional detective is responsible to no one but himself and his client. [BROWN]

    b The only English people there besides myself were a couple called Keith and Doreen. [LLC]

    c He saw himself as if he were standing apart from himself and watching the scene. [LLC]

Next, there is an extensive class of examples which introduce some sort of comparison between two referents on the one hand or an equation on the other and may therefore be referred to as 'comparative/equative structures'. In these cases, E. x-*self* usually follows the prepositions *like, as* or *than*. Here are some representative examples.

(3.138) a John thinks that physicists like him/himself are a godsend.

    b John felt that Mary was as lonely as him/himself.

    c John thinks that Mary is taller than him/himself.

(3.139) a Always a bit of a loner, Basil here found an environment of people committed like himself. [LLC]

    b Joyce hadn't expected Barry to follow her, for she knew he was as obstinate as herself. [BROWN]

    c She never felt quite at ease with people richer than herself. [LLC]

As for group five, it is made up of a group of prepositions which are typically used in topicalisations. These include *as for, as far as x is concerned, with respect/regard to*, etc. with *as for* being the most prominent context for untriggered reflexives, cf.:

(3.140) a As for me/myself, I'll never forget you.

    b Tom determined that as for him/himself, he wouldn't eat anything that Sarah cooked.

    c Ed believed that as for him/himself, he'd be spared.

(3.141) a As for myself, I had on an enormous black muff. [BROWN]

    b And as for yourself, you too should try talking to a friend or relative whom you trust – the chances are that they may already have realised that things are going badly. [BNC]

    c As for himself, he just didn't have the temperament for it. [BROWN]

Interestingly enough, untriggered reflexives as arguments of these prepositions are most commonly found in the first person singular although the
singular/plural distinction is probably of little importance in comparison
with the restriction on person. This is due to a constraint which virtually all
occurrences of untriggered reflexives share to a certain degree, namely that it
must be possible to interpret them logophorically, i.e. the referent of their
antecedent must express a belief, hope, etc. or simply make a statement from
their perspective.[9] Since a statement in the first person almost by definition
gives the perspective of the speaker(s) on a certain state of affairs, it can come
as no surprise that untriggered reflexives are most acceptable with these. This
applies particularly to *as for* x-*self* in sentence-initial position of isolated
sentences because there is no context to interpret them logophorically other
than in the first person, cf. the following examples taken from Kuno (1987:
129). Note that the examples in (3.140b,c) and (3.141b,c) are fine because
they are embedded into larger contexts.

(3.142)   a   As for myself, I won't be invited.
          b   ??As for yourself, you won't be invited.
          c   *As for herself, she won't be invited.

Moreover, untriggered reflexives can be associated with a focus particle
such as additive *even* or exclusive *only*. Let us regard these examples as
group six.

(3.143)   a   The results were a big surprise even for me/myself.
          b   She came to realise that he was thinking only about her/
              herself.

(3.144)   a   Tennyson was a poet whose emotions were so deeply
              suppressed, even from himself, that they emerged as 'the
              blackest melancholia.' [LLC]
          b   As he began to speak, he seemed to grow less and less aware
              of his audience and continually turned his head, as though
              listening to some sound, audible only to himself from the
              entrance tunnel behind him. [LLC]

When the preceding groups showed untriggered reflexives as arguments of
prepositions, group seven comprises those occurrences of them which are
part of coordinations. These can either be conjunctive or disjunctive, i.e.
contain either *and* or *or* as a conjunction or similar expressions.

(3.145)   a   This would be very difficult for Mary and me/myself.
          b   Believe me, neither your husband nor you/yourself could
              stand it.
          c   Tom believed that the paper had been written by Ann and
              him/himself.

(3.146)   a Perhaps you will give Mrs Sutton or myself the cheque to-day? [LLC]

         b What I fled from was my fear of what, unwittingly, you might betray, without meaning to, about my father and yourself. [BROWN]

         c She ended her letter with the assurance that she considered his friendship for her daughter and herself to be an honor, from which she could not part without still more pain. [BROWN]

Note that in most of the examples considered so far, alternatives are evoked to the referent of the NP the (untriggered) reflexive is in association with. This is particularly clear in groups three to seven. Comparative/equa-tive structures, topicalisations and focus particles are all contexts establishing a contrast between two (sets of) referents. In the case of coordinations (group seven), and also in various examples of the other groups, the alternative is explicitly given. Moreover, the contrast between two (sets of) referents is often essential to the acceptability of the relevant examples. When the expression denoting the alternative referent is taken away from e.g. a coordi-nation, the examples concerned turn hopelessly bad:

(3.147)   a *This would be very difficult for myself.

         b *Believe me, yourself could not stand it.

         c *Tom believed that the paper had been written by himself.

Groups one to seven have one thing in common. Reflexive and antecedent are to be found in the same sentence, though not necessarily in the same clause. This remark taken in its entirety can, of course, only apply to the third person because the antecedents of first and second person untriggered reflexives may be directly recovered in discourse as speaker and hearer, cf. e.g. (3.142a) and (3.145a). On the basis of this criterion, we can single out yet another group, number eight as it were. Here, third person x-*self* may find its antecedent outside its own sentence, cf. (3.148). (3.149) shows that group eight may mix with features of the other groups, cf. Zribi-Hertz (1989: 707, 716, 717).

(3.148)   a He [Zapp] sat down at the desk and opened the drawers. In the top-right hand one was an envelope addressed to himself.

         b There were hours when Mrs Wix sighingly testified to the scruples she surmounted (...) If the child couldn't be worse it was a comfort even to herself that she was bad (...)

         c Joyce is just holding herself together (...) Her defences are well inside herself, not where mine are, outside in clothes, hair, etc.

(3.149) a I stared at her. Her manner clearly frightened Mary much more than it did myself.

b He sat staring ahead of him with his bright blue eyes. Some thought seemed to have struck both Eleanor and himself.

c The music made her think of her life as it seldom did; it exalted no one as it did herself.

(3.150) I loved talking to him, to hear about his first wife whom he had clearly loved dearly; she had given him the exquisite Clytie and then departed. Then to England where he was fascinated by the glamorous actress who strangely enough had agreed to marry him. None had been more surprised than himself. [LLC]

In all probability, the above listing does not exhaust all possible locations of untriggered reflexives, but it gives a sufficiently correct overview and clearly shows that it is a widespread phenomenon in English. As far as German is concerned, no comparable cases exist. The G. reflexive *sich* is restricted to finding its antecedent within the same clause. All occurrences of untriggered reflexives in the examples above can be translated into German either as bare pronouns (reflexive or personal) or as pronouns modified by ANS. (3.151) gives the translation of the first example of each group.

(3.151) a John bemerkte ein Bild von sich (selbst) auf dem Postamt.

b Max bemerkte eine Schlange neben sich (selbst).

c John glaubt, daß dieser Brief an jeden geschickt worden war außer an ihn (selbst).

d John glaubt, daß Physiker wie er (selbst) ein Geschenk des Himmels seien.

e Was mich (selbst) betrifft, so werde ich dich nie vergessen.

f Die Ergebnisse waren sogar für mich (selbst) eine große Überraschung.

g Das würde Maria und mir (selbst) große Probleme bereiten.

h Er [Zapp] setzte sich an den Schreibtisch und öffnete die Schubfächer. In dem Fach ganz oben rechts lag ein Umschlag, der an ihn (selbst) adressiert war.

After having sketched the dominant areas of untriggered reflexives, let us now briefly review the proposals that have been advanced for their analysis. These are usually developed within the Binding Theory. The Binding Conditions for nominal expressions are formulated as follows, cf. Chomsky (1981: 188, 1986b: 166):

(3.152) A. An anaphor is bound in its governing category.

B. A pronominal is free in its governing category.

C. An R-expression is free.

As already mentioned, the problem with untriggered reflexives is that they alternate with ordinary pronouns (pronominals) and that if they are regarded as anaphors in the sense of the Binding Theory, the underlying assumption of complementarity between the two sets of expressions breaks down and hence either of the two must occur in violation of the Binding Conditions. We are here confronted with two kinds of violations, condition A or condition B violations. Given that governing category is defined as in (3.153) below, cf. Chomsky (1981: 188ff.), Haegeman (1991:187ff.), group two above contains condition B violations because the pronoun is bound within the governing category in these cases whereas the remaining groups mainly contain free anaphors, i.e. are condition A violations. In addition, it is usually assumed that anaphor and antecedent must enter the structural relation of c-command, cf. (3.154). In fact, Chomsky (1981) defines 'binding' as coindexation plus c-command. Hence, selection of an antecedent is restricted both in terms of distance and structure.

(3.153) The governing category of a reflexive α is the domain containing α, the governor of α and a subject.

(3.154) An anaphor is c-commanded by its antecedent.

The proposals to deal with untriggered reflexives as exemplified by the eight groups above can be divided into three groups: (i) analyses that try to motivate syntactic structures for the relevant examples that conform to the Binding Conditions, (ii) amendments to the Binding Conditions themselves and (iii) analyses taking untriggered reflexives out of the scope of the Binding Conditions altogether.

As far as the first approach is concerned, it has mainly proved useful for the resolution of condition B violations, i.e. for positions where the reflexive is correct, but the pronoun is wrong. Consider the case of picture NPs repeated in (3.155).

(3.155) a John noticed pictures of himself in the post office.
       b John noticed pictures of him in the post office.

Chomsky (1986b: 173) suggests that there are two different syntactic structures for cases like (3.155). In the case of the reflexive, it is as given in (3.155a) so that its governing category includes the subject *John*. In the case of the pronoun, by contrast, a 'hidden pronominal' in the determiner position of the NP intervenes and restricts the governing category of the pronoun (because the hidden pronominal is now the nearest subject) so that the pronoun can become free. A similar argument can make group two conform to the Binding Conditions, cf. (3.156).

(3.156) a Max noticed a snake near himself.
       b Max noticed [SC a snake near him].

Here too, it is possible to assume a structural ambiguity. (3.156a) is analysed as a normal sentence, in (3.156b), by contrast, we find a small clause which contains an extra subject thus constraining the governing category of the pronoun. Subsequently, conditions A and B are met. It is easy to see that the assumption of structural ambiguities can go a long way towards explaining the untriggered reflexives of the remaining groups.

An interesting proposal for the analysis of groups three and four within the realms of the Binding Theory comes from Keenan (1988). He suggests that the entire bracketed expression in (3.157) is to be viewed as an anaphor, a complex anaphor (CA), according to his terminology. Such an approach is based on the observation that in examples like these, complex anaphors as well as bare anaphors can be interchanged.

(3.157) John believes that letter was sent to [CA everyone but himself]/ himself.

However, it is totally inadequate for examples like (3.136b), repeated in (3.158), because the complex anaphor is a subject and does not contrast with bare anaphors.

(3.158) John asked Mary whether [CA anyone besides herself]/*herself got an A.

Alternatively, and now we are going over to discussing the amendments to the Binding Conditions, the approach taken in Chomsky (1995: 103ff.) is to relativise the notion of governing category. Consider again the case of picture NPs in (3.155). For examples like these, it is now assumed that the governing category in which the reflexive is bound is different from the one in which the pronoun is free. The governing category relevant for the reflexive extends up to the NP *John* of the higher clause, and *himself* is indeed bound in that domain. As for the pronoun, its governing category ends at the NP *pictures*, which is a governor of the pronoun and also contains a (phonetically null) subject. The pronoun is free in that domain. Chomsky says that the governing category for an expression is the domain in which it can be bound *in principle*. Note that relativising the notion of governing category boils down to saying that anaphors and pronominals are not in complementary distribution because the touchstone, with regard to which complementarity is measured, is thereby destroyed.

A more abstract version of that idea can be found in Koster and Reuland (1991: 2), cf. (3.159). Here it is assumed that the left-most boundary of the governing category, which normally is the nearest subject, is variable. This is expressed by the opacity factor F which can be assigned one of several values. One of them, of course, is 'subject', others include 'Tense', 'Agr' or 'Comp'.

Table 3.4 The distribution of nominal expressions
according to Chomsky (1982)

[–A]	[–P]	R-expressions
[+A]	[–P]	anaphors
[–A]	[+P]	pronominals
[+A]	[+P]	?

(3.159) β is a governing category for α iff β is the minimal category
containing α , a governor of α , and F (F = opacity factor)

Reinhart and Reuland (1993: 661), by contrast, depart from the observation that the complementarity of anaphors and pronominals holds only if they and their antecedent are co-arguments of one and the same predicate. They redefine the Binding Conditions as a property of predicates and regulate the distribution of anaphoric expressions outside predicates on the basis of chain theory. What we find here is a drastic restriction of the scope of the Binding Theory with the final aim of giving it up in its original formulation.

Another possible extension to the Binding Theory, which is discussed in Chomsky (1982), runs as follows. In its standard form, the Binding Theory tries to account for the distribution of three types of expressions, anaphors (reflexives like x-*self* in their referential interpretation), pronominals (pronouns like *him*) and R-expressions (referring expressions like *John*). These expressions can be described on the basis of two binary features [±A] and [±P]. This results in the distribution given in Table 3.4 which has the obvious problem that the combination [+A][+P] lacks an appropriate expression in English and also in German.

The Binding Conditions can now be restated as follows and will account for all three types of expressions in the usual way.

(3.160) A. An NP with the feature [+A] is bound in its governing category.
B. An NP with the feature [+P] is free in its governing category.

As a matter of fact, Chomsky observes that it is impossible for an overt expression with the features [+A][+P] to exist if we take these features seriously. Since [+A] means that an expression is bound in its governing category and [+P] that it is free, [+A][+P] would have to mean that it is bound and free within one domain at the same time, which is simply a contradiction.

Due to this contradiction, however, it is not possible to assign the features [+A][+P] to untriggered reflexives. The only viable option seems to be to regard the meaning of the two features not as being compositionally derived, but to view their combination as merely being a label for a group of expressions whose properties are given by a separate definition as e.g. done in

(3.161). But now, we could just as well label them 1 to 4 so that all we achieve is the generation of four different categories.

> (3.161) 1 A [+A][−P] expression is bound in its governing category.
> 2 A [−A][+P] expression is free in its governing category.
> 3 A [−A][−P] expression is free.
> 4 A [+A][+P] expression is bound.

More radical approaches, however, would try to take untriggered reflexives out of the scope of the Binding Theory altogether. One idea hinted at in Chomsky (1981: 289ff.) and taken up in Zribi-Hertz (1989: 701) sets off from the observation that most of the reflexives violating the Binding Conditions are emphasised, i.e. they carry nuclear stress. This is unexpected in view of the fact that reflexives in argument positions of verbs normally come unstressed. In (3.162) probably the least likely expression to put stress on is the reflexive whereas it is obligatory in (3.163), indeed, these examples become fairly unacceptable if an element other than the reflexive receives the main stress.

> (3.162) a He poured himself a whisky.
> b She prepared herself for a long wait.

> (3.163) a John thinks that Mary is taller than himSELF.
> b This paper was written by Ann and mySELF.

This being so, it seems possible to formulate a restriction on the Binding Conditions to the effect that they are valid only for those occurrences of reflexives, or better of the form x-*self,* which are unstressed. Such an approach has the consequence of also declaring the Binding Conditions invalid for stressed x-*self* in argument positions of the verb, i.e. in cases like the following:

> (3.164) a Liz criticised herSELF.
> b Max washed himSELF.

Zribi-Hertz, by contrast, does not link the special status of certain reflexives to a factor inherent to them, but to their antecedent. On the basis of well-known minimal pairs as e.g. (3.165), which are adapted from Kuno (1987: 123), she claims that an English reflexive may violate the Binding Conditions if it is in association with what she terms the 'minimal subject of consciousness', which means the nearest NP to the left of the reflexive which can be read logophorically.

> (3.165) a John$_i$ said to Mary that physicists like him$_i$/himself$_i$ were a godsend.

Table 3.5 Intensive expressions according to Baker (1995)

Intensive expression	Example
Adnominal intensifier	Max himself, she herself, etc.
Untriggered reflexive	myself, yourself, himself, etc.

  b Mary said about John$_i$ that physicists like him$_i$/*himself$_i$ were a godsend.

Baker (1995) also analyses untriggered reflexives outside the Binding Theory. Just as Zribi-Hertz, he departs from the idea that there must be something special about their antecedent which licenses their use. However, he also takes into consideration that untriggered reflexives themselves possess a very important property. As already mentioned, they are nearly always stressed and by virtue of being in association with a nominal antecedent, they evoke a contrast to the referent thereof.

As for the properties of this antecedent, Baker manages to show that logophoricity or being the subject of consciousness is only a subcase of the much more general property of being central or prominent in discourse. Here, Baker takes up a proposal put forward by König (1991: 87ff.) in the context of adnominal intensifiers. König claims that these expressions characterise the referent of the NP they interact with as central and oppose it to a set of peripheral referents. The details of this analysis are discussed in Chapter 6.

The actual merit of Baker lies in his drawing of a parallel between adnominal intensifiers on the one hand and untriggered reflexives on the other, i.e. between expressions of the type exemplified in (3.166a) and those in (3.166b), both of which he analyses as intensive expressions. Untriggered reflexives by and large seem to adhere to the condition on centrality.

(3.166) a He himself had been born in India, and his mother had had had two other children here and all of them had thrived. [LLC]
         b She never felt quite at ease with people richer than herself. [LLC]

According to Baker, then, there are two types of intensive expressions, adnominal intensifiers and untriggered reflexives, which obey the same underlying semantic principles. This is summarised in Table 3.5. Note that x-*self* in its function to indicate co-reference (reflexive anaphor) forms a category of its own.

On the basis of this categorisation, Baker draws a distinction between British and American English, mainly with the outcome that untriggered reflexives are a phenomenon restricted to British English. In American

Table 3.6 Intensive expressions in British English and American English

Intensive expression	British English	American English
Adnominal intensifier	Max himself, she herself, etc.	Max himself, she herself, etc.
Untriggered reflexive/ intensive pronoun	myself, yourself, himself, etc.	ME, YOU, HIM, etc.

English, by contrast, emphasised forms of personal pronouns, i.e. intensive pronouns, are used. This is shown in Table 3.6. One of the consequences of this claim is that American English almost perfectly adheres to the Binding Conditions whereas British English does not behave according to the rules.

Such a claim, of course, is much too strong. It is disputed in Zribi-Hertz (1995: 338–9) and the examples in (3.167), which are taken from the Brown Corpus, prove beyond any doubt that untriggered reflexives are a common phenomenon also in American English.

(3.167) a His patronage on this stretch was made up largely of San Franciscans – regulars, most of them, and trenchermen like himself. [BROWN]

b I have no one but myself to worry about. [BROWN]

c His sandy hair was already beginning to thin and recede at the sides, and Abel looked quickly away. Mark easily looked years older than himself, settled, his world comfortably categorized. [BROWN]

Given that adnominal intensifiers as well as untriggered reflexives can both be subsumed under intensive expressions, it appears reasonable to ask whether there is any difference between these two expressions at all. And, in fact, according to prosody and semantic contribution, they cannot be distinguished. Moreover, both are in association with an NP. Still, only ANS is an adjunct and forms an endocentric expansion of its head. Untriggered reflexives clearly behave like arguments, as the following data on omissability make clear.

(3.168) a He (himself) had been born in India, and his mother had had two other children here and all of them had thrived. [LLC]

b She never felt quite at ease with people richer than *(herself). [LLC]

Recall, now, from the previous section that English neither allows intensification of reflexive pronouns nor of object pronouns with disjoint reference. The strategies to resolve these limitations are to use stressed x-*SELF* in the former case and a semantically unspecified NP (or an alternative intensifier) in the latter. The relevant examples are repeated in (3.169).

(3.169) a Jack has tried to kill *himself himself/himself.
        b I would like to talk to *him himself/*himself/the man himself/him personally.

Moreover, we proposed that *himSELF* in (3.169a) is the reduced form of *himself himself* and that the reduction occurs on the basis of the economy principle *Π* repeated below. However, the pronominal head of the intensifier is merely made covert, namely by replacing it with an empty nominal category, so that there still is an NP the intensifier can be adjoined to. *Him himself* in (3.169b) cannot be reduced because *himself* as such in an argument position is interpreted as an anaphor by default. This is, in fact, a case of competing principles with the latter one winning out.

Π   If two expressions E_1 and E_2 form a complex expression E_c, and if the semantic features of E_1 are a subset of those of E_2, then E_1 is superfluous and can be dispensed with.

Note now that all the environments of untriggered reflexives discussed in groups one to eight above block intensification of the object pronoun in case the pronoun is used to indicate co-reference instead of the reflexive. Stressed x-*SELF* on its own, however, is grammatical and, as pointed out above, makes the same contribution as 'x x-*self*' would. (3.170) shows this on the basis of the first example of each group.

(3.170) a John noticed a picture of *him himself/himself in the post office.
        b Max noticed a snake near *him himself/himself.
        c John believes that letter was sent to everyone but *him himself/himself.
        d John thinks that physicists like *him himself/himself are a godsend.
        e As for *me myself/myself, I'll never forget you.
        f The results were a big surprise even for *me myself/myself.
        g This would be very difficult for Mary and *me myself/myself.
        h He [Zapp] sat down at the desk and opened the drawers. In the top-right hand one was an envelope addressed to *him himself/himself.

This being so, however, it again seems reasonable to argue that *himself* in (3.170) is the reduced version of *him himself* and that reduction again takes place according to the economy principle *Π*. Hence, it also becomes possible to analyse untriggered reflexives as intensifiers (ANS) with covert heads:

(3.171) a John noticed a picture of [e himself] in the post office.
b Max noticed a snake near [e himself].
c John believes that letter was sent to everyone but [e himself].
d John thinks that physicists like [e himself] are a godsend.
e As for [e myself], I'll never forget you.
f The results were a big surprise even for [e myself].
g This would be very difficult for Mary and [e myself].
h He [Zapp] sat down at the desk and opened the drawers. In the top-right hand one was an envelope addressed to [e himself].

In point of fact, the economy principle *Π* thus motivates and generalises a proposal made in Ross (1970), who suggests that untriggered reflexives in coordinations (group seven here) are derived from structures containing an anaphoric pronoun followed by an emphatic reflexive (ANS) by a rule which deletes the anaphoric pronoun. According to Ross, (3.172a) yields (3.172b). Note that this rule is meant to cover 'x x-*self*' in coordinations only. *Π*, by contrast, explains why intensification of both reflexive pronouns and object pronouns results in ANS with covert heads.

(3.172) a Tom believed that the paper had been written by Ann and him himself.
b Tom believed that the paper had been written by Ann and himself.

The above analysis of untriggered reflexives has the following consequences for the Binding Theory. First of all, by regarding a substantial amount of occurrences of x-*self* as intensifiers rather than reflexive anaphors, the scope of condition A is vastly reduced. As a matter of fact, it is reduced to unstressed x-*self* in a co-argument position of its antecedent. Second, since the co-argument position is the only position in which the claim for a complementary distribution of anaphors and pronominals really holds, cf. Reinhart and Reuland (1993: 661), no amendments (such as features, *i*-within-*i* constraint, relative governing category, etc.) nor additional syntactic stipulations are necessary in order to explain long-distance bound anaphors and short-distance bound pronominals. In other words, the Binding Conditions become robust by themselves.

Given the definition in (3.173), we can restate the Binding Conditions as done in (3.174). An obvious drawback of such an approach is that the Binding Conditions thereby become language specific and do not apply universally any longer. With regard to German, for instance, the relevant domain would be the clause.

(3.173) English x-*self* is ambiguous between
a a reflexive anaphor, which is unstressed (x-*self*) and
b an intensifier (ANS), which is stressed (x-*SELF*).

(3.174) As for English:
A. An anaphor is bound in a co-argument position.
B. A pronominal is free in a co-argument position.

Let us finally take a look at two phenomena of English which also need discussion in the present context. On the one hand, it is noteworthy that there are contexts which superficially look like cases belonging to group two, but which, however, block untriggered reflexives and require the exclusive use of a simple pronoun instead, cf. (3.175). These are mainly contexts which hinder the evocation of the necessary contrast for untriggered reflexives to work properly. Put differently, the relevant situations are bound to the referent of the antecedent and cannot be performed by an alternative referent. Looking at the examples in (3.175), it is easy to see that it is conceptually impossible to have someone beside someone else, to push a cart in front of or carry a gun with someone else or to have the whole day before another person. Also, note that the stress in these cases invariably falls on the preposition.[10]

(3.175) a She had her fiancé beside her/*herself.
b She pushed the cart in front of her/*herself.
c He carried a gun with him/*himself.
d We have the whole day before us/*ourselves.

On the other hand, we find a certain amount of examples which do pose a real problem to an analysis that aims at reducing all occurrences of untriggered reflexives to adnominal intensifiers, cf. Zribi-Hertz (1995). Here, we first of all have to mention the entire group one delineated above where x-*self* may also be read without the contrastive stress requisite for ANS, cf. (3.176). Hence, no alternatives get evoked to the referent of the antecedent and in the German translation the reflexive *sich* is sufficient.

(3.176) a John noticed a picture of himself in the post office.
b Bill likes stories about himself.

(3.177) gives another set of examples provided by Zribi-Hertz (1989: 709, 1995: 338–9). In these examples too, x-*self* does not receive contrastive stress in their most natural interpretation, although Zribi-Hertz does not want to rule that option out entirely. The sentences below, however, are unlikely to be translated into German on the basis of ANS.

(3.177) a Tell him, please, that we wish him no harm; but that it will
be better for himself if he goes away from Germany at once.
   b John couldn't resist the hunger for revenge which filled
himself.
   c. Slowly, strangely, consciousness changes, and Petworth can
feel the change taking place within himself.

What examples like (3.176) and (3.177) show is that there is still a set of
occurrences of x-*self* left which evade a proper analysis. These examples are
impossible to capture within the framework of the Binding Theory, and to
regard them as intensifiers with covert heads does not seem to make sense
either (there is no evoking of alternatives). Further research will have to show
whether it is necessary for English to assume another class of nominal expressions which are unspecified for binding, i.e. may be bound or not, as the
'UBEs' (Unspecified Bindable Expressions) discussed in Zribi-Hertz (1995:
356). Given that Old English did not know the distinction between
anaphors and pronominals and used the same expression for indicating
disjoint reference and co-reference, it should not seem too surprising to find
traces of that situation left.

3.3 ANS in role reversal structures

Edmondson and Plank (1978: 386) distinguish, apart from ANS and AVS
(*himself*₁ and *himself*₂ in their terminology), yet another use of intensifiers
which they label *himself*₃. The distinctive feature of this use type, in their
view, is to express a reversal in terms of thematic roles. The subject (referent)
of sentences containing *himself*₃ is required to explicitly or implicitly appear
in an opposite role in a similar predication. Girke (1993) even holds that the
main contribution of intensifiers in general consists in indicating the role
reversal of a referent. The examples of Edmondson and Plank are given in
(3.178) with (3.178b) showing that thematic role probably is too narrow a
concept to capture all the cases involved. (3.179) proves that role reversal is
necessary.

(3.178) a Lucrezia poisoned Lorenzo, and was herself poisoned by
Cesare. (agent ⇒ patient)
   b Smith is taller than Jones who is himself taller/shorter than
my aunt. (standard of comparison ⇒ person compared)

(3.179) *Smith is taller than Jones and is himself shorter than my aunt.
(no switch of roles)

Note, however, that Edmondson and Plank are far from being certain that
*himself*₃ is an intensifier with distinctive semantic features. This uncertainty
makes them subsume under this label a rather heterogeneous set of data

which is why we find examples in it (p. 385ff.) that clearly belong to inclusive AVS, cf.:

(3.180) a These cops know what it means to be arrested by a sheriff because they've been arrested by a sheriff themselves.
b He has himself not erased the tapes.

In the following, we will concentrate on those intensifier constructions which involve a thematic role reversal. The aim of the present section is to show that these examples can be subsumed under the established uses of SELF, mainly ANS, and that no additional category is necessary. The prosodic and syntactic properties of these structures favour such an analysis. Section 6.4 gives an explanation of why role reversal is necessary in these examples.

Note, for a start, that many of the examples involving role reversal are coordinating structures in which the subject of the second conjunct is deleted according to the well-known phenomenon of coordination reduction. Apart from the subject, role reversal is also possible with respect to the object, but this necessitates an alternative complex structure, namely a relative clause, cf. (3.181). Coordination reduction is only possible with subjects, cf. Keenan (1976: 317).

(3.181) Tom was followed by Dick who was himself followed by Harry.

The most convincing argument for our hypothesis that these examples contain instances of ANS can be drawn from the fact that all of them can be rephrased by splitting the complex structure up into two sentences of which the second contains ANS beyond any doubt. (3.182a,b) are equivalent in meaning to (3.178a) and (3.181) respectively.

(3.182) a Lucrezia poisoned Lorenzo. She herself was poisoned by Cesare.
b Tom was followed by Dick. He himself was followed by Harry.

Moreover, note that in the complex structures, ANS is positioned behind the finite verb. Although this position is indicative of inclusive AVS, it is a possible position for ANS too, provided that the relevant sentences are read with a double focus. A double focus allows ANS to either move before its head or after the finite verb. (3.183) repeats the relevant examples for the sake of convenience.

(3.183) a MySELF // I had no clue at ALL.
b I had mySELF // no clue at ALL.

Taking into consideration that all the examples involving role reversal discussed so far are in fact double focus structures with two tone groups, we have another point in favour of an analysis according to ANS. Reading them with a single focus on the intensifier clearly yields unacceptable results. Consider the contrast between (3.184) and (3.185).

(3.184) a Lucrezia poisoned Lorenzo, and was herSELF // poisoned by CeSAre.
         b Tom was followed by Dick who was himSELF // followed by HArry.

(3.185) a ?Lucrezia poisoned Lorenzo, and was herSELF poisoned by CeSAre.
         b ?Tom was followed by Dick who was himSELF followed by HArry.

At this point, a word of caution is in order because not all role reversal structures necessarily involve ANS. Under a single focus, SELF is forced into its inclusive interpretation (inclusive AVS) which underlines that there is no need for the assumption of an additional category in the sense of Edmondson and Plank's *himself*₃. The examples in (3.185) above are odd because the inclusive reading of the intensifier is blocked by the surrounding context. The examples in (3.186) below, by contrast, are perfectly well-formed. In (3.186a) the contradictory sequence *by Cesare* is now outside the scope of inclusive AVS.

(3.186) a Lucrezia poisoned Lorenzo, but was herSELF poisoned, namely by Cesare.
         b ... comprehension involves the joint processing of a set of assumptions, and in that set some assumptions stand out as newly presented information being processed in the context of information that has itSELF been previously processed. [Sperber and Wilson 1986: 118; my emphasis]

The difference between ANS and inclusive AVS in the context of role reversal also explains the contrast between (3.187a,b). Whereas (3.187a) presents an arrangement of the three objects book, keyboard and screen which can be described as 'book before keyboard and keyboard before screen', (3.187b) also denotes a scenario with both book and keyboard placed before the screen; however, the position of the book relative to the screen is not determined relative to the keyboard, but must be inferred directly with respect to the screen. The underlying arrangement rather is 'book before keyboard, both before screen'.

(3.187) a The book is in front of the keyboard which is itSELF // in front of the SCREEN. (adnominal) b The book is in front of the keyboard which is itSELF in front of the screen. (inclusive)

Another argument for our claim that the role reversal structures under discussion involve ANS can be derived from the observation that in structures which reverse the role from the object NP, and hence need a relative pronoun, the intensifier cannot only occur behind the finite verb, but also right adjacent to the relative pronoun without any change in meaning, cf. (3.188). The position adjacent to the head, however, is one of the prominent features of ANS.

(3.188) Tom was followed by Dick who himself was followed by Harry.

That the intensifier is bound to the post-finite position in examples involving coordination reduction can be exploited for a more indirect argument proving the same point. In its standard non-dislocated position adjacent to its head NP, the adnominal intensifier needs this NP as a syntactic carrier because it is an adjunct and cannot project a phrase on its own. When the head NP is deleted in the course of coordination reduction, ANS must also get deleted, because it is a part of it. Thus, the ungrammaticality of (3.189) strongly suggests that it contains ANS.

(3.189) *Lucrezia poisoned Lorenzo, and herself was poisoned by Cesare.

In sum, the above arguments seem to prove beyond any doubt that it is not necessary to assume a further use of SELF and that those instances contained in role reversal structures can be subsumed under the known varieties. As indicated at the beginning, why role reversal is to be found at all in the examples discussed will be explained in section 6.4.

Notes

1 Note that there is a number of fairly idiosyncratic cases in which the particle may intervene between a preposition and its complement, cf. Jacobs (1983: 69):

  (i) The rocket exploded due to only a minor mistake.

2 Not all predicates are suitable for this test, particularly those allowing arguments other than NPs, cf. *Kate amazes me/makes me happy* versus *That Kate phoned tonight amazes me/makes me happy.*

3 Note that these restrictions cannot be accounted for within the Barriers framework, cf. Chomsky (1986a), because barriers block extraction out of subjects, but permit extraction out of objects. Topicalisation of *selbst* from a subject NP crosses two barriers (NP, IP) and hence violates subjacency.

4 Note, though, that in most cases, ANS will not have to bear the burden of making precise which interpretation is intended. After all, there is agreement in

number between verb and subject in many cases. However, when number agreement is missing, as e.g. with the majority of verbs in the past, ANS can serve a useful function, provided, of course, that it is necessary and adequate in the relevant context. It would be totally beside the point to regard ANS as a means for clearing up the desired interpretation of such NPs.

5 McKay (1991: 372) observes that (3.114b) can receive another interpretation in which *himself* is in association with the NP *Rupert* and not with the pronoun. This occurrence of *himself* he regards as a displaced adjunct. According to our classification, *himself* in this interpretation must be analysed as AVS, more precisely, as inclusive AVS. The example below provides context to make the adverbial reading more easily accessible.

    (i) Derek and Gareth wanted Peter to think well of Rupert. But Rupert was not unduly worried about Peter's opinion of him himself.

6 The figures in Table 3.3 exclude ambiguous examples like the one below so that the actual difference between subject and object pronouns could turn out to be a little less.

    (i) I need hardly say that if Gillian's arrest had been anything other than a trick there would have been no question of my confronting him personally. [LOB]

7 It is relatively straightforward to motivate such an economy principle independently of the present phenomenon because reduction due to overspecification or redundant information is a common occurrence in natural language, take e.g. coordination reduction, ellipsis, etc. A phenomenon that can be directly explained on the basis of Π is the reduction of the subject pronoun in *pro-drop* languages. These pronouns can be discarded because their ϕ-features are fully specified on the VP. Using them must be justified on grounds of information not provided by the VP, as e.g. topicalisation, deixis, etc.

8 Notice that in spite of the fact that pronouns and reflexives are interchangeable, the binding domain of x-*self* is generally more restricted than the one of pronouns. A parallel situation can be found in languages which allow long-distance binding. Here too, using a complex expression containing the intensifier reduces the binding domain.

    Norwegian (Nynorsk)
    (i) Karin$_i$ hørte han snakke om seg$_i$.
       'Karin heard him talk about her.'
    (ii) Karin hørte han$_i$ snakke om [seg sjølv]$_i$.
       'Karin heard him talk about himself.'

9 Thus, logophoric binding can be viewed as a special way of binding which, apart from co-reference, imposes semantic restrictions on the binder/antecedent. The term 'logophoric pronouns' was introduced by Hagège (1974) to cover parts of the pronominal systems of West-African languages like Ewe, Yoruba and Igbo (cf. also Frajzyngier 1985, 1989).

10 Notice, however, the existence of examples like *She was pushing the cart along, in front of herself.*

4   Adverbal intensifiers

Adverbal intensifiers (AVS) are always stressed and bear the sentence accent. Moreover, in English, they show agreement with some NP in person, number and gender so that there are at least two properties which they share with adnominal intensifiers:

(4.1)   a Mary Fisher earned all her money herSELF.
        b They try to compute the results themSELVES.

Whereas ANS occurs right-adjacent to the NP it is in association with and can be analysed as an endocentric expansion of that NP, AVS is nearly always separated from it and occurs in a non-juxtaposed position. In actual fact, AVS and the NP it interacts with favourably tend to turn up at almost opposite ends of a sentence so that there appears to be little point in even trying to analyse them as a single constituent. AVS seems to belong to a different constituent, namely the VP, and indeed, there are a number of arguments in support of such a view.

With x-*self* being in sentence-final position, (4.1) shows an extreme case of distance between AVS and its interacting NP. Still, it would not be correct to claim that this is universally the case with AVS. As already hinted at in section 2.1, there is no need for AVS to be sentence-final. Syntactically speaking, occurrences of the intensifier can be regarded as adverbal as long as they appear behind the finite verb.

(4.2)   I have myself come to the conclusion that the upper limit for the average amount of capital investment per workplace is probably given by the annual earnings of an able and ambitious industrial worker. [LLC]

However, even such a weak generalisation cannot be maintained for all the sentences under consideration. Recall from section 3.1.2 that ANS can also turn up behind the finite verb provided that there are two foci and subsequently two tone groups:

(4.3)   a She had herSELF // no clue at all. (adnominal)
         b She had herSELF no clue at all. (adverbal)

In contrast to adnominal intensifiers, adverbal intensifiers cannot interact with just any NP. There are tight conditions on both its type and its function. Recall that ANS can potentially interact with common nouns and proper nouns, subject and object NPs, NPs inside PPs or as part of adverbials, in fact, any NP independent of type and function. As for AVS, it is by and large confined to interacting with subject NPs denoting human referents although there are additional constraints as well as differences between English and German, as we will see.

(4.4)   a Phil has sharpened the pencil himself_adverbal.
         b *I sent George the letter himself_adverbal.
         c *The new aircraft seats 500 passengers itself_adverbal.

In several cases, the positional variation of AVS between post-finite and sentence-final position is accompanied by a semantic distinction which can be characterised as inclusive versus exclusive. Such a distinction can be drawn because inclusive AVS can more or less be replaced by postfocal *also* whereas exclusive AVS rather displays some affinity to *alone*. (4.5a) is inclusive and says that someone besides Kate had seen the movie in question three times whereas the preferred reading of (4.5b) is exclusive and states that on all three occasions Kate was present in the movie theatre rather than relying on her boyfriend for telling her what the movie was about. Nevertheless, (4.5b) is also possible with an inclusive interpretation.

(4.5)   a Kate remarked that she had herself seen 'Sense & Sensibility' three times.
         b Kate remarked that she had seen 'Sense & Sensibility' three times herself.

Still, any statement concerning the syntactic distribution of inclusive and exclusive AVS must be taken with a pinch of salt and, on the whole, it will turn out that we can talk of no more than a certain tendency. Neither inclusive nor exclusive AVS is bound to a particular syntactic position. But we will discuss this issue in detail later on. As for the validity of the assumption that AVS is polysemous between an inclusive and an exclusive usage, recall the discussion in section 2.1.

This chapter is organised as follows. In the subsequent section, we will try to bring forward some watertight facts to show that (i) AVS is part of the VP, that it is not a co-constituent of the NP it is in association with, and that it is a co-constituent of the VP itself and not of some other element inside it, and (ii) that AVS must be analysed as an adjunct and not as an argument of the verb, i.e. that AVS can be regarded as an endocentric expansion of the

VP. Section 4.2 deals with the pros and cons of analysing AVS as an adverb. Although it does behave in many respects like an adverb, more precisely a focus adverb, there are also differences which seem to obstruct such an analysis. Section 4.3 is concerned with syntactic restrictions and peculiarities of AVS as well as a brief review of the major English-German contrasts. All these considerations apply to both varieties of AVS. In addition to that, we will try to list representative syntactic environments of inclusive as well as exclusive AVS.

4.1 AVS – the VP-adjunct

As far as co-constituency of the intensifier with the VP is concerned, it is first of all noteworthy that clefting is an operation that does not affect AVS at all. This is in sharp contrast to ANS. Independently of whether the NP the intensifier is in association with – or any other NP present – is put into an *it*-cleft, the relative position of AVS remains stable:

(4.6) a Paul felled the tree himself.
       b It was Paul who felled the tree himself.
       c It was the tree that Paul felled himself.

It is difficult to make a similar point in connection with pseudo-clefts because, in contrast to *it*-clefts, they usually block human NPs as complements, cf. (4.7a,b). What can be done, though, is to cleft the object NP of (4.7a) which at least shows that AVS is not a co-constituent of it, cf. (4.7c). Recall that co-constituency must be kept apart from interaction.

(4.7) a Max wrote the letter himself.
       b *Who wrote the letter himself was Max.
       c What Max wrote himself was the letter.

What examples like (4.6) and (4.7) certainly show is that AVS stays in a fixed position while other elements are being displaced, but it is hard to accept that as a proof for the claim that AVS is part of the VP. What we are really looking for is a means to either extract or replace the entire VP including AVS. Note, however, that the above examples make it unlikely for AVS to belong to one of the NPs present, although it clearly interacts with one.

Pseudo-clefts in a slightly different usage can be used as such a test. In contrast to *it*-clefts, pseudo-clefts make it possible to cleft the entire VP or parts thereof and turn it into a complement of *be*. Since this kind of clefting leaves the subject without a VP, it has to be replaced by an appropriate pro-form, usually *do*, cf. (4.8). Here, *do* functions as a substitute for the entire VP including AVS and this can be taken as an indication that the latter is part of the former. What clefting also shows is that the intensifier is not adjoined to a node above VP. In (4.8) the entire VP is clefted, in (4.9) only a part of it.

(4.8)   a She sent the message herself.
         b What she did was send the message herself.
         c Send the message herself was what she did.

(4.9)   a He wanted to clean the bathroom himself.
         b What he wanted to do was clean the bathroom himself.
         c Clean the bathroom himself was what he wanted to do.

So far we have restricted our attention to cases of exclusive AVS; however, this is due to properties inherent to the cleft construction. We usually cleft elements in order to highlight them, i.e. to set them apart from others. The resulting effect is one of exclusion rather than inclusion, which is why pseudo-clefts involving inclusive AVS are somewhat difficult to construct. Moreover, the prevalent pro-form to replace the clefted VP is the verb *do* which, for reasons to be made precise in section 7.2, mostly functions as a trigger for exclusive AVS. Still, if we resort to other possible substitutes apart from *do*, such as e.g. *achieve*, and put them into adequate context, it becomes possible to use pseudo-clefts as a means for showing that inclusive AVS belongs to the VP too, cf. (4.10) within the context provided.

(4.10)   Francis could not stop making fun of Maggie, pointing out to her how stupid she was. What Francis achieved was to look pretty stupid himself.

Another test showing that AVS can be analysed as part of the VP consists in forming questions containing AVS and then formulating answers to them with a VP pro-form such as *have* and *do*. Since these pro-forms again replace the entire VP, it follows that AVS belongs to it, cf. (4.11). Notice also, as shown in (4.12), the differing degrees of acceptability between AVS and ANS in such examples.

(4.11)   a Have you done that yourself? Yes, I have.
          b Who mowed the lawn himself? John did.

(4.12)   a Has he himself done that? He himself, no, but …
          b Has he done that himself? ?He himself, no, but …

Exactly the same point can be made with the following test. It is possible in English to topicalise or left-dislocate the entire VP on condition that the position left vacant is filled with a replacement. Naturally, we can again use the pro-form *do*. Here, AVS clings to the topicalised VP and hence can be considered a co-constituent of it.

(4.13) a I would never mow the lawn myself.
  b Mow the lawn myself, I would never do.

German allows for a similar observation; however, here, due to the relatively free word order, no pro-form for the topicalised VP is necessary. (4.14) below is the translation of (4.13). Since there can be only one constituent before the finite verb in German, the example below yields another point in favour of the co-constituent analysis.

(4.14) a Ich würde den Rasen niemals selbst mähen.
  b Selbst mähen würde ich den Rasen niemals.

More indirect evidence for the claim that AVS should be analysed as a co-constituent of the VP can be drawn from the fact that certain occurrences of sentence-final SELF are ambiguous between an adnominal and an adverbal interpretation. Depending on whether the intensifier is in association with subject or object NP, the following example can be read both ways, and provided that we assume that, other things being equal, a difference in meaning must go hand in hand with a difference in structure, then the ambiguity in meaning of (4.15) can be put down to a structural ambiguity as shown below:

(4.15) a The leader of the opposition [VP attacked [NP the Prime Minister himself]].
  b The leader of the opposition [VP attacked [NP the Prime Minister] himself].

As far as this ambiguity is concerned, English sentences often specify the desired interpretation unequivocally. Due to its overt agreement features, sentence-final SELF can clarify whether it is in association with the object or with the subject, hence whether we deal with ANS or AVS. It is sufficient for subject and object NP to differ in one feature: person, number or gender.

(4.16) a I [VP invited [NP the author himself]].
  b I [VP invited [NP the author] myself].

(4.17) a They [VP invited [NP the author himself]].
  b They [VP invited [NP the author] themselves].

The parallel German sentences, by contrast, must remain ambiguous since *selbst* lacks inflection. (4.18) gives the translation of (4.16).

(4.18) a Ich [VP habe [NP den Autor selbst] eingeladen].
  b Ich [VP habe [NP den Autor] selbst eingeladen].

Examples like (4.16)–(4.18) also support the claim that AVS is a co-constituent of the VP and not of some element inside it, such as e.g. the object NP. This point is underlined by the observation that AVS readily occurs with intransitive verbs:[1]

(4.19) a The president came himself.
          b I will go there myself.
          c How can he complain about the snoring of other people when he snores himself?

The fact that AVS combines with intransitive verbs makes it likely to be analysed as an adjunct. At least three additional points can be brought forward to support this view. For a start, recall from section 3.1.1 that ANS could convincingly be shown to be an adjunct. Since, for all their differences, ANS and AVS share a wide variety of properties – they look the same formally, inflect in the same way, are in association with an NP, etc. – one should assume by extension that AVS also shares this feature of ANS. Second, AVS combines with transitive verbs only if all their argument slots are saturated. Otherwise, it is interpreted as the reflexive pronoun and, where that reading is barred for semantic reasons, the relevant examples simply become ungrammatical:

(4.20) a She wanted to solder the wires together herself.
          b *She wanted to solder herself.

Finally, and this again is implicit in what has been stated so far, AVS is always optional. Leaving it out never affects the grammaticality of a sentence. Semantically speaking, sentences with AVS imply those without intensifiers:

(4.21) a I don't believe that (myself).
          b She was (herself) surprised at the news.
          c They had to repair the car (themselves).

It is important to bear in mind that the preceding remark applies in principle only. Saying that AVS is optional should not give rise to the implication that it is superfluous (the same holds for ANS). As soon as one takes a look at attested examples, which are not made up to prove a point of linguistic interest, it becomes apparent that deleting AVS can indeed make otherwise impeccable sentences extremely hard to interpret:

(4.22) a The experience of watching someone lecture to a live audience is very different from being there yourself. [BNC]
          b It will you know, you see it done once and do it once yourself. [BNC]

c Elizabeth waited for a moment as though for someone else to open the door and then rose and went to do so herself. [BNC]

Section 3.1.1 showed that ANS always occurs right-adjacent to the NP it modifies and that additional arguments and adjuncts must be placed to the left of the intensifier, never to its right. A similar observation can be made in the case of AVS. Here too, adjunction occurs at the right periphery of the VP, cf. the data in (4.23) through (4.25).

(4.23) a I have been to London myself.
       b ??I have been myself to London.

(4.24) a He has hoovered the carpet himself.
       b ??He has hoovered himself the carpet.

(4.25) a I have given her advice myself.
       b ??I have given her myself advice.
       c ??I have given myself her advice.

Nevertheless, in complex VPs, AVS can also occur behind the finite verb (modal, auxiliary, etc.), and here, additional adjuncts are more acceptable behind the intensifier and not before it, cf. (4.26) and (4.27).

(4.26) a I have myself been to London.
       b He has himself hoovered the carpet.
       c I have myself given her advice.

(4.27) a I have (??often) myself (often) been to London.
       b He has (??quickly) himself (quickly) hoovered the carpet.
       c I have (??frequently) myself (frequently) given her advice.

Let me briefly summarise the main points. So far we have shown that AVS is a co-constituent of the VP. It is not a co-constituent of the NP with which it interacts and with which it shows agreement, nor is it part of any of the internal arguments of the VP. Moreover, it is not adjoined to a node above VP. It is an adjunct and must be analysed as an endocentric expansion of the VP. Figure 4.1 depicts these results.

Recall that the present study assumes threefold polysemy of the intensifier. This approach assigns separate meanings to ANS, on the one hand, as well as to inclusive and exclusive AVS, on the other. Consequently, the lexicon will have to provide three different entries. As far as ANS is concerned, this is a straightforward approach because its entry can be kept relatively simple. Neglecting the semantic side of the coin for the time being, all it has to specify is that ANS modifies NPs. The entries of AVS, inclusive and

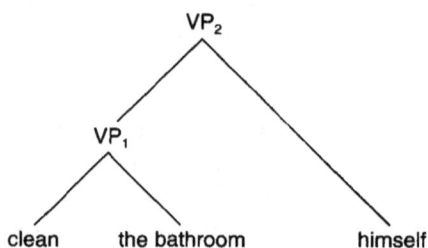

Figure 4.1 Adverbal SELF.

exclusive, look slightly more complicated because in these cases, it has to be made sure that although they modify VPs, they are at the same time in association with an NP. Given that all three intensifiers have their own entries, they can be generated in their final positions right from the beginning.

Whatever the actual entries of the three types of usage might look like, the disadvantage of this approach lies in the fact that three separate entries are necessary. Hence, one might want to consider the possibility to restrict the entries necessary to just one, yielding the basic use type, and to derive the remaining two related uses from the basic one with the help of some syntactic operation (transformation, movement, or the like). Such an approach presupposes that there is a core meaning of the intensifier which the three uses can be reduced to.

A likely scenario would be to regard the adnominal intensifier as the basic use type because here, syntax and semantics go neatly hand in hand. On that account, the adverbal intensifiers would come to be analysed as ANS which has been moved into the VP (or which floated there by itself), and indeed, such proposals can be found in the literature, cf. Moravcsik (1972), Keenan (1996). The prerequisite for such an account is the assumption of more than one level of representation, as e.g. done in frameworks such as Government & Binding. Given this proviso it becomes possible to regard AVS as being generated right-adjacent to the NP it interacts with, which means that it is generated in the syntactic position of ANS. In a subsequent step, ANS (AVS) is moved into the VP and adjoined there. It is then said to leave a trace or simply an empty position in the location where it was generated. Figure 4.2 depicts such a scenario.

However, an analysis according to Figure 4.2 is unlikely because syntactic operations are generally thought to be meaning-preserving.[2] This is plausible in so far as the lexicon is the place where meaning is specified. A movement analysis predicts that ANS and AVS make the same contribution modulo differences due to the context. In particular, ANS and AVS should be equivalent with respect to which constituent they interact with, namely an NP. However, there are good reasons to believe that AVS is in association with both the VP and an NP. This will become clear in the chapters on semantics.

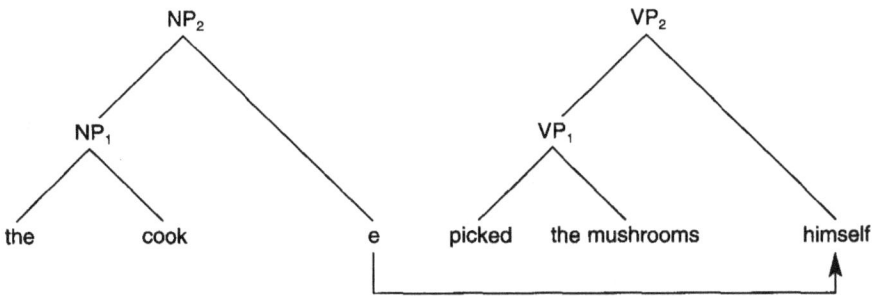

Figure 4.2 Movement to the right.

4.2 AVS as an adverb

The conclusion that AVS is an adjunct of the VP, i.e. that it modifies the VP, calls for a few remarks on how it compares with the traditional concept of an adverb. The question is which additional features AVS shares with expressions of that group and where it differs. It is also of interest whether AVS can be subsumed under one of the established adverb groups, as e.g. focus adverbs, adverbs of manner, frequency, time, degree, location, etc., although only the first two can be regarded as serious contenders. As pointed out in section 2.2, the stance taken here is that AVS, and of course ANS, belong to the group of focus adverbs or focus particles. However, it will turn out that there is no easy answer possible for either of the two questions posed above because although AVS clearly possesses some properties typical of adverbials as well as properties making it a likely candidate of some particular group, it is equally apparent that it also lacks important ones. Here are some pros and cons.

As for the pros, we already know that AVS is part of the VP, that it is optional and that it somehow modifies the VP semantically. These are central properties of adverbs. Moreover, it can occupy standard adverb positions, namely between auxiliary and main verb as well as at the end of a sentence.

(4.28) a I could easily win the match.
        b I could win the match easily.

(4.29) a I could myself win the match.
        b I could win the match myself.

In addition, AVS is not allowed in positions where adverbs are forbidden too. The following examples show that neither of the two can take up the position between the verb and its internal argument and, what is more, it is equally ruled out for either to intervene between two arguments, cf. also (4.23) to (4.25).

(4.30)   I could win *easily/*myself the match.

(4.31)   He could buy her *easily/*himself the diamond.

Note that in contrast to adverbs like *cleverly, probably, slowly*, etc., AVS cannot occur in sentence-initial position. However, this is not a point against an adverb analysis because many adverbs block this position too, cf. (4.32). The restriction to only occur after the auxiliary or in sentence-final position would make AVS an adverb of group four according to the classification of adverbs put forward in Jackendoff (1972: 49ff.). Note, however, that AVS can neither be used as a sentence adverb nor as a modifier for adjectives.

(4.32)   a   *Easily I could win the match.
         b   *Myself I could win the match.

The list of the pros can be extended by the fact that, just as ordinary adverbs, AVS can be the focus of particles such as *only, even*, etc. This property, however, is restricted to exclusive AVS.

(4.33)   You can make this decision only yourself/quickly.

(4.34)   I can do that even myself/quickly.

Another property which is frequently mentioned in connection with adverbs is that they are invariable, i.e. that they do not inflect. This point brings us to a discussion of the cons, simply because that property can justly be claimed only for German. As we have mentioned above, English AVS inflects for person, number and gender, which is extremely untypical of adverbs, even when looked at from a typological perspective, and moves it more into the direction of adjectives.

A related point concerns the fact that AVS is always in association with an NP. Being part of the VP, this is rather reminiscent of secondary predicates, but can hardly count as a central adverb property.[3] To regard AVS as a secondary predicate is, however, difficult from a semantic point of view. Whereas it is easily possible to view *tired* in (4.35a) as a predicate and to interpret 'tired(x)', it seems rather hard to figure out what 'himself(x)' could possibly mean.

(4.35)   a   He drove the car tired.
         b   He drove the car himself.

Also, if AVS is to be analysed as an adverb, it is not easy to decide which semantic subclass it is supposed to belong to. This brings us to the second question. Apart from focus adverbs, the most likely group under which one could subsume AVS is manner adverbs, and indeed, Browning (1993) suggests an analysis along these lines, at least for exclusive AVS. However, standard tests for manner adverbs, as e.g. the paraphrases according to (4.36), reveal that there is no paraphrase possible with AVS, cf. (4.37). This suggests that AVS is not a manner adverb, but does not dispute its membership of the adverb class itself.

(4.36)   a Liz answered the letter cleverly.
               b The manner in which Liz answered the letter was clever.

(4.37)   a Liz answered the letter herself.
               b *The manner in which Liz answered the letter was herself.

Note further that AVS cannot be coordinated with manner adverbs. Although there are probably many manner adverbs which cannot be coordinated for semantic reasons, it is not obvious why *efficiently* and *quietly* in (4.38a,b) should be incompatible with AVS. Among themselves, *efficiently* and *quietly* are easily compatible, cf. (4.39).

(4.38)   a ??He had done it himself and efficiently.
               b ??She spoke to him quietly and herself.

(4.39)   He had done it quietly and efficiently.

A similar point can be made with a slightly different type of coordination, namely the list structures in (4.40). (4.40a) is only acceptable with an intonational break between *herself* and *discreetly* which serves to clarify that the two expressions are not coordinated. This is only possible with AVS heading or terminating the list. If it is contained somewhere in the middle, a successful interpretation is hard to achieve, cf. (4.40b).

(4.40)   a She was assuring the headmaster that she could handle it herself, discreetly, quickly, and well.
               b ?She was assuring the headmaster that she could handle it discreetly, herself, quickly, and well.

The only option there is for coordinating AVS with anything at all is to use an expression similar to it in meaning as e.g. *alone* or *on one's own*. Although it is possible to interpret these structures, they do not make much sense semantically since the same information is conveyed twice.

(4.41)   He had done it all himself and alone/on his own.

Notice also that manner adverbs are not affected by syntactic operations such as passivisation or anticausative formation. AVS, by contrast, becomes ungrammatical:[4]

(4.42)   a The captain sank the ship quickly/himself.
         b The ship was sunk quickly/*himself.
         c The ship sank quickly/*himself.

If exclusive AVS is a dubious manner adverb, it appears to make no sense at all to try to subsume inclusive AVS under that class. Paraphrases with adjectives as in (4.36) are doomed to failure right from the beginning and coordinating it with manner adverbs, in fact all adverbs, would result in equally unacceptable constellations.

From what was said above, it appears that mainly two points argue against an adverb analysis of AVS. On the one hand, it is unusual for adverbs to show inflection. On the other, adverbs are not supposed to be in association with an NP. Still, adverbs are an extremely large and heterogeneous class and if there is a class to subsume adverbial intensifiers under, then this one should probably be it. At least its syntactic position as well as the distributional facts support such a decision.

However, inclusive and exclusive AVS are clearly not members of any of the core groups of adverbs, they are not manner adverbs, nor of time, place, degree, etc. Where they could be reasonably well placed is in the group of focusing adverbs. Being always stressed, in association with an NP and, moreover, evoking alternatives to the denotation thereof definitely points into that direction, cf. (4.43).

(4.43)   a She has been happily married twice herself.
         b They usually do quantitative research most efficiently them-
            selves.

Such a move also aligns adverbal with adnominal intensifiers. Nevertheless, that intensifiers are restricted to nominal foci as well as the fact that English intensifiers show agreement with their focus remain mysterious properties which would almost justify our regarding them as expressions *sui generis*.

4.3 Syntactic restrictions

The following discussion concerns the syntactic restrictions applying to adverbal intensifiers as well as a review of the major English-German contrasts. These two areas will often turn out to be closely intertwined. Let us start with a comparison between ANS and AVS. These observations are mainly based on Moravcsik (1972) and Edmondson and Plank (1978).

First of all, it is noteworthy that AVS readily interacts with indefinite NPs, cf. (4.44) below. Recall from example (3.47) that ANS cannot modify such NPs. Moreover, AVS also interacts with quantified NPs, cf. (4.45), as well as with interrogative pronouns, cf. (4.46).

(4.44)   a A chieftain could lead the onslaught himself.
         b A president should sign all important documents himself.

(4.45)   Some/many/all presidents were uneasy about the contract themselves.

(4.46)   Who/which president came himself?

However, when considering additional data it turns out that indefinite pronouns are a little difficult to judge. Whereas *anyone* and *nobody* certainly interact with AVS, the judgements about *someone* are not unanimous. (4.47b), in contrast to (4.47a), appears to require a more extensive contextualisation before it can be made sense of.

(4.47)   a Anyone/nobody would do such a thing himself.
         b Someone has obviously repaired the car himself.

By and large, interaction with indefinite and quantified NPs seems to be restricted to exclusive AVS. The examples in (4.44) are likely to be read this way. However, it is not entirely clear whether inclusive AVS blocks these NPs as such or whether it is simply a little difficult to produce an inclusive effect with them. At least (4.44a,b) seem to allow inclusive AVS, but it is hard to think up adequate context.

As a matter of fact, with regard to indefinite NPs, inclusive AVS appears to be more similar to ANS than to exclusive AVS. As soon as the indefinite article is forced into its specific interpretation, as done in (4.48c), inclusive AVS suddenly becomes much more acceptable, as was the case with ANS. To get the desired reading of (4.48c), imagine a set of presidents as well as a set of worried people.

(4.48)   a The president was worried himself.
         b ??A president was worried himself.
         c A certain president/one of the presidents was worried himself.

Something similar also seems to be true of exclusive AVS. Note that both examples in (4.44) involve generic indefinite NPs, which are much better with ANS than non-generic indefinites. Sentences containing non-generic indefinite NPs in combination with exclusive AVS suffer a decrease in acceptability too:

(4.49)   a ?A postman delivered the parcel himself.
         b ?A pilot landed the aircraft himself.

The present point carries over to the generic or indefinite pronoun *one* which we also found barred from interacting with ANS other than in its specific reading, cf. (4.50).

(4.50)   a ??One oneself will need to grow the plants and prepare the drink.
　　　　 b That is to say they constructed a picture of the world, a picture which one oneself no longer believes to be viable. [BNC]

Again, E. *one* as well as G. *man* seem to require a specific reading to allow inclusive AVS. Here, in contrast to indefinite NPs in general, we know for certain that they can be constructed not only with exclusive, but also inclusive AVS, cf. (4.51). (4.51b) is taken from Plank (1979a: 270), (4.51c) from Dirven (1973: 291).

(4.51)   a One will need to grow the plants and prepare the drink oneself. (exclusive)
　　　　 b Es ist beunruhigend zu wissen, daß man eines Tages selbst dort enden wird. (inclusive)
　　　　　　'It is disquieting to realise that one will sooner or later end up there oneself.'
　　　　 c It's nice to know that one will sleep there oneself one day. (inclusive)

(4.52) is an example of inclusive AVS from a corpus.

(4.52)   And if one started to lust after it oneself, as much as the men – and let them see that one lusted – then what weapon had one left? [LLC]

Another property in which AVS and ANS differ is that the former is fine in imperatives whereas the latter is not, cf. the contrast between (4.53) and (4.54). Moreover, although there again seems to be a certain preference for the exclusive reading, inclusive AVS is also possible in imperatives, cf. (4.53b).

(4.53)   a Go yourself! (exclusive)
　　　　 b Be confident yourself! (inclusive)

(4.54)   a *Yourself go!
　　　　 b *Yourself be confident!

These data are easily explained on the basis of the syntactic analyses developed so far. On the assumption that the subject NP is deleted in imperatives and replaced by a pro-form, it is obvious that ANS cannot occur either because it is part of the subject NP. The assumption of the pro-form, in turn, allows AVS to remain grammatical since it needs an NP to interact with. Note that this explanation is based on the condition that modification of an

NP by ANS occurs prior to imperative formation or, viewed from a different angle, that adjunction to a pro-form is impossible.

Finally, Moravcsik (1972: 275) observes that AVS is different from ANS in so far as only in sentences with AVS can both the intensifier and the NP it interacts with receive contrastive stress:

(4.55)   a   I // went mySELF, but JOHN // sent his SECretary.
           b   ???I // mySELF went, but JOHN // sent his SECretary.

(4.55b) is not acceptable for two reasons. First, the parallel focus is not equally balanced. It is concentrated on one constituent in the first part of the sentence whereas it is dispersed on to two in the second. Semantically, this must lead to incongruity since incompatible entities are contrasted – the same referent twice versus two different referents. Second, the intonational break between subject NP and intensifier excludes an interpretation according to ANS and triggers AVS. However, for AVS, the intensifier is syntactically misplaced. Notice, however, that Moravcsik's claim holds only if the contrastive stress is placed on NP and intensifier. ANS in general is far from being inadequate with parallel focus as (4.56) makes clear.

(4.56)   I mySELF // WENT, but JOHN // sent his SECretary.

4.3.1 Passivisation and passives

Next, let us have a look at data from passivisation. Recall that passivisation can be used as a test to show that ANS and the NP it interacts with are co-constituents because it follows this NP into the optional *by*-phrase. AVS behaves differently. Browning (1993: 84) demonstrates that passivisation of adverbal intensifiers is not possible. (4.57b) below is ungrammatical for two reasons. First, the position between the verb and its arguments is not a possible one for AVS, and the *by*-phrase can be considered an argument of sorts (cf. Grimshaw 1992: 143ff.). Second, and more important, the intensifier precedes the NP it interacts with. Such sequences, however, are possible only under topicalisation.

(4.57)   a   The cook picked the mushrooms himself.
           b   *The mushrooms were picked himself by the cook.

Given that the passive sentence in (4.57b) is ungrammatical because the intensifier precedes the NP it is in association with, it would appear reasonable to assume adjunction of AVS to take place after passivisation so as to allow for AVS to occur behind this NP, i.e. in its usual sentence-final position. Example (4.58) gives the relevant passive sentence.

(4.58)   The mushrooms were picked by the cook himself.

However, note that after deriving (4.58) this way, it becomes very hard to decide whether it contains an instance of ANS or AVS. As a matter of fact, the intensifier is now adjacent to the NP and obviously a co-constituent of it. If the *by*-phrase is put into an *it*-cleft, *himself* cannot be left behind:

(4.59)   a It was by the cook himself that the mushrooms were picked.
       b *It was by the cook that the mushrooms were picked himself.

The above observations might give rise to the suspicion that AVS does not only hinder passivisation, but that it is not available in English passive sentences at all. And indeed, in a context requiring the use of ANS as e.g. (4.60a), (4.60b) is much better than (4.60c).

(4.60)   a Who picked the mushrooms for the cook?
       b I believe, the cook picked them himself.
       c ?I believe, they were picked by the cook himself.

More indirect evidence for the inability of AVS to occur in passives can be obtained from replacing it by near paraphrases. It has already been mentioned that *alone* and *on one's own* can be regarded as possible glosses at least for exclusive AVS. Now, consider (4.61). In (4.61a) *alone* means that Fred is able to repair the car without help from a third party. This would be the adequate gloss for exclusive AVS. After passivisation and adjunction of *alone*, (4.61a) must receive a totally different interpretation, namely, that Fred is the only one who is able to repair the car, cf. (4.61b).

(4.61)   a Fred can repair this car alone. (≈ Fred does not need help to repair this car.)
       b This car can be repaired by Fred alone. (≈ Only Fred can repair this car.)

On one's own in (4.62) is a similar case. In (4.62a) it is a very good gloss for exclusive AVS, probably the best there is. Moreover, this is the only meaning it can have, it is not available in the sense of ANS. When (4.62b) is less acceptable, a possible conclusion is that passives block AVS.

(4.62)   a Sarah showed me the room on her own.
       b ??I was shown the room by Sarah on her own.

So far we have considered examples of exclusive AVS only. However, what we find is that sentences containing inclusive AVS behave in exactly the same way. Passivising such examples leads to ungrammatical results. (4.63) gives a modified mushroom example in the context necessary to trigger inclusive AVS and (4.64) shows the actual passivisation.

(4.63)   The cook knows what it means to pick mushrooms because he has picked some himself.

(4.64)   a The cook has picked some mushrooms himself.
          b *Some mushrooms have been picked himself by the cook.

Adjoining inclusive AVS directly to a passive sentence, again, yields grammatical output, however, the inclusive effect is lost during the process. (4.65) rather seems to be an instance of ANS, and indeed, when put into the context inducing inclusive AVS, the example becomes less acceptable, cf. (4.66).

(4.65)   Some mushrooms have been picked by the cook himself.

(4.66)   ?The cook knows what it means to pick mushrooms because some have been picked by the cook himself.

Notice, again, that there is a difference between saying that adverbal intensifiers do not permit passivisation and that they are not possible in passive sentences. Although inclusive AVS obstructs passivisation, it can nevertheless be found in passives, cf. (4.67a) taken from Browning (1993: 85). With regard to this property, it is different from exclusive AVS which neither allows passivisation nor can it be adjoined to passive sentences, cf. (4.67b).

(4.67)   a John has himself been hit by Bill a few times.
          b John has been hit himself.

The reason why English disfavours adverbal intensifiers in passives is not easy to discern. Judged from a purely structural point of view, the necessary ambiguity is provided for. In examples like (4.68) below, x-*self* can be thought of as adjoined to either the NP or the VP. The former gives ANS, the latter would result in AVS. The problem might simply be that the NP with which x-*self* is in association intervenes between the verb and the intensifier, thereby becoming the closest and hence preferred node for adjunction. Be that as it may, what appears to be the case is that English adverbal intensifiers are restricted to interacting with the subject. The following sections will confirm this hypothesis.

(4.68)   a The mushrooms [VP were picked by [NP the cook himself]].
             (ANS)
          b The mushrooms [VP were picked by [NP the cook] himself].
             (AVS)

German is entirely different in this respect. Here, the adverbal reading of the intensifier is easily available under passivisation, cf. (4.69).

(4.69)   a   Der Koch sammelte die Pilze selbst. (=(4.57a))
         b   Die Pilze wurden vom [Koch selbst] gesammelt. (ANS)
             (= (4.68a))
         c   Die Pilze wurden vom Koch [selbst gesammelt]. (AVS)
             (= (4.68b))

That this is so becomes clear when these passives are put into context necessary for exclusive AVS. (4.70) is the German equivalent of (4.60), and here, the c-sentence is perfectly acceptable.

(4.70)   a   Wer hat denn die Pilze für den Koch gesammelt?
         b   Ich glaube, er hat sie selbst gesammelt.
         c   Ich glaube, sie sind von ihm selbst gesammelt worden.

The above contrast becomes even more clearly visible under negation. Depending on the scope of the G. negative element *nicht*, either ANS (4.71a) or AVS (4.71b) is triggered. In the former case, *nicht* has scope over the *by*-phrase plus intensifier, in the latter, intensifier plus verb are in its scope. In actual fact, it should be possible to restrict the scope of *nicht* in (4.71a) so as to exclude the intensifier. This reading of AVS is indeed available though it takes some effort to get it. Its meaning can be paraphrased by *It was not the cook who picked the mushrooms himself.*

(4.71)   a   Die Pilze   wurden [nicht vom Koch   selbst] gesammelt. (ANS)
             The mushrooms   were   not   by the cook himself picked
         b   Die Pilze   wurden vom Koch [nicht selbst   gesammelt]. (AVS)
             The mushrooms   were   by the cook not   himself picked

That German should be less restricted than English could be due to the following reason. In German passives, the *by*-phrase as well as the intensifier find their natural place within the so-called '*Satzklammer*' (sentence brace), i.e. in between two verbal elements. This is by no means peculiar to passives. As is well-known, a German complex VP, i.e. a VP consisting of more than two elements, will always open up a so-called '*Mittelfeld*' (middle field) where arguments and adjunctions to the VP go. Given that the intensifier follows the NP it interacts with, although preceding the main verb, passive structures like (4.69b,c) emerge and it is obvious that they are structurally ambiguous.

As far as inclusive AVS is concerned, German behaves in the same way as English. Here too, we find that the inclusive reading is totally lost after passivisation. Where it differs is in the fact that the intensifier in the derived passive sentence can be interpreted either as adnominal or adverbal exclusive. (4.72a) is the German counterpart to (4.64a) and (4.72b) to (4.65).

(4.72) a Der Koch hat selbst einige Pilze gesammelt. (inclusive)
        b Einige Pilze sind vom Koch selbst gesammelt worden.
           (adnominal, exclusive)

It should seem that passivisation tells us three things. First, sentences containing adverbal intensifiers can be passivised in German, but, in all probability, not in English. Second, in German, only exclusive AVS can be passivised. And third, adjunction of intensifiers to English passive sentences results in ANS.

Let me finally point out again that although AVS is a co-constituent of the VP, it is still in association with an NP so that those operations on the argument structure of a verb which eliminate (or suppress) the argument position of this very NP are not applicable to the relevant examples unless the intensifier is itself dropped. This holds for passivisation, cf. (4.73), and is equally true of anticausatives as in (4.74), in fact, all valency-changing operations.

(4.73) a The cook picked the mushrooms himself.
        b *The mushrooms were picked himself.

(4.74) a The captain sank the ship himself.
        b *The ship sank himself.

4.3.2 Topicalisation

Another area where syntactic restrictions can be encountered and English-German contrasts can be observed is topicalisation. Recall that restrictions on topicalisation also apply in the case of ANS, cf. section 3.1.2. Put in a nutshell, it is only possible to topicalise adnominal intensifiers if they interact with the subject NP and, what is more, in English, topicalisation of ANS is by and large confined to the first person. As far as adverbal intensifiers are concerned, there is a very sharp contrast observable between inclusive and exclusive AVS as well as between English and German. In brief, AVS does not topicalise in English, but only in German, and topicalisation in German is confined to exclusive AVS. But let us look at these issues in more detail.

As for English, consider the examples in (4.75). (4.75a) is a valid occurrence of exclusive AVS. (4.75b), by contrast, is a valid topicalisation, but it is not an example of exclusive AVS any longer.

(4.75) a I didn't repair the roof myself.
        b Myself, I didn't repair the roof. ≠ (4.75a)

(4.76) shows (4.75) in the context necessary to induce exclusive AVS. The topicalised example, however, is not adequate.

(4.76)   a   I asked the tiler to repair the roof. I didn't do it myself.
         b   I asked the tiler to repair the roof. ?Myself, I didn't do it.

The question that remains to be answered is in what kind of SELF the topicalisation exclusive AVS results. Obviously, it is not inclusive AVS so that ANS can be the only valid alternative. And indeed, put into adequate context, (4.75b) manifests itself as a clear example of ANS, cf. (4.77).

(4.77)   It was my brother who repaired the roof. Myself, I didn't do it.

Further support for this state of affairs comes from topicalising near paraphrases of exclusive AVS. (4.78b) is less acceptable than (4.78a) because *on one's own* does not allow the adnominal reading.

(4.78)   a   I didn't repair the roof on my own.
         b   ?On my own, I didn't repair the roof.

German, by contrast, readily allows topicalisation of exclusive AVS, cf. (4.79), which is the translation of (4.75).

(4.79)   a   Ich habe mein Dach nicht selbst repariert.
         b   SELBST habe ich mein Dach // NICHT repariert.
             = (4.79a)

The prerequisite is that the sentence in question has two tone groups each containing a focus accent and that it is read with a special intonation contour. Without the double focus, an interpretation is not possible:

(4.80)   *SELBST habe ich mein Dach nicht repariert.

Due to its particular intonation, this type of topicalisation is sometimes referred to as 'I-Topikalisierung' or 'I-topicalisation' (cf. Jacobs 1982, 1986, 1996). The 'I' is shorthand for 'intonation'. Under this particular intonation, which, roughly speaking, requires a rise on the first focus and a fall on the second, *selbst* comes into the scope of the negative element *nicht* which makes the interpretation of (4.79b) equivalent to that of (4.79a).[5] A more extensive discussion of 'I-Topikalisierung' in connection with intensifiers can be found in König and Siemund (1999a).

In parallel order to the English examples above, (4.81) gives the translation of (4.76) and, as one would expect, the topicalised example is perfectly acceptable in the context necessary to induce exclusive AVS.

(4.81)   a   Ich habe den Dachdecker beauftragt, das Dach zu reparieren. Ich habe das nicht selbst gemacht.
         b   Ich habe den Dachdecker beauftragt, das Dach zu reparieren. Selbst habe ich das nicht gemacht.

(4.82), in turn, is the German equivalent of (4.77), which again shows that the adnominal reading is possible too, i.e. German topicalised *selbst* is in fact ambiguous.

(4.82)   Mein Bruder war derjenige, der das Dach repariert hat. Selbst habe ich das nicht gemacht.

To sum up, topicalisation of adverbal intensifiers is not possible in English, but it is in German. Topicalised *selbst* is ambiguous between exclusive AVS and ANS, context permitting. It remains to be asked what happens when inclusive AVS is topicalised. As the examples below show, inclusive AVS does not permit this operation and the intensifier escapes into either the adnominal or exclusive interpretation, depending on the surrounding context.

(4.83)   a Ich habe selbst Kopfschmerzen. (inclusive AVS)
         b SELBST // habe ich KOPFschmerzen. (ANS)
           'I've got a headache myself.'

(4.84)   a Er hat sein Fahrrad selbst nicht geputzt. (inclusive AVS)
         b SELBST hat er sein Fahrrad // NICHT geputzt. (exclusive AVS)
           'He did not clean his bike himself.'

The reason for this restriction is not easy to see, but it may be due to the fact that topicalisation is a contrasting device whereas inclusive particles are equalising devices. Notice, at least, that the glosses for inclusive and exclusive AVS behave in exactly the same manner, cf. (4.85).

(4.85)   a *AUCH hat er sein Fahrrad // NICHT geputzt.
         b ALLEIN hat er sein Fahrrad // NICHT geputzt.

Note, finally, that the constraint on sentences with topicalised exclusive AVS to have two foci may be slightly relaxed under certain conditions. (4.86) is just about acceptable with a single focus in the context given (cf. König and Siemund 1996a: 13). What these conditions are is not entirely clear, but it might well be that the explicit introduction of the two alternative actions in the previous context has a stake in it.

(4.86)   A: Willst du das machen oder willst du fremde Hilfe in Anspruch nehmen? – B: SELBST will ich das machen.
           'A: Would you like to do that yourself or rather have somebody else assist you? – B: I would like to do it myself.'

4.3.3 Scope bearing elements

Further interesting properties of AVS emerge in connection with scope bearing elements, cf. Plank (1979a: 276), König (1991: 92). The resulting effects are particularly clearly visible in the case of the German negative element *nicht*. To cut a long story short, if *nicht* precedes and thus has scope over AVS, this linear order of elements results in the exclusive interpretation of AVS. If, by contrast, AVS precedes and has scope over *nicht*, the resulting interpretation is invariably an inclusive one:

(4.87)   Paul hat die Aufgabe nicht SELBST gelöst. (exclusive)
          'Paul has not solved the problem himself.'

(4.88)   Paul hat die Aufgabe SELBST nicht gelöst. (inclusive)
          'Paul has not solved the problem himself.'

The above effect can be observed with other scope bearing elements too, in fact, it manifests itself in all of them. (4.89) can only mean that Laura phoned her boss three times and that she did so on her own, whereas (4.90) states that Laura as well as somebody else both phoned their boss three times.

(4.89)   Laura hat ihren Chef dreimal SELBST angerufen. (exclusive)
          'Laura has phoned her boss three times herself.'

(4.90)   Laura hat ihren Chef SELBST dreimal angerufen. (inclusive)
          'Laura has phoned her boss three times herself.'

A comparable effect cannot be found in English. Note that the English translations of (4.87) and (4.88) as well as of (4.89) and (4.90) are equivalent. Here, we find no correspondence between syntactic and semantic scope. However, since all the relevant examples are ambiguous between inclusive and exclusive AVS, it should seem reasonable to attribute the ambiguity to a difference in semantic scope. The contrastive evidence from German also supports such a conclusion. (4.92) explicates the two possible readings of (4.91).

(4.91)   Paul didn't notice the error himself.

(4.92)   a Somebody had to tell Paul that there was an error.
             (exclusive)
          b Paul was not the only one who did not notice the error.
             (inclusive)

As a matter of fact, the phenomenon under discussion is much more general than it might appear to be because exactly the same ambiguity in scope can be observed with scope bearing expressions apart from AVS too.

(4.93) and (4.94) exhibit the same contrast. In the former example, *nicht* has scope over *ein*, whereas *ein* has scope over *nicht* in the latter. Again, this differentiation is lost in English which makes the relevant translations ambiguous. König (1991: 50) points out that English cannot disambiguate relative scope due to its comparatively fixed word order. Descriptive negation in English is confined to the position behind the first auxiliary.

(4.93)   Ich habe nicht ein Buch gelesen.
         'I have not read one book.'

(4.94)   Ich habe ein Buch nicht gelesen.
         'I have not read one book.'

The different scope relations that inclusive and exclusive AVS induce are also reflected in their paraphrases. (4.95) demonstrates that *allein* has narrow scope whereas *auch* takes wide scope.

(4.95)   a Paul hat die Aufgabe nicht allein gelöst. ≈ (4.87)
         b Paul hat die Aufgabe auch nicht gelöst. ≈ (4.88)

Recall, nevertheless, that in English complex VPs, adverbal intensifiers may occur either immediately after the auxiliary or in sentence-final position. Recall further that exclusive AVS is highly unusual right behind the auxiliary whereas inclusive AVS can occur in either position. This means that in negative complex VPs, even English can, at least to a certain extent, reflect relative scope correctly in the linear order of constituents, cf. the contrast between (4.96) and (4.97).

(4.96)   a He blames me for not having found the answer although he
            has not found it himself. (inclusive)
         b I will have to tell him the answer. He will not find it himself.
            (exclusive)

(4.97)   a He blames me for not having found the answer although he
            has himself not found it. (inclusive)
         b I will have to tell him the answer. ?He will himself not find
            it. (exclusive)

If inclusive AVS cannot occur within the scope of scope bearing elements whereas exclusive AVS cannot acquire scope over them, it should follow that these restrictions can be used as a tool for singling out predicates which are confined to either of the two types of AVS. Naturally, this will work only for German. In case an example containing AVS becomes unacceptable under negation with *selbst* taking narrow scope, it can be followed that the relevant predicate is restricted to inclusive *selbst* (provided that the relevant predicate allows adverbal intensifiers at all), cf. (4.98a). If the scope relations are reversed, the example becomes acceptable, cf. (4.98b). Hence, *snore* must be regarded as a predicate disallowing the exclusive intensifier. Conversely, if, under negation, an example becomes unacceptable with *selbst* taking wide scope, it cannot be the adequate context for inclusive *selbst* so that the relevant predicate must be bound to the exclusive intensifier, cf. (4.99).

(4.98) a ???Paul schnarcht nicht selbst.
        b Paul schnarcht selbst nicht.
           'Paul does not snore himself.'

(4.99) a ???Der Papst hat die Osterbotschaft selbst nicht verlesen.
        b Der Papst hat die Osterbotschaft nicht selbst verlesen.
           'The Pope did not read the Easter Message himself.'

In sum, in the presence of additional scope bearing elements, inclusive and exclusive AVS are in complementary distribution. The former always takes wide scope whereas the latter is restricted to taking narrow scope. In German, scope relations are reflected in the linear order of constituents, i.e. semantic scope equals syntactic scope. English only partly disambiguates scope relations on the surface.

4.3.4 Inclusive versus exclusive AVS

Whereas additional scope bearing elements, at least in German, are an extremely sound criterion to separate inclusive from exclusive AVS, there are also a number of less precise factors which will be discussed in the following. Let us start with position.

As already indicated in section 2.1, AVS predominantly occurs in two positions, after the auxiliary (or modal), if present, and in sentence-final position. As for its distribution with respect to the inclusive/exclusive distinction, it appears to be a reasonable approximation to say that inclusive AVS can occur in either position whereas exclusive AVS is primarily to be found sentence-finally. Of course, the argument is pointless for simplex VPs.

(4.100) a I have myself read this book. (inclusive)
         b I have read this book myself. (inclusive, exclusive)

This generalisation is by and large confirmed when we put sentences like (4.100) into disambiguating contexts and thus restrict their interpretation to either use of AVS. (4.101), which gives the relevant context for inclusive AVS, allows both positions whereas post-auxiliary AVS in the exclusive context of (4.102) appears less acceptable.

(4.101) a I know what 'The Monk' is about. I have myself read the book.

b I know what 'The Monk' is about. I have read the book myself.

(4.102) a Paul did not read 'The Monk' to me. ?I have myself read the book.

b Paul did not read 'The Monk' to me. I have read the book myself.

A similar statement is possible about German. (4.103) and (4.104) are reasonable German renderings of (4.101) and (4.102) and also here the oddity appears in the same position, cf. (4.104a). Recall that there is no sentence-final AVS in German complex VPs. Instead, AVS is found either before or behind the object NP.

(4.103) a Ich weiß, worum es in 'The Monk' geht. Ich habe selbst dieses Buch gelesen.

b Ich weiß, worum es in 'The Monk' geht. Ich habe dieses Buch selbst gelesen.

(4.104) a Paul hat mir 'The Monk' nicht vorgelesen. ??Ich habe selbst dieses Buch gelesen.

b Paul hat mir 'The Monk' nicht vorgelesen. Ich habe dieses Buch selbst gelesen.

These observations square nicely with what has been said about the interplay between AVS and scope bearing elements in German. Since they occur in the middle field under normal conditions and inclusive AVS must be placed before them, it necessarily ends up after the auxiliary. Conversely, since exclusive AVS has to follow them, it takes up the position before the main verb, which is equivalent to the English sentence-final position.

(4.105) a Ich habe selbst viele Fehler gemacht. (inclusive)
b Ich habe viele Fehler selbst gemacht. (exclusive)
'I have made many mistakes myself.'

The statements made above are correct as far as theory goes. In practice, however, there are all sorts of peculiar examples, particularly in English. Nevertheless, the overwhelming majority of occurrences of AVS in post-auxiliary position is inclusive. A short glance at some authentic data will illustrate this point, cf. (4.106) through (4.108).

(4.106) a Perhaps this would be the place to take French visitors in search of authentic English food, although it must be said that I have myself always found it safe enough to take Paris friends to London-French restaurants. [LLC]

    b An establishment at Arras even serves a speciality of andouil-
lettes flambes au whisky – a faint echo of the haggis ritual
…? I find the French development encouraging, for I have
myself for years been experimenting with whisky in the
cooking pots. [LLC]

(4.107) a 'Do I understand you to say that you have yourself had some
remarkable experience?' – 'Nothing of much importance,
Mr Holmes.' [LLC]
    b He took particular care that Sir Henry did not make love to
her, as you have yourself observed. [LLC]

(4.108) a Mr Edelman has himself made an intense study of British
political novels. [LOB]
    b Fortunately John Wesley has himself left a list of the books
which he read with his pupils. [LOB]

Still, it is possible to find exclusive AVS in post-auxiliary position too, cf.
(4.109). This shows that even the weak restriction formulated here, which
disallows exclusive AVS in post-auxiliary position, has to be taken with a
pinch of salt.

(4.109) a To complete the range of work he has added problems
which he has himself devised. [LOB]
    b Henchard is not destroyed by a new and alien kind of
dealing but by a development of his own trade which he has
himself invited. [LLC]

Another criterion for separating the two varieties of AVS is their range of
possible syntactic structures. Put in a nutshell, inclusive AVS extends to a
wider range of structures than exclusive AVS. Whereas the former readily
occurs in passives and unaccusatives, the latter is by and large restricted to
active causative sentences. This restriction, however, is semantic in nature
because exclusive AVS needs an agentive NP to interact with. Recall that in
German, exclusive AVS is possible in passives since it can interact with the
agentive NP inside the *by*-phrase. The situation is less clear in English, but
in all probability, exclusive AVS is here barred from passives altogether. If we
restrict our attention to subject NPs only, German and English behave alike.
The following examples can only receive the inclusive reading.

(4.110) a Paul got hurt himself.
    b How could the Pope speak of immortality when he knew he
would die himself! [Edmondson and Plank 1978: 384]

As far as English is concerned, it would then be correct to say that
exclusive AVS can only be in association with NPs in subject position and,

excluding the *by*-phrase, the same would be true of German. Concerning inclusive AVS, however, the two languages differ substantially. English inclusive AVS behaves like its exclusive counterpart: it cannot interact with NPs other than those in subject position. German, by contrast, allows for nominative subject NPs plus dative and accusative object NPs:[6]

> (4.111)   a   Ich bin selbst betrogen worden. (nominative)
>   'I've been betrayed myself.'
>   b   Mir gefällt die Situation selbst nicht. (dative)
>   'I don't like the situation myself.'
>   c   Mich regt Eifersucht selbst auf. (accusative)
>   'I can get angry about jealousy myself.'

König and Siemund (1996a) suggest as a generalisation that inclusive AVS is always in association with the argument of a sentence that ranks highest in the case hierarchy (nominative > dative > accusative). As for English, this generalisation is trivially true because inclusive AVS interacts only with subjects and subjects are always in the nominative. It would just as well be possible to say that inclusive AVS selects the NP with the highest grammatical function from the hierarchy subject > indirect object > direct object. With regard to German, neither rule makes sense on its own since inclusive AVS can be in association with subjects and objects as well as with dative and accusative NPs. Therefore, König and Siemund postulate an additional constraint which requires the relevant NPs also to be highest in the hierarchy of thematic roles (agent > experiencer/beneficiary > patient) in case the constraint on case roles or grammatical function does not hold.

In German, inclusive AVS may even be in association with NPs inside prepositional adjuncts, cf. (4.112a) and (4.113a) below. If one decides to retain the PP when translating such examples into English, one will have to replace inclusive AVS by *also* or *too* with a subsequent loss in meaning, cf. the corresponding b-sentences. However, it is usually possible and often more adequate to render these secondary subjects as 'real' subjects in English, and then inclusive AVS becomes grammatical again, cf. (4.112c) and (4.113c).

> (4.112)   a   Für mich ist das selbst ein Problem.
>   b   This is a problem for me too/*myself.
>   c   I find that problematic myself.

> (4.113)   a   Für mich war das selbst eine große Überraschung.
>   b   This was a big surprise for me too/*myself.
>   c   I was very surprised myself.

In sum, as long as attention is restricted to German, the generalisation is that AVS in association with NPs other than subjects must be inclusive. Subject NPs allow for both types of AVS. Since English AVS in general appears to be confined to subject NPs, the present criterion is not applicable to it.

Finally, let us discuss the least decisive syntactic correlates of the inclusive/exclusive distinction. As a matter of fact, it is imperative to regard the following effects as mere tendencies. They all centre around the distinction between definiteness and indefiniteness, however, not with regard to the subject NP, but the object NP. To make a long story short, it turns out that AVS in sentences containing definite object NPs is more likely to be interpreted in the exclusive sense whereas indefinite object NPs more or less pattern with inclusive AVS. The reason is purely semantic in nature and will therefore be discussed in a separate section (7.2).

(4.114) a Ruth has posted the letter herself. (exclusive)
          b Ruth has posted a letter herself. (inclusive)

Also, verb alternations entailing partitive/holistic contrasts show a certain influence on the interpretation of AVS. The conative alternation below seems to be patterned in the indicated manner. In the holistic example (4.115a), the entire bread is cut and all of the hamburger is eaten whereas in the partitive example (4.115b), some of the bread remains uncut and some of the hamburger uneaten. To be sure, this is the definite/indefinite distinction in disguise. Whereas (4.115a) denotes a unique cutting or eating event there are several such events possible in (4.115b).

(4.115) a Sue cut the bread/ate up the hamburger herself. (exclusive)
          b Sue cut at the bread/ate from the hamburger herself.
            (inclusive)

Finally, such effects can be observed in alternations of the spray/load type because they induce a partitive/holistic contrast too.

(4.116) a Jack has sprayed the wall with paint himself. (exclusive)
          b Jack has sprayed paint on the wall himself. (inclusive)

Interestingly enough, tense and aspect can also influence the interpretation of AVS to a certain extent. In all likelihood, *himself* in (4.117a) will rather be read as exclusive AVS whereas (4.117b) is open to both interpretations.

(4.117) a Tom read the book himself.
          b Tom has read the book himself.

On the whole, then, the actual interpretation of intensifiers is confined and influenced by a wide variety of factors. On the one hand, we can observe rigid restrictions under passivisation, topicalisation, scope, etc. which force them into a specific reading. On the other hand, we find more subtle ones. These are of limited power and all they can do is make one interpretation more likely than the other. Moreover, these restrictions apply to English and German to different degrees.

Notes

1 These examples, however, do not rule out that the intensifier is adjoined to a node above VP.
2 Movement to the right is discussed in Ross (1967), Baker (1978: 206ff.), Kayne (1979), Haegeman (1991: 381ff.) and Büring and Hartmann (1995). Kayne (1994) excludes rightward movement entirely.
3 Notice, though, that there are adverbs (*willingly, consciously*, etc.) which do interact with the subject NP.
4 Those adverbs being in association with the subject NP differ from AVS in so far as they are possible in passives, but not in anticausatives:

   (i)   The captain sank the ship willingly.
   (ii) The ship was sunk willingly.
   (iii) *The ship sank willingly.

5 This is a slightly simplified picture. The peculiar property of 'I-Topikalisierung' is that it is often not sufficient to pronounce the first focus simply with a rising intonation. It rather has to be a rise-fall-rise because otherwise the scope inversion cannot be achieved and 'I-Topikalisierung' is no longer distinguishable from ordinary double focus structures (Jacobs, 1996). Alternative terms for this intonation contour are 'hat contour', 'bridge accent' and 'root contour', the latter term being motivated by the symbol '$\sqrt{}$'.
   In English, it is also possible to achieve scope inversion by changing the intonation contour of a sentence. The contour lacking scope inversion is usually referred to as 'A-accent', the one inducing scope inversion as 'B-accent', cf. Bolinger (1965), Jackendoff (1972), Büring (1995). The difference between A- and B-accent is that the former pattern terminates with a fall whereas the latter ends in a rise. Accordingly, the example below can be interpreted as either '$\forall x\neg$' or '$\neg\forall x$'.

   (i) All the boys did not come.

6 The only example for which a native speaker felt that it was acceptable to her to translate a G. inclusive AVS interacting with an accusative NP into English on a one-to-one basis that I have come across so far is the following. However, most people do not seem to like it.

   (i) German
       Seine Antwort hat mich selbst nicht besonders überzeugt.
       'His answer didn't strike me as particularly convincing myself.'

5 The meaning of intensifiers – overview

According to the proposal defended here, intensifiers are polysemous and exhibit three types of usage. It is possible to distinguish between one adnominal and two adverbal intensifiers. This differentiation can be motivated on syntactic and semantic grounds. As for syntax, Chapters 3 and 4 have shown that adnominal intensifiers (ANS) are endocentric expansions of an NP whereas adverbal intensifiers (AVS) are endocentric expansions of the VP. The subsequent chapters will demonstrate that, on the semantic level, adnominal SELF only interacts with an NP, but that adverbal SELF interacts with an NP and the VP. From a closer perspective, it becomes apparent that adverbal intensifiers further subdivide into an inclusive and an exclusive variety. Provided that intensifiers are analysed as focus particles, as done here, the former unites focus and alternatives with regard to the remaining open sentence, the latter separates them. Figure 5.1 depicts the present analysis.

This introductory chapter gives an overview of the semantic approaches to intensifiers that have so far been pursued, as well as a brief discussion of the contributions the three types of intensifiers make to the meaning of a sentence. The three subsequent chapters deal with adnominal, adverbal inclusive and adverbal exclusive intensifiers individually.

5.1 Three approaches to intensifiers

Over the past forty or so years, linguists have tried out various approaches to the semantic analysis of intensifiers, thereby arriving at basically two schemes for their classification. They range from purely structuralist to more substantialistically orientated approaches.

The group of sign-oriented approaches holds the contention that all occurrences of intensifiers should subsume under one central meaning. This semantically reflects the fact that there is only one form. According to this point of view, intensifiers are monosemous. In terms of time, this is the group with the longest tradition. Most if not all of the grammar books published in this century belong to this group. They usually admit syntactic differences, however, nowhere do they make these precise and neither do

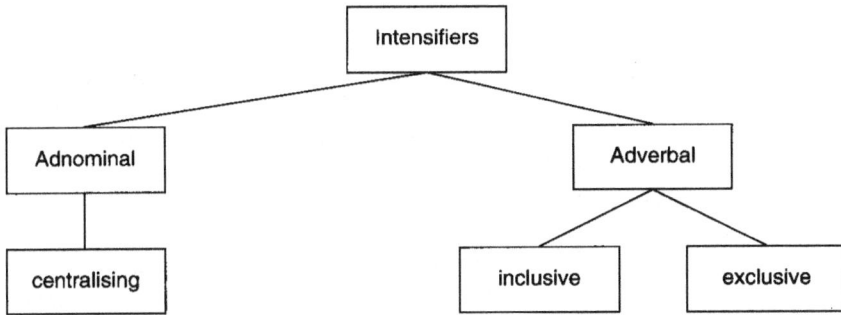

Figure 5.1 The analysis of intensifiers.

they correlate them with particular semantic contributions, or at least contexts. Poutsma (1916), Curme (1931) and Christophersen and Sanved (1969), but also more recent grammar books such as Quirk *et al.* (1985) and Givón (1993) may serve to illustrate the present point. A common theme is to say that intensifiers occur either immediately to the right of the noun or pronoun they modify, which is usually supposed to be the subject, at the end, or in the body of a sentence. Their semantic contribution is simply said to be 'emphasis', without specifying what this label exactly stands for. Hence, these approaches can provide no more than a bird's eye view of the problem.

More theoretically oriented accounts within the group of structuralists attribute a more sophisticated (unique) meaning to intensifiers. Primus (1992), for instance, analyses them as scalar adverbs or scalar focus particles; a move which links intensifiers to German prefocal *selbst* ('even'). She essentially believes them to arrange their focus and the alternatives evoked on a contextually salient scale. According to her, intensifiers invariably characterise their focus as the least likely value in the context of the remaining open sentence. They may, however, select different constituents as their focus, which in turn accounts for the two dominant interpretations intensifiers can have. Girke (1993), by contrast, thinks that thematic roles are essential for the understanding of intensifiers. He mainly argues that the NPs intensifiers modify always manifest a change in their thematic role relative to the preceding context and that the task of intensifiers precisely lies in indicating such a change. Yet another view is expressed in Kibrik and Bogdanova (1995), who regard the discourse properties of intensifiers as basic. In their view, these expressions serve to indicate to the discourse partners present that the assumptions they hold about the referent of the NP an intensifier modifies must be recalculated. Notice that the structuralist approach to intensifiers has been tried out on the levels of semantics, pragmatics and information structure. There are also approaches that see a connection between English intensifiers and reflexive anaphors and ascribe only one meaning to the form x-*self,* cf. e.g. Jayaseelan (1988) and Browning (1993). The validity of such proposals has been dealt with in section 2.4.

Approaches not committed to the one-form-one-meaning contention, however, usually acknowledge two separate meanings of intensifiers. These go hand in hand with their syntactic division into adnominal and adverbal intensifiers. If the node named 'Adverbal' is imagined without the branches below it, Figure 5.1 depicts the present scenario. Moravcsik (1972), Dirven (1973), Edmondson and Plank (1978) and König (1991) are representatives of such a view.

Moravcsik differentiates between head-bound (ANS) and sentence-final x-*self*(AVS) and lists a number of syntactic and semantic differences between them. Nevertheless, she does not venture to develop an analysis of their semantics. Dirven (1973) holds that the meaning of adnominal intensifiers can only be adequately captured on the level of discourse and subsequently labels them 'discourse emphasizers'. This mainly boils down to saying that the contribution of ANS is relevant beyond the boundaries of the sentence it is contained in. Although true, Dirven does not specify what the actual contribution is. Moreover, a similar statement could be made about adverbal intensifiers, however, these he views as 'predicate emphasizers' without making their semantics explicit either.

Edmondson and Plank propose a modal as well as a referential analysis of adnominal intensifiers (*himself*$_1$ in their terminology). As for its modal contribution, they assume ANS to place the referent of its head NP in top position on a scale of remarkability, i.e. the relevant referent is made the most remarkable or least expected value in the situation described by the sentence. Here, the inspiration for Primus (1992) can be found. Concerning referentiality, they suggest that adnominal intensifiers are restricted to nominals with an extensional or de-re reading. They consider generics and indefinites as well as some more special types of NPs incompatible with it. Adverbal intensifiers (*himself*$_2$) are also supposed to achieve an ordering, however, the relevant scale is one of involvement. Adverbal intensifiers, according to Edmondson and Plank, characterise the referent of the NP they interact with as the most directly involved in a situation.

König, finally, analyses intensifiers as clear instances of focus particles. He sees the main contribution of adnominal intensifiers in opening up a contrast between a centre and a periphery. The focus is characterised as central for the alternatives evoked and, conversely, the alternatives are marked as peripheral with regard to the focus. Concerning the analysis of adverbal intensifiers, König mainly follows Edmondson and Plank in regarding them as devices to characterise a referent, now viewed as the focus value, as the most directly involved participant in a situation.

Although it has frequently been noted that, on the one hand, adverbal intensifiers can receive an interpretation in which they are similar in meaning to *alone* and *on one's own,* they may, on the other hand, bear a certain resemblance to the additive particle *also,* cf. e.g. Hall Partee (1965),

Dirven (1973), Plank (1979a,b), König (1991), Browning (1993), Kibrik and Bogdanova (1995). The goal of the relevant studies has always been to motivate these two interpretations from a semantic contribution underlying all occurrences of AVS, as e.g. direct involvement. An analysis in which adverbal intensifiers are strictly polysemous between an inclusive and an exclusive variety, cf. Figure 5.1, has not been advanced yet (except for König and Siemund 1996a,b). Such a substantialist position is taken here, which, among other things, draws justification from the fact that the two adverbal intensifiers as well as the adnominal type can potentially co-occur, cf. section 2.1. Nevertheless, the ordering of elements into central and peripheral ones is a common characteristic of all intensifiers.

5.2 The three uses of intensifiers

According to the position taken here, intensifiers are focusing devices which interact with the information structure of a sentence. They invariably are in association with an NP, their focus as it were, to which they evoke alternatives. Focus and alternatives can be regarded as a set of elements, and what intensifiers also do is to impose a certain structure on this set. König (1991: 87ff.) proposes that the relevant structure is one of centre versus periphery. This is most clearly visible in the case of adnominal intensifiers:

(5.1)   a   The chancellor himself was surprised at the results.
        b   Nobody cared about the fans when the fire broke out, but the rock star himself was quickly whisked away.
        c   Lucy's sister is more intelligent than Lucy herself.
        d   Paul wondered where the problem was. He himself found everything crystal clear.

The alternatives most likely to be evoked to the chancellor in (5.1a) include his ministers, state-secretaries, his chauffeur, etc., in short, people who are affiliated to him and somehow depend on or are subordinated to him. Nowhere is the contrast between centre and periphery more clearly visible than in these hierarchies of the real world. (5.1b) is a special case of (5.1a) in that it exemplifies the same contrast against the background of a particular situation. A rock star is only central for the fans in the context of a rock concert. The centrality of Lucy in (5.1c) results from the fact that the identity of another character is established through her. The defining entity is central whereas the defined entity is peripheral. Finally, a character may acquire centrality by functioning as the centre of perspective in a certain piece of discourse. This is shown in (5.1d). The semantic contribution of adnominal intensifiers is summarised in (5.2), the relevant subcases (proposed in Baker 1995, König and Siemund 1996a,b) are given in (5.3).

(5.2)   Adnominal intensifiers structure a set into a central element X and peripheral elements Y.

(5.3)   a X has a higher position than Y in a hierarchy.
        b X is more significant than Y in a specific situation.
        c Y is defined in terms of X.
        d X is the centre of perspective (logophoricity).

The analysis of adnominal intensifiers on the basis of (5.2) appears to be adequate and sufficiently general to cover all cases and therefore no proposal for a new approach will be made in this study. The chapter on adnominal intensifiers is mainly concerned with finding more subcases and elucidating the properties of the NPs with which they are in association. More challenging is the analysis of adverbal intensifiers. Although there can be no doubt that inclusive and exclusive AVS represent separate uses of intensifiers, it is nevertheless reasonable to assume that there is a common denominator which all types of intensifiers share. The position taken here is that the ability to structure sets into a central element on the one hand and peripheral elements on the other is this common denominator. The main objective, then, is to generalise this idea from adnominal to adverbal intensifiers.

As for adverbal inclusive intensifiers, these characterise a referent as the central representative of a certain property and contrast it with peripheral holders of the same property. One could say that the focus referent is characterised as the embodiment of the property in question. The VP-denotation yields the relevant property. This is summarised in (5.4). In addition to that, adverbal inclusive intensifiers have become specialised to contexts in which two referents are identified against the background of a conditional schema.

(5.4)   Adverbal inclusive intensifiers structure a set of elements with a common property P into a central representative X of P and peripheral representatives Y of P.

(5.5) below gives some typical examples. Although all sentences containing inclusive AVS claim that there is a set of referents (at least one more referent apart from the focus) for which the property denoted by the predication holds, only the character marked by inclusive AVS is perceived as the prototypical holder of that property. Therefore, Max in (5.5a) does not have to be told what it means to be blind and character B in (5.5b) can decline A's request to lend him money.

(5.5)   a Max knows what it means to be blind because he is blind himself.
        b A: Could you lend me some money? – B: Sorry, but I'm a little short myself.

When inclusive AVS characterises a referent as central for or prototypical of a property or, more generally, situation, the contribution of exclusive AVS, by contrast, consists in making a referent (the one denoted by the subject

NP) central in a situation. Again, the VP denotes the relevant situation. Exclusive AVS always interacts with an agentive NP and subsequently evokes agentive alternative referents. The semantic contribution of exclusive AVS is summarised in (5.6).

(5.6)   Adverbal exclusive intensifiers structure a set of possible agents in a situation S into a central agent X and oppose it to peripheral agents Y.

The centrality of the focus referent in a situation in comparison with the alternatives evoked can rest on three characteristics. First, the focus referent may be responsible for or interested in the (result of the) situation. Second, the focus referent may be the beneficiary and third he may be the maleficiary of the situation. These points are never true of the alternative agents although they may participate in the situation. (5.7) summarises these three subcases:

(5.7)   a X is responsible for S.
          b X is the beneficiary of S.
          c X is the maleficiary of S.

The following examples illustrate these subcases:

(5.8)   a The professor devises the exam questions himself.
          b I polish my shoes myself.
          c Paul has ruined his career himself.

In the situation of arranging exam questions, as in (5.8a), it is usually the professor who bears the responsibility and not, say, his assistant, even if the former delegates this task to the latter. The occurrences of exclusive AVS in (5.8b,c) clearly interact with the NPs denoting beneficiary and maleficiary respectively. The crucial point about adverbal exclusive intensifiers is that even if the alternative agents participate in the situation instead of the focus referent itself, the latter remains central in the sense of (5.7).

6 Adnominal centralising intensifiers

The semantic analysis of adnominal intensifiers as discussed in König (1991), namely that these expressions make the referent of their focus central and oppose it to peripheral alternatives, goes a long way towards an exhaustive description of this type of intensifier. Hence, it will not and cannot be the aim of this chapter to put forward a new proposal. Nevertheless, there are several issues that have not been dealt with sufficiently.

First, it has been proposed in the literature that ANS should be analysed as a scalar focus particle, cf. e.g. Primus (1992). Although many of the examples involving adnominal intensifiers show scalar effects, it can be demonstrated that these effects are produced by the context and are not the contribution of the intensifier. This will be done in section 6.1.

Second, the existing body of sentences in the literature exemplifying the usage of adnominal intensifiers is extremely limited. As a consequence, misleading generalisations emerge with respect to the contexts in which ANS can prototypically be found. Although it is certainly true to say that those head NPs denoting personalities of high rank are the first to come to mind, these NPs are far from being representative of the entire spectrum available. Section 6.2 attempts a more comprehensive appraisal of the data.

A third issue concerns the referential properties of the NPs involved. Section 6.3 will show that Edmondson and Plank's (1978) assumptions are too rigid in this respect. The NPs with which adnominal intensifiers interact are bound by exactly two constraints: they must denote something uniquely identifiable and it must be possible to evoke a contrast to the relevant denotations.

The final section 6.4 will take up again the problem of adnominal intensifiers in the context of role reversal structures (recall section 3.3), however, this time from a semantic perspective. It will be argued that the role reversal observed is no contribution of the intensifier.

6.1 Scalar and non-scalar approaches

The basic semantic contribution of adnominal intensifiers (ANS) has been analysed in terms of remarkability/expectancy (Edmondson and Plank

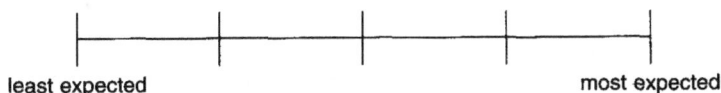

least expected   most expected

Figure 6.1 A scale of expectedness/remarkability.

1978), centrality (König 1991) and likelihood/expectancy (Primus 1992, Kemmer 1995). Moreover, it has been proposed that ANS should be regarded as a focus particle (König 1991, Primus 1992), an expression marking a thematic role reversal (Girke 1993), an operator correcting the expectations in discourse (Kibrik and Bogdanova 1995) and as an indicator of discourse prominence (Baker 1995). These approaches quite naturally divide into scalar analyses (Edmondson and Plank, Primus as well as Kibrik and Bogdanova) and non-scalar or semi-scalar analyses (König, Girke and Baker). Both approaches to analyse ANS take into account that the intensifier evokes alternatives to the referent of its head NP (its focus) in one way or another. Therefore, and for a variety of additional reasons discussed in section 2.2, it makes sense to regard ANS as a focus particle which takes the NP it interacts with as its focus.

The scalar approach holds that ANS orders its focus and the alternatives evoked on a scale. The one end is labelled 'most expected', 'most likely' or 'least remarkable', the other 'least expected', 'least likely' or 'most remarkable'. However, and this is important, the focus value and its alternatives are not ordered *per se*, but only with regard to a certain background or situation. In other words, ANS is assumed to make the focus referent the least likely participant in that situation. Figure 6.1 shows such a scale (cf. Edmondson and Plank 1978: 404).

At first sight such an analysis does indeed seem to make sense. Consider the following example:

(6.1)   The director himself attended our informal meeting.

A director being the focus in (6.1), the alternatives most naturally evoked in a situation of informal meeting attendance will comprise members of his staff. More generally, and in view of the fact that directors mostly are in top position, the set of alternatives will include all those members in the hierarchy below him. Furthermore, since (6.1) is about attending an informal meeting, it appears justified to say that the director is the least likely person to attend such a meeting and therefore his presence is the most remarkable event possible. On the further assumption that the set of alternatives evoked is heterogeneous, i.e. some members of staff are more likely to turn up at informal meetings than others, the entities present in the situation easily map onto the scale given in Figure 6.1. Accordingly, we might want to paraphrase (6.1) with (6.2):

(6.2)   Even the director attended our informal meeting.

A scalar implication for E. *even* and G. *sogar* has never been disputed. Example (6.3) strikes the same chord. Against the background that God is the ultimate source of all knowledge, it becomes extremely unlikely for anybody else to know in case God does not. Hence, one might be inclined to substitute *himself* for *even*.

(6.3)   a   God himself would not know.
         b   Even God would not know. ≈ (6.3a)

The scalar approach, which characterises the focus value as least likely with regard to the background, becomes even more forceful if we take into account that G. *selbst* can occur before and after its focus. Prefocal *selbst* is well established as a scalar focus particle being more or less synonymous with G. *sogar* ('even'), and hence, it would seem to make a lot of sense to regard the scalar implication as the common denominator linking the two. (6.4) gives the translations of (6.1) and (6.2) respectively.

(6.4)   a   Der Direktor selbst nahm an unserem informellen Treffen teil.
         b   Selbst der Direktor nahm an unserem informellen Treffen teil. ≈ (6.4a)

German prefocal *selbst*, just as E. *even*, structures a proposition into focus and background and characterises the focus value as the least likely with regard to the remaining open sentence. Example (6.5) below shows a possible representation of such a structured proposition. The variable *x* stands for the focus value and the alternatives evoked.

(6.5)   *selbst* [λx (x nahm an unserem informellen Treffen teil), der Direktor]

However, the picture is slightly more complex. Pre- and postfocal *selbst* are far away from being synonymous and so are *even* and x-*self*. Primus (1992: 72) observes quite correctly that postfocal *selbst* does not share the quantifying implication of prefocal *selbst*. The same holds for x-s*elf* versus *even*. Put differently, ANS is not an inclusive particle. Whereas *even* and prefocal *selbst* or *sogar* unite focus referent and alternatives evoked into one big set for all members of which a certain proposition holds, ANS simply is indifferent. It does not block an inclusive reading as (6.1)–(6.4) have shown, but neither does it force one as the following example makes clear:

(6.6)   John Major himself closed last year's conference in Blackpool.

Obviously, (6.6) denotes a singular, non-repeatable situation. On the assumption that there was just one Tory conference taking place in Blackpool last year, there can have been only one single person closing it: John Major in the present case. The meaning of a sentence like (6.6) should leave no room for inclusive particles, and indeed, if we extract *himself* and put *even* in instead, (6.6) becomes very hard to interpret if not even ungrammatical:

(6.7)   ??Even John Major closed last year's conference in Blackpool.

Unless we provide for several attempts at closing this particular conference, (6.7) is clearly out. If, in contrast, we allow for several conferences to have taken place last year, (6.7) immediately becomes acceptable:

(6.8)   Even John Major closed one of last year's conferences in Blackpool.

No such amendments are possible in the following minimal pair. The earth has been created once and only once and therefore (6.9b) is impossible unless we resort to imaginary worlds. The quantifying effect indeed is what separates *even* from x-*self*. They do not make different modal contributions as Edmondson and Plank (1978: 404) have it.[1]

(6.9)   a God himself created the earth.
          b *Even God created the earth.

Strangely enough, though, we also find examples where the relevant scales, i.e. likelihood, remarkability or expectancy, are suddenly inverted. Here, ANS marks the least remarkable or most expected character. Take e.g. (6.10a). In all of the current nuclear powers, it is the president, prime minister, head of state, etc. who bears the responsibility for launching a nuclear attack. Consequently, there should be nothing exceptional about him being the only one to know the necessary code. Note further that *even* in (6.10b) would appear unexpected under normal conditions which is due to the president's being placed at the wrong end of the scale involved.

(6.10)   a Only the president himself knows the secret code to start a nuclear strike.
          b ?Even the president knows the secret code to start a nuclear strike.

The examples in (6.11) confirm these observations. By and large, a coach will appoint the best player of a team as team leader. Being the best, again, there should be nothing remarkable or unexpected about him scoring a goal. Hence, *himself* in (6.11a) should be incompatible with our assumptions unless we have reason to believe that the skipper in question is a bad player. However, it is perfectly adequate. That our assumptions are correct is shown in (6.11b) which is somewhat unusual in the context evoked.

> (6.11) a The skipper himself scored the equaliser.
> b Even the skipper scored a goal.

Such a contradiction in terms of scales is not easy to explain and we may wonder if the scalar effects observed are really brought about by ANS or if they are merely the product of the context. After all, since both (6.10a) and (6.11a) are about important persons, i.e. people in top positions of hierarchies, scalar effects may creep in by themselves. And indeed, there is a large number of sentences containing ANS with no scalar implications whatsoever. In fact, the majority of occurrences of adnominal intensifiers do not show scalar effects, as only a quick glance at the data available makes clear. For many of those sentences under consideration, matters of likelihood, remarkability or expectancy are not at issue at all. Consider (6.12). From the fact that John's wife is an actress there is no way of inferring what John's job is. In other words, after uttering (6.12), we cannot have expectations concerning John's occupation. Moreover, being a musician does not seem to be more or less remarkable than the job of an actress either.

> (6.12) John's wife is an actress. John himself is a musician.

Hence, regarding a scalar implication in terms of likelihood as the basic contribution of ANS cannot account for examples like (6.12). Further evidence is provided by König (1991: 91), cf. (6.13a):

> (6.13) a (The accident happened at 5 a.m.) The front seat passenger was severely injured. The driver himself was killed instantly.
> b (The accident happened at 5 a.m.) The front seat passenger was killed instantly. The driver himself was severely injured.

In the situation of a road accident, both driver and passenger have about the same chances of getting injured or even killed. And indeed, modifying the NP denoting the driver with *himself* does not make his death remarkable or in any way unexpected. ANS does not interact with other possible scales, say a scale of affectedness, either. Otherwise (6.13b) should lose in acceptability since killing should rank higher than merely injuring on such a scale.

Finally, note that ANS need not interact with the NP denoting the most remarkable or least expected character even if such a character is available. In the situation described in (6.14b), it should appear rather unlikely that a copilot outperforms his captain so that if ANS characterised a referent as least likely/most remarkable in a situation, the copilot should be the referent of choice. Still, (6.14b) is much less acceptable than (6.14a), where our expectations are well-catered for.

(6.14)   a The copilot nearly fainted in view of the oncoming aircraft. The captain himself remained calm and composed.

             b The captain nearly fainted in view of the oncoming aircraft. ?The copilot himself remained calm and composed.

To sum up, we have seen adnominal intensifiers in four environments: (i) there are contexts in which they do seem to make a scalar contribution in terms of remarkability or likelihood, (ii) we also find cases where the scalar implication is hinged on an inverted scale, (iii) there are non-scalar cases and (iv) ANS may be incompatible with foci on the right end of the scale. I take that as sufficient evidence to reject the idea of adnominal intensifiers making a scalar contribution (remarkability, expectancy, likelihood, etc.) at all. If such effects turn up, they must be due to the context, or more precisely, the semantic properties of the focus involved. Note that examples (6.1) and (6.3) feature referents in top positions of real-world hierarchies. Therefore it should come as no surprise that all statements about them convey an air of remarkability. When the intensifier is taken away, the scalar effects persist:

(6.15)   a The diRECtor attended our informal meeting.

             b GOD would not know.

Although Primus (1992) deals almost exclusively with G. *selbst*, the gist of her argument is easily applicable to English and many other languages. She mainly follows Edmondson and Plank (1978) in her analysis of adnominal intensifiers. Her label for ANS – 'a non-quantifying scalar adverb' – plus the assumption that the relevant scale is one of likelihood can leave no doubt about what she means. According to her, ANS is in effect the same as G. *sogar* or E. *even* minus the quantifying effect.

As indicated above, Kibrik and Bogdanova (1995) consider adnominal intensifiers, and in fact all intensifiers, operators with which it is possible to correct the expectations of the participants present in discourse. Their analysis is tailored around Russian *sam*, but many of their observations are so similar to what we find in English and German that it makes sense briefly to discuss the essence of their proposal. Note that we are now dealing with what they regard to be the core meaning of *sam* because it is not clear whether the differentiation of intensifiers into ANS and AVS is really applicable to Russian. What Kibrik and Bogdanova claim, then, is that *sam* can be used by the speaker to indicate to the hearer that the latter has wrong expectations concerning the referent of the NP with which *sam*, and by extension ANS, is in association. More precisely, they say that *sam* can be used in case the hearer does not expect the relevant referent to participate in the situation under discussion. Subsequently, *sam* leads to a correction of the hearer's expectations. Translated into the familiar notion of likelihood, this, of course, means that the referent under consideration is the least likely in the predication relevant at the current stage of discourse. Note that likely/

unlikely in a predication in effect means likely/unlikely with respect to the judgement of the speaker and/or hearer. After all, the participation of a referent is always likely or unlikely with respect to someone's expectations. Consider example (6.2) again. It is only possible felicitously to relate this sentence to somebody if the hearer knows and shares the knowledge of the speaker that the director does not attend informal meetings under normal conditions. This, indeed, leads to a correction of the hearer's expectations. To cut a long story short, Kibrik and Bogdanova in effect also view the scalar effect as the central semantic contribution of Russian *sam* (or ANS).

The preceding discussion has indicated, however, that the contribution adnominal intensifiers make to the meaning of a sentence must be sought elsewhere. Here is where the non-scalar or semi-scalar analyses come in. They try to analyse the contribution of ANS not so much as the result of the interaction between a character, a situation and a scale, but mainly as affecting the properties of the character itself. In other words, for an expression to be marked with ANS, the relevant referent must possess qualities setting it apart from possible alternatives. These qualities may either be inherent or temporarily assumed. Conversely, marking an expression with ANS highlights particular qualities or attributes of its referent. A scalar particle like *even* is not bound in this respect. It always locates its focus on a scale relative to the entire proposition, it never merely assigns a value with respect to another character. Such behaviour becomes apparent under negation:

(6.16)   a Even John knew the answer.
          b Even John didn't know the answer.

Whereas (6.16a) characterises John as not particularly intelligent, he will be understood as a bright boy in (6.16b). The reason, of course, is the negation which inverts the background with regard to which John is marked as least likely. Similarly, take the slightly more complicated examples below:

(6.17)   a Even the Pope received the delegation.
          b Even the Pope didn't receive the delegation.

Even in (6.17a) characterises the Pope as the least likely person to receive the delegation. It is an adequate statement for an individual who is more likely to receive the delegation and for whom the receiving of the delegation thereby becomes a necessity, cf. *We must receive the delegation because even the Pope received it.* Again, under negation the picture is reversed. (6.17b) makes it unlikely for the Pope not to receive the delegation. Put differently, it marks the Pope as the most likely person to receive the delegation. However, the delegation is never received. Therefore, less likely persons may not receive it either, cf. *We need not receive the delegation because even the Pope did not receive it.* ANS is totally different:

(6.18) a The Pope himself received the delegation.
       b The Pope himself didn't receive the delegation.

In either sentence of (6.18), the Pope is not contrasted with more or less likely individuals to receive the delegation, but with those who bear a certain relation to him. These include holy or profane members of the papal family such as substitute, prelate or secretary. What a sentence like (6.18a) asserts is that the Pope received the delegation and not, say, his secretary. (6.18b), i.e. the negative counterpart to (6.18a), states that one of the possible alternatives of the Pope did the job. Note that the delegation is received in both (6.18a) and (6.18b), but only in (6.17a) and not (6.17b). Moreover, either sentence of (6.18) seems to say that the delegation was received just once. In (6.17a), by contrast, it was received at least twice. If there are scalar effects in (6.18), they are certainly not adequately described in terms of likelihood.

The examples in (6.16) and (6.17) have shown that negation does not influence the scale on which *even* operates. Independently of whether the remaining open sentence is negative or positive, *even* characterises its focus with respect to the background as the least likely value of all those under consideration. In (6.16a) above John is made the least likely referent with respect to knowing the answer, in (6.16b) he is least likely with respect to not knowing the answer. Note that when a focus value is the least likely with respect to a positive open sentence, it is at the same time the most likely with respect to the negative counterpart. To give an example, when John in (6.16a) is least likely to know the answer, he is, viewed from the opposite angle, most likely not to know it. No such effects can be observed with adnominal intensifiers. The relation between focus value and alternatives evoked is persistent. The remaining proposition or open sentence has no influence on it. These differences between *even* and ANS can be recovered as a difference in scope:

(6.19) *even* [λx (x received the delegation), the Pope]
(6.20) x-*self* [λx (x), the Pope]

When adnominal intensifiers do not evoke a scale of likelihood, but, nevertheless, manage to order focus and alternatives in a certain way, we are faced with the question what kind of ordering that is. König (1991: 87ff.) proposes that ANS makes its focus referent central for the alternative referents evoked. It always associates with a centre and opposes it to a related periphery or entourage. Focus and alternatives are ordered, and if one would like to project this ordering onto a scale, this would not be an ordering in terms of likelihood or remarkability, but according to importance, prestige and glamour. Moreover, the peripheral referents somehow depend on the central one which is why it is inadequate to talk of mere scalar ordering. A system consisting of concentric circles with its centre in the middle is the more adequate visualisation, cf. Figure 6.2.

Figure 6.2 Centre and periphery.

However, it is probably necessary to exclude the idea of a scalar ordering altogether. It appears more appropriate to say that ANS imposes a binary structure on a previously unordered set. ANS always picks out the central and often most important referent and contrasts it with less significant characters. What matters is the contrast between one central, important, outstanding, etc. individual and a peripheral rest. Apparently, hierarchies of the real world are very good candidates for such a contrast since their top position is of central importance for all the characters in the ranks below. That such a semantic contribution really is at work becomes apparent if we try to associate ANS with an NP whose denotation is a character of the rank and file. To be sure, these cases are not excluded or ungrammatical, but they strike us as somewhat unnatural and more often than not they carry ironic undertones, cf. the contrast between (6.21a) and (6.21b):

(6.21)   a The chancellor himself announced the budget cuts.
         b The porter himself opened the gate.

Baker (1995) mainly follows König, but tries to recover the idea of centre versus periphery as a 'condition of relative discourse prominence':

> Intensive NPs can only be used to mark a character in a sentence or discourse who is relatively more prominent or central than other characters. (Baker 1995: 80)

The two proposals are more or less equivalent and although Baker's label sounds like a purely scalar approach, this impression vanishes as soon as the details are evaluated. Their common denominator is that both attribute the appropriateness of ANS to inherent qualities of the characters concerned or, viewed the other way round, that ANS highlights certain properties of the focus referent regardless of the background. It might even be justified to say that ANS assigns certain properties to this referent. Where they seem to differ is in the assumptions they make about the relation between focus and alternatives. König holds that centre and periphery are linked through a firm bond. Characters are never peripheral with respect to some centre, but always converge on one particular centre. If the chancellor in (6.21a) cannot do the job, then it is one of *his* ministers, *his* secretaries, etc. who will replace him, never an unrelated character or the member of another centre's periphery. In one way or another the periphery is dependent on the centre or affiliated with it. We will say that there is a relation holding between centre and periphery and write 'R(centre, periphery)'.

As indicated above, the advantage of assuming a relation between centre and periphery lies in the fact that it does not rely on scalar notions such as importance, glamour, prestige, etc., although such concepts can potentially be derived from it. This opens the door for an analysis of the following examples where no scalar effects are visible at all.

> (6.22) a The lamp on the table looked antique. The table itself was very modern.
> b Kate became friendliness itself.

The idea of discourse prominence does not assume such a relation. All that is evaluated is a character's importance relative to another, however it comes about. That this is not sufficient is shown in (6.23). Whereas it is unproblematic or even more appropriate to insert *himself* into (6.23a), trying to do the same in (6.23b) makes one hesitate. The reason, of course, is that although the German chancellor outranks the Chinese foreign secretary, i.e. although the former is more prominent than the latter, they bear no relation to each other. Here, an adversative connective like *however* would be more fitting. Introducing the German chancellor and *his* foreign secretary, however, almost forces the use of *himself*. But now, the former is the centre and the latter *his* periphery. Interestingly enough, all the examples discussed in Baker and some of the subclassifications he makes show such a relation in one way or another, but taking his condition on discourse prominence at face value, we would not have a clue as to why (6.23a) is better than (6.23b).

> (6.23) a Last month, the German chancellor and his foreign secretary were considering top-level talks with the Chinese. The foreign secretary suggested Beijing as the venue, the chancellor himself favoured Berlin.
> b Last month, the German chancellor and the Chinese foreign secretary were considering top-level talks. The Chinese suggested Beijing as the venue, the chancellor however/ ?himself favoured Berlin.

Furthermore, there are numerous examples for which it is very hard to say why one referent should be more prominent than another. This is particularly true of non-human referents. Consider the examples given in (6.24). Indeed, it should turn out to be fairly difficult to explain in what respect the lake in (6.24a) or the castle in (6.24b) can be considered more prominent in discourse than the beach or the valley to Penhill respectively. The label 'discourse prominence', it appears, cuts no ice with the true semantic contribution of ANS. However, let me emphasise again that this is mainly a problem of adequately naming the thing. In their essence, the proposals by König and Baker differ in degree at most, but certainly not in kind.

(6.24)   a Even on a quiet mid-week summer's day the beach is fringed with people picnicking or sleeping in their cars, while the lake itself is often used for windsurfing or water-skiing. [LLC]

b In Wensleydale, Bolton Castle looks across the broad valley to Penhill, which, legend has it, was once the haunt of a fierce giant, while the castle itself is the place where Mary Queen of Scots was placed under house arrest before she was taken to London to be executed. [LLC]

Coming back to the qualities of the characters concerned, both König and Baker seem to agree that there are no absolute values involved. Although examples out of context like (6.21) or those embedded into a relatively rigid frame as in (6.25) could give such an impression, adequate context can nearly always put matters right.

(6.25)   a A: Who signed the treaty? – B: The president himself did.
b A: Who typed the letter? – B: The secretary herself did.

Both the president as well as the secretary in (6.25) are placed in natural contexts, however, (6.25a) appears to be more appropriate than (6.25b). One might jump to the conclusion that (6.25a) is better because presidents rank higher than secretaries in absolute terms. Now look at (6.26):

(6.26)   The part-timer made the coffee. The secretary herself typed the letter.

Here, the secretary is contrasted with someone she has authority over, i.e. relatively speaking, she now ranks highest. The sentence immediately gains in acceptability. (6.25b) is marked because secretaries do not possess a natural periphery.

The semantic contribution of adnominal intensifiers can be particularly well observed when they are put into the scope of additional focus particles like e.g. *even* or *only*. Whereas these particles as such add elements to or extract them from rather unspecific and heterogeneous sets, these very sets become well ordered or polarised between centre and periphery as soon as the intensifier becomes involved. John in (6.27a) without *himself* could refer to any of the alternatives evoked by *even*, adding it makes him a leading personality and the remaining elements his periphery. The same is true of (6.27b). *Himself* present, Richard will be understood as the leader of the attack (or defence). Take it away and he will be shifted to grass roots level.

(6.27)   a Even John (himself) didn't know what to do.
         b Only Richard (himself) survived the attack.

What examples like (6.27) also show is that ANS is compatible with both inclusive and exclusive particles. Put differently, it is not specified in this respect. In some cases, the ordering of the set can go hand in hand with a change in quantity. A statement like (6.28a) may plausibly include the entirety of mankind. It basically ascertains that everybody is doomed to die including the Pope in spite of the fact that he is the head of the Catholic church. This sentence characterises the Pope as the least likely to die, if that were possible. (6.28b), in contrast, will hardly be interpreted as opposing the Pope to mankind in its entirety. Here, he is contrasted with his periphery, i.e. his staff, the papal family, etc. As a consequence, the resulting set is much smaller. Moreover, (6.28b) could receive a deontic reading which is clearly excluded for (6.28a).

(6.28)   a Even the Pope must die.
         b Even the Pope himself must die.

To sum up, from a most general perspective, adnominal intensifiers contribute two things: (i) they evoke alternatives to their focus, and (ii) they build up a relation which is best characterised as one of centre versus periphery – R(centre, periphery) – between focus and alternatives. Centre and periphery are relative notions. Moreover, scalar implications in terms of remarkability, expectancy, likelihood, but also glamour, prestige, etc. must be considered side effects which do not reflect the essence of ANS. Baker's notion of discourse prominence, taken at face value at least, has turned out to be too narrow a concept. Semantically speaking, adnominal intensifiers could be referred to as 'centralising intensifiers'. They may also be considered set structuring devices.

Before turning to a detailed analysis of the possible instantiations of the centre-periphery contrast, let us briefly draw attention to the proposal put forward by Girke (1993), which also belongs to the group of non-scalar approaches presently under discussion. Similarly to Kibrik and Bogdanova, Girke's focus is on Russian *sam*, but it is nevertheless possible to apply the relevant points to English and German adnominal intensifiers. Girke distinguishes three types of *sam*, numbered 1 to 3, and it is *sam* 3 that comes closest to our notion of ANS. Typically, *sam* 3 involves contrasts of the type shown in (6.29) below.

(6.29)   a the wife of the director – the director himself
         b the aunt's eyes – the aunt herself.

The two contrasted expressions are usually found in relative proximity, i.e. either in the same sentence or in two consecutive sentences, the important point being that the expression on the right is partly contained in the one on the left. According to Girke, then, *sam 3* signals that an aforementioned expression is taken up again and that the referent of that expression changes its role although it is left open what kind of role that is supposed to be. Moreover, these contrasts often involve part-whole relations, cf. (6.29b). We will see shortly that Girke's examples represent an important usage of adnominal intensifiers which, however, can be easily subsumed under the concept of centre and periphery.

6.2 Possible instantiations of centre and periphery

In the following, we will discuss the notions of centre and periphery in more detail. We will also try to describe the different types of relations holding between the relevant referents. The key issue here is the question of what the semantic properties of central referents are. Put differently, we will ask which conditions have to be satisfied for an NP to be modified by ANS. This section draws heavily on ideas and observations put forward in Baker (1995).

Before we start, a word of caution seems to be necessary. English and German, in fact all languages which have possessed intensifiers for extensive stretches of time, allow an enormous amount of NPs in even more different contexts to be modified by ANS. As a consequence, the relation of centre versus periphery turns up in a wide variety of guises and it might become difficult to decide for which subrelations a separate class should be established and for which it should not. Hence, the following classification cannot claim to give an exhaustive account of what is possible, but rather tries to list the dominant patterns in an orderly fashion.

Note, for a start, that both English and German allow intensification of NPs denoting human as well as non-human referents. This is by no means obvious. Many languages such as e.g. Turkish define a cut-off point there, cf. example (6.30) below, where modification of a non-human NP results in ungrammaticality. The same is true of Japanese, Korean and Mandarin.

(6.30)   Turkish
 a müdür-ün   kendi-si
   director-GEN   self-POSS.3P.SG
   'the director himself'
 b *ev-in   kendi-si
   house-GEN   self-POSS.3P.SG
   'the house itself'

Consequently, languages establish different cut-off points on the well-known animacy hierarchy (Silverstein 1976, Comrie 1981), cf.:

(6.31)   1,2 > 3 > proper nouns > common nouns [+human] > common nouns [-human]

In view of the cross-linguistic importance of the [±human] distinction, it seems to make sense to incorporate it into the present classification. Moreover, it will become apparent that [+human] referents force a different subclassification from [-human] ones. (6.32a) shows ANS in association with an NP denoting a human referent, (6.32b) gives a non-human example:

(6.32)   a   Amnesty also has its own checks which ensure that all its major reports are passed through several levels of approvals, often up to the Secretary General himself. [BNC]

          b   A rash of illegally printed revolutionary pamphlets was followed in May 1862 by the outbreak of alarming fires in several cities, including the capital itself. [BNC]

Let us concentrate on human referents for the time being. Here, it is possible to distinguish between referents that are central due to their rank, position, status or degree and those that are central because another referent is defined, identified or referentially accessed through them, cf. Baker (1995: 81). (6.33a) highlights the former point with the Tsar heading the Russian nobility, (6.33b) defines or accesses other referents through Jackie, namely his grandfather, father and brother and may hence serve as an example of the latter.

(6.33)   a   In any case, the majority of senior officials, as well as the Tsar himself, had imbibed from childhood a sense of personal and national honour inextricably bound up with Russia's military might and international status. [BNC]

          b   Jackie's grandfather was a gamekeeper, his father owned a garage, his brother Jimmy raced before him – until a bad accident at Le Mans in 1954 and Jackie himself started at twenty-one, in 1960. [BNC]

As a rule, sentences of the (6.33a) type can more readily dispense with a periphery overtly given in the surrounding context than those similar to (6.33b). (6.33b) would be less natural than (6.33a) without the relevant context. This is plausible in so far as referents of NPs like *tsar, president, director*, etc. possess by definition a number of properties which make them central. Proper names, by contrast, are not specified and need context to make clear what the relevant properties are. Whereas *tsar* can easily evoke a periphery by itself, *Jackie* needs explicit context with respect to which it can be viewed as central.

We will expand (6.33a) in the following. When we categorise human societies, there are at least two ways of recovering the idea of centre versus periphery. At the one end of the spectrum we find hierarchies of the real world. Here, the highest rank qualifies as the centre, everything below it as its periphery. They mostly are independent of the actual human beings involved. These systems or organisations are the product of a process of conventionalisation evolving in time spans stretching from decades to centuries. No matter whether the humans involved leave, change their position, pass away or stay on, the system itself is not affected and remains in the same state, cf. *The king is dead, long live the king*. Examples of such hierarchies are the nobility, politics, political parties, the military, the clergy, commerce, education, in fact, any form of organisation. Referentially accessing members of these systems often leads to logical puzzles such as *The president of the US is bald* – true or not true? We will call the top positions of these systems organisational centres and contrast them with situational centres which can be located at the opposite end of the spectrum. King and queen in (6.34a) are examples of organisational centres, the bride in (6.34b), however, should be regarded as a situational centre, cf. Baker (1995: 82).

(6.34) a The king and the queen themselves watched the test match.
        b The congregation was close to tears. The bride herself smiled.

Apart from rigid forms of organisation like the military, the nobility, etc., people also tend to assemble on a more informal basis. Nevertheless, one particular person can become central and make the remaining crowd their periphery. (6.34b) depicts a wedding situation. Here, of course, it is the bride (or, alternatively, the bridegroom) who is of central importance. For all the wedding guests present she is the ultimate cause of attendance. She also is the centre of attention. A means for detecting the centre of both an organisation and a situation would be to scan the entire population under consideration for the individual one has the most difficulty taking away. Their removal usually leads to the disintegration of the organisation or situation concerned. As there can be no nobility without a king or a queen, there can be no marriage ceremony without a bride or a bridegroom. Where they clearly differ is in their independence from personalities. There is no continuous marriage ceremony with different people entering as bride and bridegroom and exiting as a couple as there is, say, a stable and static political establishment. Marriage ceremonies are personalised events. They always emerge anew and then fall apart. Political systems and organisations, in comparison, are impersonal and tend to be extremely persistent.

(6.35) strikes the same chord. Here, we are in the situation of a quiz show. As one would expect, it is the quiz master who is central for such a show. Taking him away makes the show break down. The guests, by contrast, serve as his periphery.

(6.35) The guests were very carefully dressed. The quiz master himself looked like a clown.

It is also possible to recover the contrast between centre and periphery in a communication situation. Here, the prototypical centre is the speaker and the hearer will usually serve as his periphery. (6.36) gives an example. ANS modifies the expression referring to the speaker thereby opposing this referent to the hearer as well as to a third party.

> (6.36)   John may go shopping while you can walk the dog. I myself will stay with the kids.

However, the speaker is not necessarily the only character entitled to being made central. There is also the option to make the hearer central. (6.37) underlines the present point. Now, the hearer is made central and contrasted with the speaker plus the third party, however, this example appears to be slightly less natural than (6.36).

> (6.37)   John may go shopping while I walk the dog. You yourself can stay with the kids.

Interestingly enough, it is much more difficult to make the third party central without having sufficient reason to do so. (6.38) is a lot less acceptable than the previous example. Apparently, centralisation is restricted to speaker and hearer because it is only they who belong to the communication situation.

> (6.38)   You may go shopping while I walk the dog. ??John himself can stay with the kids.

Only if we make the third party central for a different reason, say by making it an organisational centre, can we focus it with x-*self*, cf. (6.39).

> (6.39)   You take the Ford, I take the VW. The director himself will take the Mercedes.

As for the speaker, an explanation for his role is certainly not hard to find. In a communication situation, he is the source of information whereas the hearer is merely the goal. Put differently, the hearer depends on the speaker in terms of the information conveyed. Therefore, we can regard the hearer as peripheral from the perspective of the speaker and the speaker as central from the hearer's perspective, cf. Figure 6.3.

Although it seems reasonable that it should be less straightforward to make the hearer central in comparison with the speaker on the basis of what was said in the preceding paragraph, it is more difficult to think of a convincing explanation to account for the only marginal decrease in acceptability. After all, in any communication situation the speaker will be the source, the hearer the goal and the latter will depend on the former for information. Hence, the distribution of roles is clear. However, it should be borne in mind

Figure 6.3 Centre and periphery in a communication situation.

that a communication situation is an extremely dynamic event and that the speaker/hearer roles can change frequently between the two interlocutors. As a consequence, the distinction between centre and periphery might be blurred. Moreover, the speaker's current statement might somehow reflect a past speaking event on the part of the hearer or anticipate such an event in the future. It is probably no coincidence that precisely these examples allow for centralising the hearer most easily, cf. (6.40). Note finally that the animacy hierarchy given in (6.31) can also be used as a possible means of explanation although it would predict that speaker and hearer do not differ with respect to ANS.

(6.40)   a 'But, as you yourself said, this is not New York.' [BNC]
         b 'If you remember,' she began, and gave a mighty hiccup,
            'you yourself refused to have poor Harrison indoors.' [BNC]

(6.37) shows yet something else. Recall from section 4.3 that Moravcsik (1972) suggests that ANS in general is inadequate in imperatives. This is certainly correct in view of examples like * *Yourself go!*. However, note that, pragmatically speaking, (6.37) is in fact an imperative (directive) and well formed. Hence, the restriction disallowing such structures cannot be semantic or pragmatic in nature, but must be sought in syntax, i.e. in the absence of an NP to which the intensifier can adjoin.

Note finally that the idea of a situational centre might encounter the following objection. In many cases, one might argue, it is exactly the referent of the expression not being modified by ANS that must be considered central for the situation. Recall the quiz show example in (6.35). Here, we could just as well hold that the guests must be central because it is for their sake that the entire show takes place in the first place. Something similar could be put forward for (6.41):

(6.41)   Most tourists survived the bus accident. The driver himself was
         killed instantly.

In the situation of a bus journey, it should again be the tourists who are central because such a journey is clearly initiated for their sake. The driver should be considered peripheral because he is merely employed to do the job. However, such a line of argument misses the essential point. However true it may be that the tourists are central for the bus journey considered as a whole – without them it would not take place – for the actual act of driving the bus, and subsequently, for any accidents caused, it is the driver who is responsible. And this is precisely what is under consideration in (6.41).

Let us now turn to the quiz show example again. We said that in its entirety the show depends on the quiz master, hence he is central. However, dispensing with all the guests does not work either. Although a TV show can go on if, say, one out of ten guests is missing, as a group they can become at least as important as or even more important than the show master himself. And indeed, the intensifier is sensitive to such a state of affairs. TV viewers, for example, want to see both the quiz master and the guests. Failing to portray them properly leads to a sudden increase in their importance, cf. (6.42) below.

(6.42)   The cameraman showed only the quiz master. The guests themselves, he completely failed to portray.

Slightly modifying the situation of a bus journey in (6.41) leads to similar observations, cf. (6.43). Here, the driving as such is no longer under consideration, the focus rather is on the bus journey as an event for the tourists to derive pleasure from. Whether there is beautiful scenery or not usually does not matter to a bus driver, but to tourists it may matter a lot, particularly if they have paid for it. Hence, for the situation of an intentional bus journey along a scenic route, the tourists are central and the driver is at most peripheral, if he is involved in the relation at all.

(6.43)   a Having made the trip for at least fifty times, the bus driver did not notice the beautiful scenery any longer. The tourists themselves were enjoying it very much.
          b ?Having made the trip for at least fifty times, the bus driver himself did not notice the beautiful scenery any longer. The tourists were enjoying it very much.

To sum up, for a situational centre to emerge, the following prototypical scenario is necessary. Previously unrelated people enter a temporary relation of mutual dependence in which one (or more than one) of them becomes of central importance to the rest, who usually form the majority. Situational centres may be mountain guides for a climbing party, bride or bridegroom for a wedding ceremony, quiz masters for a TV show and so on. A particular subtype of a situational centre is the speaker in a communication situation. Its periphery is formed by the hearer, although this pattern may be reversed under certain conditions. Situational centres are in a way centres of temporary mini-organisations. An important difference to organisational centres is that a situational centre, and hence its periphery, can be relatively easily passed on to another referent. More often than not, all that is necessary is a change in perspective.

There is a relation of dependence between a centre and its periphery. This is particularly obvious in the case of organisational centres. They determine what their periphery has to do, often even what it is allowed to say and what their economic situation looks like. Situational centres are usually less powerful. They may merely be the focus of attention as e.g. in a wedding situation or in a TV show. However, they may also be able to influence the fate of their periphery. Mountain guides and bus drivers are cases in point. In a communication situation, the hearer depends on the speaker for relevant information.

As already indicated, the differentiation between organisational centres, i.e. referents whose centrality depends on their top position in some hierarchy of the real world, and those emerging from particular situations is due to Baker (1995: 80ff.); (but see also König and Siemund 1996a,b). In the former case, Baker assumes that intensification of an NP has discourse-external justification, in the latter case, he suggests that the justification for doing so must be recovered from within the discourse. Therefore, it is called discourse-internal. Put differently, if justification for ANS comes from outside the discourse, then the expression ANS modifies is on its own sufficient to pick a central referent. If additional information is necessary, then it must be taken from within the discourse, hence justification for ANS is discourse-internal. Obviously, there is a continuum of intermediate cases between these two extremes.

Baker further subdivides what we have named situational centres into those involving 'most directly responsible agents' and 'most directly affected persons or entities'. In terms of thematic roles, this would translate into agents on the one hand and patients on the other, but this is not exactly what Baker has in mind. The thematic role of an NP is defined with regard to the verb it is an argument of, however, what is under consideration here is the role of a referent in a larger context. (6.44) is one of his examples of the former class (agents), (6.45) of the latter (patients).

(6.44)   a   The obstacle that Bill tried to set up for the opposing lawyer ultimately caused major difficulties for Bill himself.

b   Martha refused to consider indicting the organisation that had withheld evidence about the murder until she was sure that she could convict the triggerman himself.

(6.45)   a   Of all the people who were in the courtroom yesterday morning, only the defendant herself remained completely calm when the judge handed down her sentence.

b   I'm surprised that the patient himself hasn't had a bit more to say about the proposed liver transplant.

Although (6.44) and (6.45) indeed are examples of situational centres, the differentiation between central agents and patients does not seem to be helpful. This is because a referent's role has to be judged against the background of a larger context (discourse) and here, not surprisingly, a number of options arise. At least three of the four sentences under consideration are difficult to judge with respect to whether the NP the intensifier modifies denotes an agent or a patient in the given situation. Consider (6.44a). Here, it is not clear if Bill's centrality rests on the assumption that he tried to set up problems for the opposing lawyer (agent) or, if it is due to the fact that he ended up with major difficulties (patient). Similarly, (6.44b). On the one hand, the triggerman can be seen as the agent of the murder event, on the other, he could be viewed as the patient of the conviction situation. Finally, in (6.45b), although it is certainly true to say that the patient is also thematically the patient during the liver transplant, in the event of giving his opinion about the proposed transplant, he would have to be characterised as agentive. (6.45a) seems to be the only clear case.

In addition to that, Baker proposes that ANS can also be used to intensify NPs denoting characters who are 'the primary topic of concern'. This is shown in (6.46).

> (6.46)   a We got the details of Martha's unfortunate accident from Martha herself.
>
>   b Although I have heard from several of their friends about Beth and Sam's current situation, I haven't heard anything from Beth and Sam themselves.

Although this notion is much too imprecise to criticise it substantially, note at least that (6.46a) seems to be more about the details of Martha's accident than about Martha and that Beth and Sam's current situation in (6.46b) could also be regarded as an issue of concern.

Since neither 'most directly responsible agents' nor 'most directly affected persons or entities' nor 'the primary topic of concern' seem to be notions applicable to the classification of adnominal intensifiers in a straightforward way, we will not be concerned with them any further. Nevertheless, (6.44) and (6.45) easily classify as situational centres. Bill in (6.44a) is central because he is a lawyer in a trial situation. The opposing lawyer is his periphery. Here, centre and periphery could easily be interchanged. The central triggerman in (6.44b) is contrasted with peripheral accomplices. The defendant in (6.45a) is central because she is being sentenced. In (6.45b) the patient is central because he is going to be operated upon. The examples in (6.46), however, seem to belong to a particular subtype and should not be subsumed under situational centres.

As a matter of fact, (6.46) is extremely reminiscent of (6.33b) to which we will now backtrack. The common denominator of these and the subsequent examples is that one referent is defined, identified or referentially accessed through another. We will call this 'defining centrality' or 'identifying central-ity'. The general formula can be stated as follows:

(6.47)   y OF x – x SELF

OF in (6.47) does not denote a relation of possession in a straightforward sense, but must be regarded as a relation of dependence, association or affil-iation, i.e. as possession according to a more general understanding. The dash in (6.47) must be read as 'in contrast to' or 'in opposition to' and merely reflects the established property of ANS to oppose a centre to a related periphery. In the formula given above, x stands for the central refer-ent, y for the peripheral one. Note that if we regarded dependence as the essential property of a periphery with respect to its centre, (6.47) would denote the prototypical centre-periphery relation from which all the others could potentially be derived. This relation can comprise several subtypes.

First, of course, there is possession itself as exemplified in (6.48a). Second, we find possession as a result of a process of creation (6.48b). Third, in (6.48c) inalienably possessed body parts show dependence on the entity to which they belong. This is, generally speaking, a part-whole relation in which the part cannot be detached from its superstructure. And finally, fourth, we can recover the formula given in (6.47) in the area of family rela-tions, cf. (6.48d).

(6.48)   a Paul's car is very new. Paul himself is very old.
          b All her books have become best-sellers, but she herself is a rather insipid figure.
          c The doctor says that although Paul himself is in a good condition, his teeth leave much to be desired.
          d John's brother inherited the money. John himself got the estate.

Whereas the centrality of situational centres is relatively tightly geared to the actual situation, centrality resting on the property of one referent to identify another is totally independent of it. All that matters is the relation of dependence or affiliation between two referents and that this relation is overtly expressed or can at least be easily inferred. Given these provisos, ANS is restricted to the defining referent, i.e. to the referent another is accessed through. Trying to make the identified referent central renders the relevant examples inadequate:

(6.49)   a ??Paul's car itself is very new. Paul is very old.
          b ??All her books themselves have become best-sellers, but she is a rather insipid figure.
          c ??The doctor says that although Paul is in a good condition, his teeth themselves leave much to be desired.

d ??John's brother himself inherited the money. John got the estate.

Again, the idea that adnominal intensifiers can be used to establish a relation according to (6.47) is already expressed in Baker (cf. p. 81). (6.47) is a particularly nice representative of what Baker calls 'discourse internal justification' of ANS because the acceptability of most examples crucially depends on the surrounding discourse. (6.50) shows one of Baker's examples (cf. p. 82).

(6.50)   Giuliani has achieved a public profile higher than any New York prosecutor since Thomas E. Dewey. Not all of the publicity has focused on the work of his office and its cases. Giuliani himself has been the subject of major profiles in most New York publications; nearly all of them have bordered on the adultery.

Another possible usage of ANS, which can potentially be subsumed under defining centres, can be found in (6.51). The intensifier is adequate in these examples because it is in association with an NP denoting a subject of consciousness (SC) in the sense of Kuno (1987) and Zribi-Hertz (1989).

(6.51)   a Paul wondered where the problem was. He himself found everything crystal clear.
          b After dinner Paul proposed to Mary. She herself had expected something completely different.

The situations in (6.51) are presented through Paul's and Mary's eyes respectively, i.e. an evaluation is given judged from his/her point of view. One could say that a subject of consciousness is the centre of perspective in a given portion of discourse. In many cases, subjects of consciousness are subjects of verbs of saying, believing or perceiving. The parallel to identifying centres consists in the following. Just as one referent can be identified or accessed through another in the case of identifying centres, an entire situation is identified or accessed through a referent in the case of a subject of consciousness. (6.52) and (6.53) below exemplify the parallel.

(6.52)   Paul's brother – Paul himself

(6.53)   a Paul's assessment of a situation – Paul himself
          b Mary's expectations towards a situation – Mary herself

NPs modified by ANS as in (6.51) might also be described as logophors in the sense of Hagège (1974). Alternatively, one could regard the relevant sentences in their entirety as logophoric. Be that as it may, what can be safely stated is that reducing the logophoric content impairs the acceptability of these sentences, cf. (6.54).

(6.54)   a   Paul was pointing out to Mary where the problem was. ?He himself had read everything about it.
         b   After dinner Paul proposed to Mary. ?She herself proposed to wait for another year.

Consider (6.55) below as a further proof that logophoricity is involved. In (6.55a) the situation is related from Paul's perspective. The verbs involved – *notice* and *decide* – are indicative of that fact. Consequently, the corresponding pronoun can be modified by *himself*. (6.55b), by contrast, introduces Paul and Mary with a thetic sentence. No perspective is taken. In this case, the intensifier is less acceptable, or less straightforward to make sense of, unless some sort of relation between Paul and Mary is presupposed.

(6.55)   a   Paul noticed Mary in the cafeteria. She was having coffee. He himself decided to have tea.
         b   There were two people in the cafeteria, Paul and Mary. ?Mary was having coffee while Paul himself was having tea.

At this point, it appears adequate to briefly take up situational centres as found in communication situations again. Although it is certainly true to say that the speaker serves as the source of information for the hearer and that therefore the speaker can be considered central with respect to the hearer, it is also possible to regard the speaker as the referent from whose perspective a certain state of affairs is narrated. After all, whatever a speaker asserts about himself or his environment will somehow represent his own point of view and any statement on the part of the speaker could be thought of as being preceded by the introductory formula *I think/believe/expect that ...* Hence, it should be possible to regard the speaker as a subject of consciousness which offers an alternative means to account for his centrality. However, the same claim can hardly be made with respect to the hearer. Since we have seen that ANS can also be in association with the NP denoting the hearer, we will adhere to regarding them as situational centres although the speaker could alternatively be subsumed under defining centres, more precisely, those identifying or accessing entire situations.

Let us now turn to those NPs modified by the intensifier which denote non-human referents. As a matter of fact, we will only be concerned with non-animate NPs and totally disregard non-human animate NPs since nothing is to be gained from such considerations. Here too, it is possible to draw a distinction between organisational and situational centres, i.e. we find stable, static and permanent centres on the one hand and those emerging out of particular situations on the other. Nevertheless, talking of organisations in the non-human, in fact non-animate world does not sound entirely convincing. It appears much more appropriate to talk of systems and we will therefore refer to the central object of such a system as the 'systemic centre'. One such system is the solar system. As we can oppose the king as the head of an organisation (society) to his subjects, we can set the sun against the planets.[2] Whereas (6.56a) with *itself* modifying the sun appears to be a fairly natural sentence, trying to make the earth central renders the sentence less acceptable.

(6.56) a The earth revolves around the sun. The earth is called a planet, the sun itself is a fixed star.
       b The earth revolves around the sun. ?The earth itself is called a planet, the sun is a fixed star.

(6.57) may serve as an example of a non-human situational centre. It is about a communication situation and contrasts language with related factors such as gestures, acting, facial expressions, intonation, etc.

(6.57) When we receive a linguistic message, we pay attention to many other factors apart from the language itself. [BNC]

In addition, there are spatial and temporal centres:

(6.58) a However, he also stresses the differences that exist within disciplines, for example, physical geography may be placed on the hard side of the line, but human geography on the soft side, and in any case the line itself is not sharp. [BNC]
       b Tickets for the event will be available at spectator entrances on the day itself. [BNC]
       c From the Creation of the World to Doomsday itself, he spoke them over, and sometimes he would recite in French. [BNC]
       d There's nothing remarkable about the place before and after midnight. But at midnight itself, it is like hell.

Note that we still deal with relative centrality and that there are no absolute values. Similarly to human forms of organisation, there are usually several possible centres in inanimate systems. Provided that there is still some periphery left, the centre may move down right through the hierarchy, as it were. Just as a secretary can become central for a part-timer (recall (6.26)), the earth can be considered central for the moon:

(6.59) The moon revolves around the earth. The earth itself revolves around the sun.

Apparently, there is little sense in looking for an equivalent of the speaker/hearer distinction in the inanimate world and logophoric cases seem equally impossible. However, referents that are central due to the fact that they define or identify another referent are a very common phenomenon. Still, the number of possible relations between defining and defined entity is more restricted. Of course, we cannot expect to find family relations, and the idea of possession also seems to be bound to human referents. We can mainly observe two scenarios.

First, we find a relation of association or affiliation between defining and defined referent, i.e. the latter somehow belongs to the former. The garden given in (6.60) is clearly felt as pertaining to the house. We might even get the impression that the house is enclosed by the garden.

(6.60)   The garden looks relatively well tended, but the house itself is in a desolate state.

(6.61) underlines the present point with a minimal pair. It is only in (6.61b) that we are forced to understand the chapel as somehow belonging to the church. (6.61a), by contrast, could be about two disconnected buildings.

(6.61)   a The chapel was erected long after the church was built.
          b The chapel was erected long after the church itself was built.

A similar observation can be made in (6.62) below. Here, it is overtly expressed that the chapel belongs to the church. As expected, the sentence containing ANS appears slightly more natural than the one without the intensifier and this is certainly due to the forced association of the two objects.

(6.62)   a Only after the church had been finished could the chapel be annexed.
          b Only after the church itself had been finished could the chapel be annexed.

The association of two referents may also be of causal or temporal nature. Consider (6.63a). Here, one might argue that the revolution is an identifying centre for the war. Such a view is viable since the war led to the revolution which was an immediate result of it. The revolution is causally and temporally linked to the war and therefore the two events are associated with each other. On this account we would understand (6.63a) as being equivalent to (6.63b).

(6.63)   a During the war and the revolution itself, Lenin's word was by no means accepted as holy writ. [BNC]
          b During the war leading to the revolution and the revolution itself, Lenin's word was by no means accepted as holy writ.

Second, and this seems to be an extremely frequent constellation, the defined entity is properly included within the defining entity. Put differently, there is a part-whole relation similar to the one found in (6.48c). The bitter elements referred to in (6.64a) are contained in the wine and each fish in (6.64b) is a proper part of the school.

(6.64)   a   Very old red wine is often decanted so that the puckering, bitter elements which have settled to the bottom will not be mingled with the wine itself. [BROWN]

          b   Each fish moved so rapidly – though the school itself moved slowly – that it was impossible to focus on an individual. [LLC]

In most of the cases involving part-whole relations, ANS seems to be modifying the NP denoting the whole and not the part. Since a part can be seen as being defined through the whole, i.e. the relevant superstructure, the whole is central for a part and hence these constellations are in concord with the assumed semantic contribution adnominal intensifiers make.

A rather interesting scenario emerges when a certain part becomes central for the whole. Then, either the part or the whole can be characterised as central, cf. (6.65). Berlin is central for Germany because it is the capital of that country. Germany, by contrast, is central for Berlin because the city is a part of it.

(6.65)   a   Germany is a rich country. Berlin itself is rather poor.

          b   Berlin is a poor city. Germany itself is rather rich.

Similarly in (6.66). Here, the boss is central for the company due to his position whereas the company is central for the boss because he is a part of it.

(6.66)   a   The company is based in Germany. The boss himself is an American.

          b   The boss is an American. The company itself is based in Germany.

Under these conditions, ANS comes to be an expression which can be used to indicate a conceptual shift from either whole to part or part to whole, cf. Figure 6.4 where the black area represents the current focus of attention, i.e. the character in the foreground. The grey area stands for the background. (6.65a) and (6.66a) exemplify the shift from left to right, (6.65b) and (6.66b) from right to left.

The fact that ANS is able to define or identify one referent through another can also be exploited for stylistic effects. In the following example taken from Baker (p. 81, n. 18), the laugh under consideration is associated with the sea via the attributes 'rough', 'harsh' and 'frank':

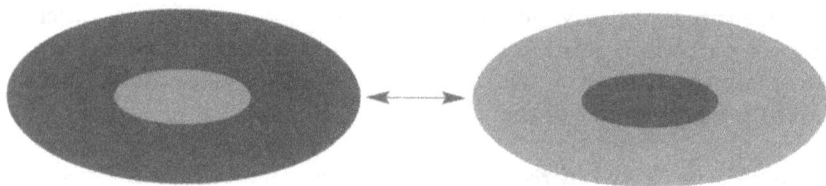

Figure 6.4 Conceptual shift between part and whole.

(6.67)   A laugh went up at my appearance – a laugh that was not less-
          ened or softened by the dead man stretched and grinning on
          the deck before us; a laugh that was as rough and harsh and
          frank as the sea itself ...

Consider also the example in (6.68). Here too, one referent is identified
through another, namely the result of a mathematical operation through
its input.

(6.68)   In other words, mod x is x itself if x is positive and is -x if x is
          negative. [LLC]

Let us finally take a look at a set of examples which appear a little puzzling
at first sight. They all are assignment constructions or predicatives involving
a copula and work according to the simple formula given in (6.69) below.
There are some representative examples in (6.70).

(6.69)   y C x itself (C ∈ {be, become, seem, look like, ...})

(6.70)   a Mary is/looks like beauty itself.
          b Ever since they had known one another, Otto had been
             kindness itself to Jean-Claude. [BNC]
          c She was friendliness itself as she ushered them into the main
             lounge, already half packed with a representative collection
             of Rupert's numerous friends. [LLC]
          d The material of the Porter film is simplicity itself. [Brown]

Note, for a start, that the above sentences have one thing in common.
They all seem to state that the subject referent is the embodiment of some
abstract concept like beauty, kindness, etc. Hence, such paraphrases can
count as adequate glosses for them, cf. (6.71). These glosses are particularly
useful for human subjects, however, they are less convincing for non-human
ones, cf. (6.71d). Here, it might be more appropriate to say that the subject
referent represents the prototype of the relevant concept. This contrast shows
that the idea of embodiment has to do with the human subject referent and
cannot be completely attributed to the intensifier.

(6.71) a Mary is beauty in person.
        b Otto was the incarnation of kindness.
        c She embodied the concept of friendliness.
        d The material of the Porter film is the prototype of simp-
           licity.

Note further that the sentences in (6.70) become ungrammatical when the intensifier is left out. However, replacing the NP denoting the abstract concept by an adjective denoting the corresponding property makes them grammatical again, cf. (6.72). The replacement entails a slight change in meaning. The adjective makes a weaker statement than the NP modified by ANS. Being beautiful is less than being beauty itself and to be kindness itself means more than just to be kind.

(6.72) a Mary is *beauty/beautiful.
        b Otto was *kindness/kind.
        c She was *friendliness/friendly.
        d The material of the Porter film is *simplicity/simple.

Therefore, we can contrast a property or, to be more precise, an entity possessing that property, with the corresponding abstract concept. In a way, we can regard the latter as the superlative of the former, cf. (6.73). The relevant intuition seems to be that if, say, a referent is beautiful, this property might be limited to certain parts of the referent or may be subject to change. If, by contrast, the referent is beauty itself, it possesses this property out and out, through and through, in fact, to the highest possible degree.

(6.73) a Mary is not just beautiful, she is beauty itself.
        b Otto was not just kind to Jean-Claude, he was kindness
           itself.
        c She was not just friendly, she was friendliness itself.
        d The material is not just simple, it is simplicity itself.

This is already reminiscent of the opposition between centre and periphery for at least two reasons. On the one hand, the property is less important or glamorous than the corresponding concept. In all probability, this mainly is the achievement of the intensifier, however, there does seem to be a slight difference in degree between *beautiful* and *beauty* or *simple* and *simplicity*. On the other hand, and more important, the property can be thought of as being defined or identified through the relevant concept which again makes the former the periphery of the latter. This is because we need a concept or an idea of property p in order to be able to say or verify that an object has property p:

(6.74) a the property of being beautiful – beauty itself
        b the property of being kind – kindness itself

c the property of being friendly – friendliness itself
d the property of being simple – simplicity itself

If it is true to say that the concept identifies the corresponding property, it would, by extension, also be true to say that it identifies an entity holding that property. This is due to the fact that we can understand properties as functions returning entities. Thus, 'beautiful(x)' can be regarded as a function returning all those elements for which holds *x is beautiful.* In short, the concept identifies a property which in turn identifies a set of elements. Due to transitivity, the concept can identify all those elements which partake in it:

(6.75)   a a beautiful person – beauty itself
         b a kind person – kindness itself
         c a friendly person – friendliness itself
         d a simple thing – simplicity itself

Such reasoning begins to indicate that expressions like *beauty itself, kindness itself*, etc. should best be analysed as defining or identifying centres. Just as e.g. *John himself* potentially evokes all sorts of entities which bear whatever relation to him (part-whole, association), cf. (6.76), *beauty itself* evokes all those entities which partake in the concept, i.e. beautiful persons, things, men, women, cars, etc. Therefore, the contrast given in (6.77) is feasible.

(6.76)   a John's teeth – John himself
         b Kate's books – Kate herself

(6.77)   a I have met beauty itself, not just a beautiful person.
         b I have found kindness itself, not just a kind person.

The parallel is properly spelt out in (6.78) and (6.79) below. The only difference between (6.78) and (6.79a) consists in the fact that, in the former, the object can be identified in one step whereas two steps are necessary in the latter. If we equate property and object of that property, we arrive at the simplified (6.79b).

(6.78)   an object related to referent x – referent x himself

(6.79)   a an object of property y – property y identified through
            concept x – concept x itself
         b the property identified through concept x – concept x itself

Still, another step is necessary to derive the meaning of examples like (6.70). What we have done so far is to uncover where centre and periphery are hiding. However, in addition to that, sentences like (6.70a,b,c,d) assert that Mary, Otto, the person referred to by *she* as well as the material of the

Porter film equate with the concepts of beauty, kindness, friendliness and simplicity respectively and do not simply belong to the sets of beautiful, kind, friendly and simple entities. They thereby become the structure itself, not just an ingredient. Consider the following paraphrases, which are slightly different from (6.73), and where we find two assignments to Mary, etc., one being peripheral to the other.

(6.80) a Mary is not just a beautiful person, she is beauty itself.
        b Otto was not just a kind person, he was kindness itself.
        c She was not just a friendly person, she was friendliness itself.
        d The material is not just a simple object, it is simplicity itself.

To sum up, the meaning of the examples in (6.70) can be derived in two steps. First, the NP modified by ANS denoting an abstract concept must be interpreted. This results in a contrast between the concept, the property that can be derived from that concept and, by extension, the entities which possess that property. Since the entities holding that property are defined through the concept, they are peripheral to it or, put the other way round, the concept is central for them. Second, the subject referent is equated with the concept which is why we get the impression of an embodiment of that concept.

Note finally that the above examples often convey additional ideas like admiration, appreciation or surprise, but also irony, ridicule or mockery. This follows immediately from the explanation given above since by equating entities with a concept or an idea and not just attributing the corresponding property to them, we state that they cannot be exceeded with regard to the quality under consideration. Depending on the size of the factual gap between reality and what we state, we either create admiration, esteem or respect (no gap) or irony, mockery and derision (big gap).

Figure 6.5 gives a summary of the classification arrived at so far. Central entities are divided into a human as well as a non-human branch. The subsequent level gives the basis on which their centrality rests. Referents can be central in comparison with other referents for mainly two reasons. On the one hand, they may have, in relative terms, a higher rank or be in a higher position. On the other hand, the centrality of a referent may be due to the fact that other referents are defined, identified or referentially accessed through it. The remaining levels give prominent instantiations of this general dichotomy. Notice that the relevant nodes could be expanded infinitely.

6.3 Unique identifiability

At least since Moravcsik (1972) it has been known that adnominal intensifiers cannot be in association with just any NP. After having seen in the previous section what contrasts or oppositions ANS can evoke to the referent of the NP it modifies, we will now turn to a discussion of the

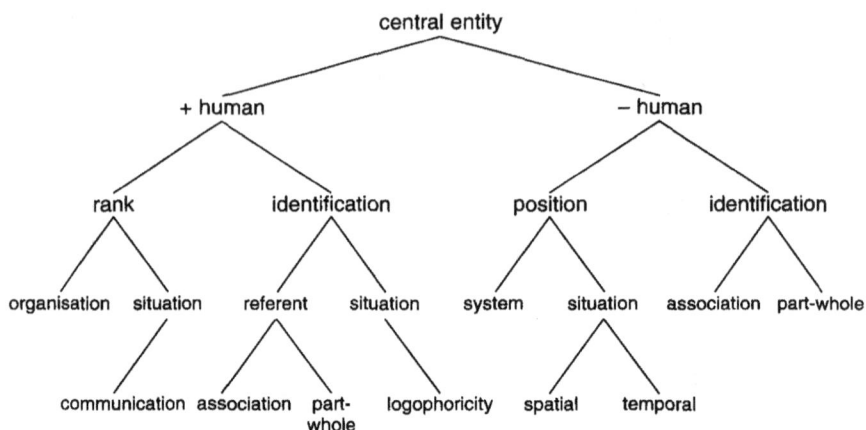

Figure 6.5 A typology of central entities.

properties of these NPs themselves. There are two well-defined constraints which an NP must fulfil in order to be successfully modified by ANS. On the one hand, it must denote a uniquely identifiable referent where referent can be understood in the broadest sense of the word. On the other hand, the NP must allow for the evocation of a periphery related to the relevant referent in any of the senses discussed above. Since the indefinite NPs in (6.81) do not obey the first constraint, the relevant examples are ungrammatical. The definite NPs shown in (6.82), by contrast, pick unique referents and can subsequently be intensified.

(6.81)   a *A linguist himself wouldn't know.
         b *She is seeking a true friend himself.

(6.82)   a God himself wouldn't know.
         b I have met the Pope himself.

Notice that only the first constraint can lead to true ungrammaticality since, given a sufficient amount of adequate context or some imagination on the part of the decoder, almost any referent can be thought of as being central and hence associated with another referent which forms its periphery. The relevant examples begin to become unacceptable as soon as the association becomes too far-fetched judged against the background of our world-knowledge or simply does not conform to it. (6.83) is odd because we do not expect caretakers and butlers to have subordinates. Since this constraint has been sufficiently illuminated in the previous sections, we will focus almost exclusively on unique identifiability in the following. In other words, this section is mainly about the referential properties of the NPs involved.

(6.83)   a ?The caretaker himself is watering the flower beds.
           b ?The butler himself ironed the morning paper.

So far, Edmondson and Plank (1978: 398) have put forward the most detailed description of the properties pertaining to the head NPs of adnominal intensifiers. As a matter of fact, apart from them, nobody else has directed much attention to this issue. They arrive at the following generalisation:

(6.84)   1 The NP must denote something that is identifiable.
          2 The NP cannot be a head of an imperative, a vocative, a generic, a general term or a nonreferential indefinite description.
          3 The NP cannot be a predicate nominal in identity sentences.

The above three points reflect a number of relevant intuitions about ANS. However, some of the predictions (6.84) makes are too strong whereas others follow from more general principles. As will be shown below, generic NPs should be considered appropriate heads for ANS and so should predicate nominals in identity sentences, although both need a well-tailored context to become fully acceptable. Moreover, although it is true that imperatives, vocatives as well as nonreferential indefinite NPs block ANS, these restrictions can be derived and need not be listed separately. In the following, we will try to account for the points listed in (6.84) on the basis of the two constraints formulated above.

(6.85) through (6.87) list some examples to illustrate (6.84). Let us discuss these cases separately, though in a slightly different order, taking up related bits and pieces on our way.

(6.85)   She is in love with Colonel Brandon himself.

(6.86)   a *Yourself go!
           b *May I ask you, Mr President himself, how do you intend to handle the situation in Bosnia?
           c ?The dodo itself is extinct.
           d *She needs a husband himself.

(6.87)   *De Gaulle was the King of France himself.

As far as identifiability is concerned, this constraint is best fulfilled with definite NPs because they pick unique referents. Therefore, definite NPs are the most common type of NP to be modified by ANS. Within the group of definite NPs, in turn, it is proper names that are frequently encountered. Here, reference can be to persons, places, times, etc., cf. (6.88) below.

(6.88)   a The work led Russell himself to conclude that the teaching of the subject had no effect whatsoever on pupils' political outlook. [BNC]

b The Montreal into which Leonard was born was deeply segmented, as is Canada itself in its famous 'two solitudes', the legacy of its Franco-British history; a difficult dimension for those outside its rivalries to understand. [BNC]

c In other words, there are marvellous projects going on which really stimulate the interest of everybody, and it's, the Engineering Council's still trying to push them along into the twenty first century itself. [BNC]

From proper names it is only a small step to definite NPs in general and ANS takes it without problems. Since German and English explicitly mark definite NPs by prefixing the relevant NPs with the definite articles *der, die, das* and *the* respectively, it is by and large possible to say that if an NP is headed by the definite article, it will allow intensification by ANS.

(6.89)   a On this model I get the best of both worlds and yet, for me, the sound of the stick itself is more unique than any MIDI sounds I've ever heard. [BNC]

b This can be tested both by examining the structure of the pot itself and by making a similar pot in this way to see if the result matches the pot being studied. [BNC]

Notice, however, that such a rule is not without exceptions. Definite NPs can be used in a way in which they are much more similar to indefinite descriptions than to definite ones, cf. (6.90a), which essentially means *We wanted to call a doctor* because it is left open who exactly the doctor is. Here, two things are noteworthy. First, if ANS is added to these examples, the reading according to the definite description is triggered, cf. (6.90b), where a specific doctor is under consideration. Second, if context is supplied to force the indefinite reading, ANS becomes inadequate, cf. (6.90c). Apparently, this is due to the fact that no particular doctor can be identified in this example, cf. Edmondson and Plank (1978: 382).

(6.90)   a We wanted to call the doctor.

b We wanted to call the doctor himself.

c *We wanted to call the doctor himself, but we didn't know any.

Section 3.1.1 showed that ANS is always a sister of a maximal projection. This can come as no surprise because every adposition makes the interpretation of an NP more precise, cf. (6.91a). Provided that the maxim of quantity holds, a less specific NP would not be enough to pick the referent correctly. Since ANS expects a uniquely identifiable referent, it cannot intervene between a noun and its adpositions, cf. (6.91b).

(6.91)   a the house next door with the red windows itself
         b *the house itself next door with the red windows

The same argument holds for defining relatives as in (6.92).

(6.92)   a The man who I met yesterday himself.
         b *The man himself who I met yesterday.

Moreover, there are definite common nouns lacking an overt article (Chesterman 1991: 44), however, as it turns out, ANS seems to reject such NPs, cf. (6.93). Why this should be so is not entirely clear to me, but it appears as if an explanation would rather have to be hinged to constraint number two since the NP in question clearly identifies a referent. What is missing in (6.93) is the necessary contrast to another referent.

(6.93)   *Lunch itself is ready.

Nevertheless, precisely this incompatibility can result in clearing up otherwise ambiguous cases. Complex NPs as in (6.94a) may fail to specify whether x-*self* interacts with the embedded NP or with the NP as a whole, i.e. in this example, it may either be in association with *the issue* or with *the discussion of the issue*. (6.94b), in contrast, leaves no questions open. Here, ANS can only be interpreted as interacting with *the issue*.

(6.94)   a The discussion of the issue itself continued for several hours.
         b Discussion of the issue itself continued for several hours.

Apart from singular NPs as in (6.89), definite NPs can also occur in the plural. Number does not pose a problem for ANS, however, it can have consequences for the way in which it makes a referent central and opposes it to a related periphery. Essentially, a plural definite NP denotes a set of equal referents so that if *the horse* refers to just one particular object which happens to be a horse, *the horses* refers to a set of more than one object each having the property of being a horse. What we would expect, then, is that ANS characterises each of these referents as central and opposes every single referent to a separate periphery. In other words, after intensification there should be as many peripheries as there are centres. This is indeed what happens in many examples. (6.95a) contrasts poets with their respective work, (6.95b) images and their counterparts in experience and (6.95c) dreams and their interpretations. The number of central referents matches exactly the number of peripheral referents in all three cases.

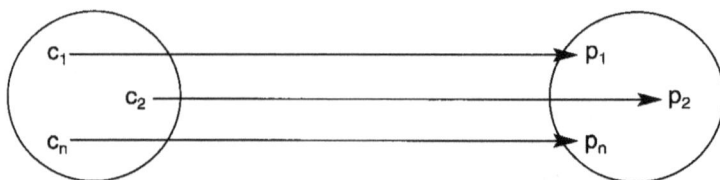

Figure 6.6 Multiple centres and peripheries.

(6.95)   a Plato is, at times, just as suspicious of the poets themselves
          as he is of their work. [BROWN]
       b The images themselves, like their counterparts in experi-
          ence, are not neutral qualities to be surveyed dispassionately.
          [BROWN]
       c Interpretations were not offered by these priests – rather, the
          dreams themselves were thought to be curative. [LLC]

Figure 6.6 gives a schematic representation of the centre-periphery oppositions (c = centre, p = periphery).

But let us return to definite NPs in general. On the basis of the few cross-
linguistic remarks made so far, one might suspect that English and German
adnominal intensifiers also show some incompatibility with the nominal
class at some point, recall (6.30). Likely candidates could be nouns denoting
abstract referents since in terms of immediacy to the real world, they are
farthest away from proper nouns. That ANS interacts with concrete nouns
has been documented sufficiently. Still, there is no problem. However
abstract the concept denoted by the relevant NP is, as long as a relation to
another referent (concept) can be built up, intensification is not obstructed,
at least not in English and German.

(6.96)   a Thus too often we think of form as a relation of A to B, of
          a movement being fine if C, instead of D, follows B at a
          certain point; sometimes this pseudo-explanation may in
          fact support truth, but we grasp the symbols of the truth
          instead of the truth itself. [LOB]
       b That was the fallacy of the death-bed repentance – peni-
          tence was the fruit of long training and discipline. And the
          sin itself was so old that like an ancient picture the defor-
          mity had faded and left a kind of grace. [LLC]

Finally, and this will conclude our brief discussion of definite NPs, note
that ANS also allows NPs denoting situations or events, i.e. NPs denoting
relations between referents rather than the referents themselves. Such NPs
are the nominal equivalents of sentences and have the semantic status of a

proposition. They are sometimes referred to as 'action nominalisations', cf. Chomsky (1970), Grimshaw (1992).

(6.97) a The destruction of the city itself caused numerous deaths.
b I don't mind Paul's fondness of Mary itself. But that he wants to marry her simply is too much.
c Luna, almost overcome by the heat, breathing through her mouth like a dog, her hair plastered with sweat to her head, kept looking straight ahead, and walking as if the walking itself was her reward. [LLC]

Although all sorts of definite NPs allow intensification, it is obvious that as far as frequency is concerned, nouns denoting personalities of high rank play a somewhat distinguished role in that they are most commonly encountered. Not only are they the preferred object of exemplification in the relevant literature, these NPs are also the first to be produced by informants when asked for possible contexts of SELF.[3] This impression is supported by evidence taken from casual reading as well as from the corpora. Why should this be so? There are two reasons that immediately spring to mind. First, nouns denoting personalities of high rank most easily license the evocation of the contrast necessary to make ANS acceptable. In terms of the constraints formulated above, this means that these NPs readily fulfil constraint number two. Some languages even have expressions related to SELF which are explicitly confined to referents of high rank, cf. Swedish *självaste* which is the superlative of *själv* (SELF):[4]

(6.98) Swedish
Självaste kungen kunde inte ha det bättre.
'The king himself could not be better off.'

Second, and this is a diachronic observation, such nouns were in all likelihood the first to be modified by ANS. Among the intensified expressions in Old English, there is a relative abundance of nouns like *God, Crist, cyning,* etc. From there, the intensifier appears to have expanded its territory to the remaining members of the nominal class. Recall that Turkish, Japanese, Korean and Mandarin disallow non-human NPs, cf. (6.30). Hence, intensifiers in these languages can be viewed as not as advanced in the chain of grammaticalisation as e.g. in English and German.

Edmondson and Plank (1978: 398ff.), by contrast, argue that proper names are the type of NP most likely to be encountered with ANS because they have a high degree of referentiality, i.e. they denote individuals rather than their properties. On that account, ANS comes to be an expression that preferably interacts on the level of extensions and not intensions. Since proper names are bound to an extensional interpretation, so the argument goes, they represent the lion's share of all NPs modified by ANS.

Many definite NPs, however, allow both an intensional as well as an extensional reading, and here, Edmondson and Plank's prediction is that ANS will disambiguate the two possible interpretations and pick the extensional one. To give a practical example, in the sentences of (6.99) below, the NPs *the president, the chairman of the hospital board* as well as *my wife*, can either be understood as referring to the role their referents play or to the office they hold (intensional or type reading) or, alternatively, they can pick the referents or individuals themselves (extensional or token reading). Only the latter type of reference would result in a particular individual.[5] According to Edmondson and Plank, ANS 'functions like a filter that passes terms denoting constant individual concepts [cf. Montague 1974] and rejects all others.'

(6.99) a The President is going to be elected by the Senate.
        b Most people are going to vote for the President.
        c I want to talk to the chairman of the hospital board.
        d My wife must be an heiress.

When these NPs are modified by the intensifier, it seems, in certain examples at least, indeed to be the case that the extensional interpretation is preferred over the intensional one. Consider (6.100b) which in all likelihood means that the current president is reelected and (6.100c) where some particular individual rather than any chairman is under consideration. However, (6.100a,d) are less clear in this respect because the former could well mean that the office of the president is elected by the Senate whereas the latter rather seems to express that the role of *my wife* must be filled with an heiress independently of who exactly will finally take it up.

(6.100) a The President himself is going to be elected by the Senate.
         b Most people are going to vote for the President himself.
         c I want to talk to the chairman of the hospital board himself.
         d My wife herself must be an heiress.

To be sure, Edmondson and Plank themselves point out that the extensional interpretation is a matter of preference rather than necessity. Their examples in (6.101) below (taken from p. 399) clearly must be read intensionally. The contrasts evoked are between roles and not between individuals.

(6.101) a I want to talk to the chairman of the hospital board himself, whoever he is.
         b My girlfriend can be poor, but my wife herself must be an heiress.

Note that we are also able to construct minimal pairs to show that both the intensional and the extensional interpretation of a definite NP is possible with ANS. Whereas the ministers and the chancellor in (6.102a) refer to abstract roles, i.e. here the relevant posts are being contrasted, the *current* in (6.102b) adds the extra bit to force the extensional reading. Only (6.102b) will evoke a particular individual, say Helmut Kohl. The availability of the two interpretations is totally independent of *himself.*

> (6.102) a Ministers in the German political system lead a quiet life in comparison to the chancellor himself.
>
> b The current ministers lead a quiet life in comparison to the chancellor himself.

Furthermore, Edmondson and Plank claim that intensified anaphoric pronouns must receive an extensional interpretation too, cf. (6.103). Here, *they themselves* in (6.103a) is strictly extensional, the simple *they* in (6.103b) is ambiguous between intensional and extensional reading whereas the *chairmen* in (6.103c) can only be made sense of in an intensional way. Thus, there is a decreasing degree of extensionality to be noted from (6.103a) to (6.103c).

> (6.103) Some chairmen of the hospital board believe that
> a they themselves ⎫
> b they   ⎬ should preside at board meetings.
> c chairmen   ⎭

Note, however, that the verb in the matrix clause influences the range of possible interpretations. In (6.104), where *believe* has been replaced by *have been told*, the intensional reading of *they themselves* is in fact available and hence there is a contrast possible to, say, the deputies of the chairmen. The reason for this behaviour is not easy to understand, but it could have something to do with the fact that the subject of a verb like *believe* is a subject of consciousness (SC). Given that subjects of consciousness tend to be extensional and that ANS readily interacts with them, this could be the reason why the intensional reading in (6.103a) is blocked, but available in (6.104a).

> (6.104) Some chairmen of the hospital board have been told that
> a they themselves ⎫
> b they   ⎬ should preside at board meetings.
> c chairmen   ⎭

To sum up, although there appears to be a certain tendency of ANS to trigger the extensional reading of definite NPs, this can by no means count as a rule. Definite NPs in their intensional interpretation are clearly available for modification by ANS, and hence, it seems to be more likely that the relative abundance of ANS with NPs referring to personalities of high rank is due to the fact that they readily allow for the evocation of an appropriate periphery rather than to their high degree of referentiality. Note that the first constraint – identifiability – is not violated by intensional definite NPs. Just as extensional definite NPs, they denote something unique. This brings us to the discussion of generic NPs which can be regarded as the prototype of intensional NPs.

Recall from (6.84), that Edmondson and Plank suggest that ANS cannot be in association with generic NPs. However, to formulate a restriction in this way is probably much too rigid even in view of their own data which are repeated in (6.105), cf. their p. 382. The picture that presents itself is far from homogeneous so that it seems to make sense to look into that matter in slightly more detail.

> (6.105) a *Unicorns themselves exist.
> b ?The dodo itself is extinct.
> c Man himself is a product of his environment.

Let us first of all try to make clear what it means for an NP to be interpreted generically. Here, essentially two options arise. On the one hand, this can mean that a certain property holds for the referent of that NP at all points in time. The generic effect is due to the fact that the property of the referent is not assumed to change, cf. (6.106a). On the other hand, a generic effect can occur when a property exhaustively holds for all elements of a set. Consider (6.106b) which means that if there is a referent such that he is a Scotsman, then he drinks whisky.[6]

> (6.106) a The earth is a globe.
> b Scotsmen drink whisky.

It appears possible, then, to analyse genericity as universal quantification, cf. Hawkins (1978). In the one case, quantification ranges over points in time, in the other, it ranges over the elements of a certain set. (6.107) gives a possible formalisation of (6.106).

> (6.107) a $\forall t\ (Q(x)_t)$
> b $\forall x\ (P(x) \Rightarrow Q(x))$

As far as temporal quantification is concerned, we are most likely to find NPs involved which denote single referents or refer to a set on the whole, i.e. proper names, NPs denoting substances as well as exhaustive collectives, cf. (6.108).

> (6.108) a San Diego is very hot.
> b Water consists of hydrogen and oxygen.
> c Mankind has always been confronted with great problems.

As for universal quantification over individuals, a necessary prerequisite is the existence of a set of such individuals. What is needed is an NP denoting one element of a larger set. Here, animal terms such as dodo, lion, unicorn, etc. have turned out to be useful for exemplification. They allow a generic interpretation in either the definite or indefinite singular or the indefinite plural, cf. (6.109).

(6.109) a The dodo is big.
         b A dodo is big.
         c Dodos are big.

Interestingly enough, the definite plural of such NPs is not available in a generic reading as (6.110) makes clear.

(6.110) The dodos are big.[7]

Although this cannot be the place to investigate in detail why a generic reading is possible in exactly these cases, note at least that in the case of indefinite NPs, we appear to conclude by induction that what is true of one element or some elements holds for all elements of the relevant set, cf. (6.111), where (6.111b) is inductively inferred from (6.111a). Why definite singular NPs allow the generic reading is not entirely clear to me and neither is it transparent why definite plurals disallow it.

(6.111) a $\exists x \ (P(x) \ \& \ Q(x))$
         b $\forall x \ (P(x) \Rightarrow Q(x))$

Be that as it may, intensifying such NPs yields the following picture. Generics which are due to quantification over time points pose no problem for ANS. This is shown in (6.112).

(6.112) a The outskirts of San Diego are even hotter than San Diego itself.
         b Water consists of hydrogen and oxygen. Hydrogen and oxygen are gases, but water itself is a liquid.
         c Most other species live a pleasant life, but mankind itself has always been confronted with great problems.

Those which involve universal quantification over the elements of a set can also be intensified although the relevant examples do not exactly gain in acceptability, cf. (6.113). Nevertheless, these intensified generic NPs are not ungrammatical and this is in contradiction to what Edmondson and Plank propose.

(6.113) a The offspring of the dodo is small. The dodo itself is big.

　　b　The offspring of a dodo is small. A dodo itself is big.

　　c　The offspring of dodos is small. Dodos themselves are big.

Evidence taken from the corpora available appears to confirm these intuitions:

(6.114)　a　Similarly, I suggest, a sentence itself has only vague significance of sentences intended to convey a factual communication. This requirement is fulfilled by a prefixed assertion sign. [LLC]

　　b　This brings us on to the second of Dworkin's grounds for excluding such background policy issues from the jurisdiction of the courts, for if no one has a right to any particular form of decision-making process – whether a right to a hearing itself, a right to cross-examine witnesses or to be given reasons for a decision – this can only be because such a right can not be derived from the master principle of equal concern and respect. [BNC]

　　c　A plant and its flower may look beautiful to our human eyes, but a plant itself has no eyes with which to perceive itself or its fellows. [BNC]

　　d　It will be noticed that in all of this the term 'correlate' is being used in a way consistent with our previous uses of 'event', 'cause', 'condition', 'causal circumstance', and 'effect': not for a type of thing, but for a thing itself, more particularly an individual property or set of such properties rather than a type. [BNC]

To be sure, given that identifiability of the referent and the existence of a peripheral alternative to it are the two constraints limiting the range of NPs the intensifier can modify, there seems to be no reason why generics should be barred from it. Quantification over time points is entirely unproblematic because it does not influence the referential properties of an NP. Quantification over a set, by contrast, might seem more problematic. However, if we bear in mind that an exhaustively quantified set can be reinterpreted as a single identifiable referent, it becomes possible to understand why intensification is not obstructed.

　　Whereas it is certainly true to say that indefinite NPs in a generic interpretation can be intensified by ANS, it must, however, be taken into consideration that this is not a property of indefinite NPs in general. Consider the following examples where ANS modifies indefinite NPs thereby turning the relevant sentences ungrammatical. This constraint is most certainly semantic in nature.

(6.115)　a　*A prince himself appeared in her dreams.

    b *She is seeking a friend himself.

    c *This crown is meant for a king himself.

In contrast to indefinite generics, it is impossible to uniquely identify the referents of the intensified NPs in (6.115). Hence, constraint number one is violated. Ungrammaticality arises as soon as indefinite NPs function as true indefinite descriptions, i.e. when they state the existence of an element with a certain property plus the existence of additional elements with the same property without specifying which referent they pick, cf. (6.116).[8] Applied to (6.115) this means that there are three sets of individuals, namely a set of princes, a set of friends and a set of kings.

    (6.116) $\exists x_1 \, (P(x_1)) \; \& \; \exists x_2 \, (P(x_2)) \; \& \; \ldots \; \& \; \exists x_n \, (P(x_n))$

As a matter of fact, (6.115b,c) are ambiguous between two interpretations and only in one of them will the indefinite NPs in question pick a referent at all. In the other, which is commonly referred to as 'oblique construction' or 'referentially opaque construction', cf. Dowty *et al.* (1981), there is no referent whose existence is claimed in the first place. Under this interpretation, the relevant sentences can be true without there being any referent.[9]

Notice the difference to generics. These express that a certain state of affairs holds for all members of the set under consideration. The indefinite NPs in (6.115) merely make a statement about one element of that set, i.e. only one member of these sets is involved in the situation described by the predication, but we do not know which it is. To give an example, the statement *A dodo is big* applies to all dodos, but *A prince appeared in her dreams* is only true of one prince.

Notice also the difference to definite NPs. These claim the existence of only one element which results in the contrasts shown in (6.117).

    (6.117) a John blotched the cover/*the page of the book.

              b John blotched *a cover/a page of the book.

An alternative explanation for why indefinite NPs are inadequate with adnominal intensifiers could run as follows. Since indefinite NPs claim the existence of more than one referent for all of which the same property holds, characterising one as central boils down to characterising all as central. However, this is at variance with the very idea of a centre, cf. (6.118).

    (6.118) *The sun is a centre of the solar system.

We have seen so far that an indefinite NP can either receive a generic interpretation or be used as an indefinite description in the sense of (6.116). The former is compatible with ANS whereas the latter clearly is not. Apart from that, there is a third way to use indefinite NPs, namely in a so-called specific reading. The difference to (6.116) lies in the fact that in addition to the existential claim of more than one element, one particular referent appears to be picked or identified. Consequently, such examples are acceptable under modification by ANS, cf. (6.119).[10] Here, speaker A can identify the individual he is talking about, but speaker B cannot.

> (6.119)   A: All Cretans lie.
> B: Where did you hear that?
> A: A Cretan himself told me.

Another example is provided in (6.120), where a specific partnership is under consideration:

> (6.120)   Given the number of curriculum tasks which the school needed to address and the limited resources available to make a response with, the case had to be made not only for a partnership itself, but also for the prioritisation of this task over other needs which had been identified. [BNC]

Recall from section 3.1.1 that the German indefinite pronoun *man* can be easily intensified whereas its English counterpart *one* bars modification by ANS, cf. (6.121b) which is the attempted translation of (6.121a).

> (6.121)   a   Man selbst kann da überhaupt nichts machen.
> b   ??One oneself can do nothing at all in that matter.

In all likelihood, the German example is more acceptable because *man* preferably receives a specific interpretation referring either to speaker, hearer or both. Note that the adequate translation of (6.121a) can be any of (6.122). English *one*, by contrast, seems to be more strictly tied to the non-specific indefinite interpretation. This may have to do with the fact that it has been derived from the numeral 'one', which is a well-known source of markers for indefiniteness (as e.g. the indefinite article).

> (6.122)   a   I myself can do nothing at all in that matter.
> b   You yourself can do nothing at all in that matter.
> c   We ourselves can do nothing at all in that matter.

Again, this shows that identifiability is a useful concept for capturing the distribution of the possible head NPs of ANS. On that basis it also becomes possible to explain why quantified NPs, interrogative pronouns as well as indefinite pronouns are not suitable, cf. (6.123) through (6.125) and Edmondson and Plank (1978: 381ff.). None of these NPs denotes an identifiable referent.

(6.123) *Some/*many/*several/*all cooks themselves spoil the broth.

(6.124) a *Who himself answered the phone?
       b *What itself do you need?
       c *When itself do you intend to come?

(6.125) a *Someone himself spoiled the broth.
       b *Nobody himself came to my party.

Let us now come to predicate nominals in identity sentences. Edmondson and Plank claim that these nominals are impossible to intensify and cite the example given in (6.87) which is repeated in (6.126) for the sake of convenience.

(6.126) *De Gaulle was the King of France himself.

However, although the above example as such does indeed appear unacceptable, its oddity must arise from factors other than ANS. If (6.126) is rephrased as a hypothetical sentence, it seems to gain in acceptability, cf. (6.127a). Consider also (6.127b). This sentence can be understood in a theatre context with John and Peter being actors. What (6.127b) does is to assign roles to these referents, Horatio and Hamlet respectively. Since Hamlet is the protagonist, it would indeed be strange if intensification were obstructed.

(6.127) a De Gaulle ruled as if he was the King of France himself.
       b John was Horatio and Peter was Hamlet himself.

That such sentences do occur was also shown in (6.70) and that they are by no means a rare species is further underlined in (6.128) below.

(6.128) a Mary was innocence itself.
       b It looked as old as the Church of England itself. [LLC]
       c Siegmund is Wotan himself at one remove. [LLC]

To sum up, predicate nominals in identity sentences do not block ANS. To be sure, it would be unexpected if they did because neither the constraint on identifiability nor the one requesting a possible contrast is violated.

It seems, then, that most of the restrictions Edmondson and Plank postulate, recall (6.84), are formulated in too rigid a way or can, as in the case of indefinite NPs, be reduced to the general constraint of identifiability. What remains to be shown is that the ungrammaticality of intensified NPs in imperatives as well as vocatives follows from more general considerations. The case of imperatives is easily explained and can be motivated syntactically (cf. section 4.3). In brief, since imperatives are structures in which the

subject NP is deleted, ANS must be deleted too because it is part of this NP.
It is not necessary to assume a semantic (or pragmatic) constraint, in fact,
semantically speaking, ANS is permissible in imperatives, recall (6.37).

(6.129) a *Yourself go!
         b *Yourself sing!

The ungrammaticality of adnominal intensifiers in vocatives, by contrast,
can be attributed to constraint number two, i.e. that there must be a contrast
to another referent possible. Being a form of address, vocatives delimit the
referents present in the universe of discourse to the one or the ones being
addressed. Since ANS tries to evoke alternatives to the addressee(s) which,
however, do not exist, the relevant utterances break down.

(6.130) a *Can I ask you a question, Mr. Miller himself?
         b *Play it again, Sam yourself!

That ANS cannot build up the necessary contrast between two referents
is also responsible for what can be observed in (6.131), cf. Baker (1995),
Zribi-Hertz (1995). (6.131a,b) are perfectly well-formed with the intensifier
characterising Rod and Liz respectively as somehow superior to the other.
However, trying to intensify both NPs at the same time results in an unacceptable constellation, cf. (6.131c).

(6.131) Liz and Rod were discussing a new business strategy.
         a Liz expected the DOW to rise. Rod himself thought it
            would fall.
         b Rod expected the DOW to rise. Liz herself thought it would
            fall.
         c Liz herself expected the DOW to rise. ???Rod himself
            thought it would fall.

As a matter of fact, the reason why (6.131c) is unacceptable is slightly more
subtle than the one brought forward to explain (6.130). Whereas the latter
cannot be interpreted because there are no alternatives whatsoever, the
former breaks down due to a contradictory characterisation of centre and
periphery. In the context of (6.131), the first sentence in (6.131c) makes Liz
central and Rod peripheral to her whereas the second sentence claims exactly
the opposite, namely that Rod is central in comparison to Liz. Given that
there can be only one central referent within a certain domain, it is clear
where the oddity of (6.131c) comes from: it contains competing centres.

Exactly the same explanation can be used to account for the impossibility
of having multiple occurrences of ANS in so-called list expressions as
mentioned in Zribi-Hertz (1995: 341). Again, multiple ANS leads to multiple centres and this is prohibited by definition, cf. (6.132).

(6.132) a You_i clean the windows, you_j polish the shoes and you_k hoover the carpet.
   b *You_i yourself clean the windows, you_j yourself polish the shoes and you_k yourself hoover the carpet.

Scenarios with more than one intensifier in one and the same piece of discourse or even sentence are, nevertheless, feasible. All that has to be made sure is that the centres do not take each other as periphery, i.e. that they do not interfere. In other words, it must be ruled out that two or more referents compete for the status of being central within the same domain.

(6.133) a He was not particularly tall, a little taller than Jemima herself perhaps, but his shoulders in the tweed suit were broad, giving an air of authority, and he himself, if not exactly heavy, was certainly a substantial man. [ASR: 88]
   b But it was Barth himself who really carried this programme through, insisting that even the doctrines of creation and sin must be grounded in christology, that there is no predestination of God apart from Jesus Christ, that on the cross Jesus himself is the one rejected and abandoned by God, and that both judgement and mercy, reprobation and election, must be seen as worked through in him. [BNC]

Let us now come to a summary of the main points. In the previous discussion, we have argued that the restrictions on the type of head NP adnominal intensifiers can interact with as formulated in Edmondson and Plank (1978), cf. (6.84), are much too rigid and that the only constraint that definitely has to be fulfilled concerns the identifiability of the referent of that NP. There is no need for a referent in a material sense. Consequently, nearly all definite NPs can be intensified and so can generic NPs (definite and indefinite), indefinite NPs in a specific reading and predicate nominals in identity sentences.

The relevant generalisation seems to be that adnominal intensifiers can only intensify NPs which are definite descriptions in the sense of Russell (1905), cf. (6.134) adapted from Hawkins (1978: 94). In other words, adnominal intensifiers can interact with NPs which claim the existence of a referent and the uniqueness of that referent. (6.134) says that there is an entity x satisfying P and that there is no entity y which satisfies P and is not identical to x.

(6.134) $\exists x \, (P(x) \, \& \, \neg\exists y \, (P(y) \, \& \, \neg(x=y)))$

(6.135) is another way of expressing the same thing: there is an x such that it satisfies P and if there is a y satisfying P, then it is equivalent to x.

(6.135) $\exists x \ (P(x) \ \& \ \exists y \ (P(y) \Rightarrow x=y))$

The constraint on unique identifiability also explains why ANS cannot interact with indefinite NPs in the sense of (6.116) above. These do not make the claim on uniqueness and subsequently fail to identify a particular referent. On the other hand, we have seen that the opposition of a centre to a related periphery, as formulated in König (1991), must be regarded as the basic semantic contribution of ANS. Hence, it can come as no surprise that adnominal intensifiers cannot modify NPs whose referents fail to allow the evoking of alternatives according to these specifications for one reason or another. Generally speaking, this failure can be put down to mainly three sources. First, there is only one referent available in the universe of discourse, i.e. no alternatives can be evoked at all. Second, the referent is so low on every possible hierarchy that no periphery can be thought up. And third, the NP to be intensified already denotes a referent peripheral to some centre. (6.136) gives some final examples.

>   (6.136)   a   ?Adam himself was the only human on earth. (said before
>   the creation of Eve)
>   b   ?I have seen the caretaker himself.
>   c   ???Max himself and Tom himself met for lunch.

These considerations finally converge into the two constraints formulated at the beginning. They are once again given in (6.137) below. Notice that the constraint on a uniquely identifiable referent and the semantic contribution of adnominal intensifiers, namely to make a referent central, are intimately connected.

>   (6.137)   1   The NP must denote something that is uniquely identifi-
>   able.
>   2   It must be possible to evoke a periphery to the referent of
>   that NP.

6.4 ANS in role reversal structures

This section takes up a phenomenon already discussed in section 3.3, namely ANS in the context of role reversal. The distinctive property of this usage of ANS is that the NP the intensifier interacts with undergoes a change in its thematic role relative to the preceding context. In the previous literature, it has been assumed that the main semantic contribution of intensifiers in general lies in marking such a role reversal (Girke 1993) or, at least, that there is such a subtype, cf. Edmondson and Plank's (1978) *himself₃*. (6.138) repeats the relevant structures. The discussion pursued in section 3.3 showed, however, that it is not necessary to assume a separate type of usage, but that examples like (6.138) can, on syntactic and prosodic grounds, be reduced to ANS.

(6.138) a Lucrezia poisoned Lorenzo, and was herself poisoned by Cesare. (agent ⇒ patient)

b Smith is taller than Jones who is himself taller/shorter than my aunt. (standard of comparison ⇒ person compared)

What is left and will be dealt with in this section is to find a motivation for the role reversal, which, after all, is clearly visible in these examples. Only when we are able to attribute it to an external factor can we be sure that it is no contribution on the part of the intensifier. We will show that the role reversal observed is an effect which follows from the fact that the relevant sentences contain an S-topic in the sense of Büring (1997).

But before we come to that, let us take a closer look at the phenomenon of role reversal and examine possible patterns of reversal. A valid starting hypothesis might be to say that role reversal can occur only in one direction of the thematic role hierarchy. (6.139) portrays such a hierarchy.

(6.139) agent > experiencer > patient > theme

Consider now (6.140) which is an example of downward reversal. The NP *Paul*, which bears the role of an agent in the first clause of the coordination, is reduced to a patient in the second. The formalisation below the sentence reads as follows. The role of NP_1, $R(NP_1)$, is further up in the hierarchy than the role of NP_2 (*Mary*), $R(NP_2)$. In a next step, the two roles are exchanged ('⇔' indicates the actual reversal) resulting in the opposite constellation, namely that the role of NP_2 is now higher up than the one of NP_1. SELF here marks the NP whose thematic role was lowered.

(6.140) Paul insulted Mary and was himself insulted by Fred.
$R(NP_1) > R(NP_2)$; $R(NP_1) ⇔ R(NP_2)$; $R(NP_1) < R(NP_2)$; $SELF(NP_1)$

However, the opposite pattern is feasible too. ANS in (6.141) marks exactly the NP whose role has been elevated. NP_2 (*Mary*) bears a patient role before the reversal, but emerges as an agent afterwards. In brief, role reversal structures are not bound with respect to the directionality of the reversal.

(6.141) Paul insulted Mary who herself insulted Fred.
$R(NP_1) > R(NP_2)$; $R(NP_1) ⇔ R(NP_2)$; $R(NP_1) < R(NP_2)$; $SELF(NP_2)$

The only watertight restriction observable in role reversal structures is that roles must reverse. ANS does not allow interaction with an NP which was previously used with the same role:

(6.142)   a   ??Paul insulted Mary and himself insulted Fred.
        b   ??Paul insulted Mary who was herself insulted by Fred.

It should also be pointed out that a true role reversal is absolutely essential. A mere switch of roles as in (6.143) is not sufficient. Role reversal must be understood as a role switch pertaining to one and the same predicate. The examples in (6.143) are inadequate because although there is a switch from agent to patient in both sentences, it is not performed on the same predicate; these are changed too, from *leave* to *stab* and *insult* to *fire* respectively.

(6.143)   a   ??Lucrezia left Florence and was herself stabbed on the road.
        b   ??Paul insulted Mary and was himself fired by the manager.

In point of fact, it is sufficient if the NP undergoing the role reversal appears in a cognate predicate. Observe the decrease in affinity of the two predicates involved from (6.144a) to (6.144c). They are alike in (6.144a), namely *turn*, roughly synonymous in (6.144b), *assassinate* versus *shoot dead*, and only conceptually related in (6.144c) where the common denominator is the fixing of an object to another.

(6.144)   a   The shears were sharpened on a stone which was turned by a wheel, which was itself turned by a handle. [BNC]
        b   In a bizarre incident on April 29, Nodar Imiadze, the Vice-President of the Adzhar autonomous republic (ASSR) in south-west Georgia, attempted to assassinate the acting President, Aslan Abashidze, and was himself shot dead by security guards. [BNC]
        c   However, in our application, the aircraft, which has no undercarriage of its own, travels on a trolley which is itself tethered to the rotating pylon head. [BNC]

After having sketched the properties of role reversal structures, we will now attempt an explanation why role reversal has to occur and show that it has nothing to do with the semantics of ANS. Consider once again a typical role reversal structure and its prosodic features. For the subsequent discussion, the second sentence of (6.145) is of importance. The equivalence of (6.145) to structures like (6.140) was shown in section 3.3.

(6.145)   Paul insulted Mary. He himSELF was insulted by FRED.

Sentences like these contain two stressed syllables. Together they form a so-called 'bridge accent'. The stressed constituents evoke alternatives and can therefore be analysed as foci. In addition to that, the first focus takes up previous information and can hence be regarded as a topic, an S-topic, as it were. As for their meaning, an adversative implicature is characteristic of such sentences. Due to these properties, it should appear possible to analyse role reversal structures according to the proposals put forward in Büring (1997).

Büring analyses sentences with the properties sketched above as topic-focus structures and assumes three semantic values for the relevant structures: 1) the actual proposition which reflects the truth-conditions of the sentence under consideration; 2) the focus value, which according to Rooth (1985), can be derived from inserting alternative values into the focus position; and 3) the topic value, which is produced by putting alternative values into the topic position. Both focus value and topic value can be regarded as open propositions or questions. We will exemplify Büring's analysis on the basis of example (6.146) where subscript T marks the topic and subscript F the focus.

(6.146) [T ALL] politicians are [F NOT] corrupt.

1) propositional content (truth-value of sentence)

(6.147) ^all politicians are not corrupt

2) focus value (insertion of alternative values into the focus position; is equivalent to an open proposition)

(6.148) {^all politicians are not corrupt, ^all politicians are corrupt}

3) topic value (insertion of alternative values into the topic position of the focus value; is equivalent to a twofold open proposition)

(6.149) {{^all politicians are not corrupt, ^all politicians are corrupt}, {^many politicians are not corrupt, ^many politicians are corrupt}, {^some politicians are not corrupt, ^some politicians are corrupt}, ... }

On the basis of this interpretation, Büring formulates the well-formedness conditions of structures containing S-topics as follows:

(6.150) a Given a question–answer sequence Q A, $[[Q]]^\circ$ must be an element of $[[A]]^t$.
         b Given a sentence A containing a Topic, there must be at least one disputable element in $[[A]]^t$ after uttering A.

Let us now consider the question-answer sequence in (6.151).

(6.151) Q: Are all politicians corrupt?
         A: [T ALL] politicians are [F NOT] corrupt.

Obviously, (6.150a) is satisfied because the semantic value of the question (^all politicians are corrupt) is contained in the topic value. (6.150b) is satisfied too because (6.151A) implicates that a topic value holds which is different from the truth value of the sentence. In other words, there is a residual topic which explains the adversative implicature these sentences have. Moreover, although this point is not vital for the present discussion, Büring can explain why sentences with S-topics typically show scope inversion. In (6.151A) the negative element has wide scope over the quantifier. Note that if it had narrow scope, there would be no residual topic and (6.150b) would be violated. This is because under *in-situ* scope, the focus value implies the topic value. In the case that all politicians are corrupt, many, some, etc. politicians are corrupt too.

Let us now apply this analysis to role reversal structures. Topic and focus in (6.152) are assigned in the same manner as above.

(6.152) Paul insulted Mary. [T Paul himSELF] was insulted by [F FRED].

1) propositional content

(6.153) ^paul was insulted by fred

2) focus value

(6.154) {^paul was insulted by fred, ^paul was insulted by john, ^paul was insulted by paul, ... }

3) topic value

(6.155) {{^paul was insulted by fred, ^paul was insulted by john, ^paul was insulted by paul, ... }, {^john was insulted by fred, ^john was insulted by john, ^john was insulted by paul, ... }, {^mary was insulted by fred, ^mary was insulted by john, ^mary was insulted by paul, ... }, ... }

It is easy to see that the resulting topic value satisfies both conditions required in (6.150). The topic value abounds with disputable elements (residual topics) and the first sentence of the sequence in (6.152) is one of them. But why does that account for the role reversal?

The role reversal observed is due to the fact that the alternative adversative statement to the second sentence in (6.152), i.e. the first sentence, must be derived from the topic value and cannot be picked from the focus value. Since the topic value is a set of propositions in which the topic position is filled with *alternative* values, the original topic value cannot appear in the same position or thematic role twice, but only in another one. Moreover, since the predicate does not change, the original topic value is bound to occur in a different position or role of the same predicate which results in the role reversal effect observed.

Note that this line of argumentation in effect claims that the intensifier does not contribute to the role reversal. And indeed, all relevant effects (role reversal, adversative implicature) can be detected in equivalent structures lacking the intensifier as (6.156) makes clear.

(6.156)   Paul insulted Mary. [T HE] was insulted by [F FRED].

This brings us to the final question in the present context, namely, what the contribution of the intensifier in these structures is. Of course, it would be convenient if the contribution of ANS in role reversal structures could also be captured with the notions of centre and periphery. However, the relevant examples never show comparable restrictions on the head NP of the intensifier. What we appear to be confronted with here is a contrast between centre and periphery on a more abstract level. Notice that ANS in these structures is always in association with the NP denoting the topic and that the topic, from the perspective of information packaging, can be regarded as the central piece of information because this is what a sentence is about. According to this account, then, the comment is peripheral with regard to the topic.

Notes

1   Edmondson and Plank provide the following minimal pair:
    (i)   The president himself ordered the executions.
    (ii) ?Even the president ordered the executions.
2   This used to be a widely accepted metaphor in Elizabethan society, cf. Tillyard (1943).
3   In fact, there is another hierarchy observable when discussing intensifiers with unprejudiced informants, namely that nearly all of them spontaneously produce examples featuring ANS instead of the adverbial varieties.
4   The Scandinavian languages form one group in this respect. The equivalent form in Norwegian (Bokmål) is *selveste* and so it is in Danish.
5   As a matter of fact, Edmondson and Plank try to differentiate between intensional and extensional reference as well as extensional reference to the role, office, etc. of some individual. The reason for that move is not easy to see because intensional reference of such NPs is usually held to go to the role of the individual so that another category does not seem necessary.
6   This, in fact, is an oversimplification. A sentence like (6.106b) only says that a significant number of Scotsmen drink whisky.
7   A notable exception are nationality terms as in *The Italians have a marvellous sense of humour*.
8   Compare the discussion in Hawkins (1978: 172ff.).

9 The oblique reading of (6.115b,c) is said to contradict Leibnitz's Law which says that 'the result of substituting in any formula one name for another name denoting the same individual results in a formula that is true if and only if the original formula was true.', cf. Dowty *et al.* (1981: 142).
10 This example is taken from Edmondson and Plank (1978: 381).

7   Adverbal inclusive intensifiers

Inclusive AVS is the first of the two types of adverbal intensifiers we are going to deal with in the following. At first sight, it seems to have a lot in common with the additive particle *also* since, in a wide variety of cases, the latter can be regarded as a suitable paraphrase of it. Recall that exclusive AVS can be glossed best by *alone* or *on one's own*. However, the similarity to *also* is only the tip of the iceberg. When looked at in slightly more detail, it quickly becomes apparent that reducing inclusive AVS to the meaning of *also* cannot be the whole story. Whereas use and distribution of *also* are relatively independent of external factors, inclusive AVS imposes tight conditions on the make-up of the larger context, the NP it interacts with as well as on the kind of verb present. If one of these factors is not properly adjusted to the semantics of inclusive AVS, the sentences under consideration can easily become unacceptable or even ungrammatical.

There are also various features that clearly distinguish adverbal inclusive intensifiers from adnominal intensifiers. Recall, first of all, that the two cannot be mutually exchanged, which indicates that they make different semantic contributions and constitute a clear case of polysemy (section 2.1). Moreover, although both are in association with an NP, only ANS also belongs to that NP; inclusive AVS has to be analysed as part of the VP. As far as their semantic contribution is concerned, ANS can be viewed as structuring an unordered set of entities (referents) into a central element and peripheral elements related to it. The structuring is based on the inherent qualities of the referents concerned. Inclusive AVS also orders referents in terms of centre and periphery, however, the ordering crucially depends on the relevant situation. In other words, focus and alternatives are structured against the background of the VP-denotation.

The chapter is built up as follows. Section 7.1 provides a brief comparison of inclusive AVS and ANS, mainly in order to show that although the former evokes alternatives to the referent of the NP it interacts with in the same manner as ANS, inclusive AVS does not force a relation of centre versus periphery between them in any of the senses discussed in section 6.2. This section will also include a discussion of the properties of the referents concerned. After that, in section 7.2, the properties of the relevant situations will be under scrutiny. Here, it will be discussed which situations trigger inclusive AVS and which exclusive AVS, i.e. their necessary contextual conditions. Next (section 7.3), there will be an attempt at an informal description of the contribution which inclusive AVS makes to the meaning of an utterance followed by a comparison of inclusive AVS and its near equivalent *also* in section 7.4. Finally, several possible analyses of inclusive AVS will be contrasted, followed by a discussion of the analysis defended here. This will be done in sections 7.5–7.8.

As far as previous accounts of inclusive AVS are concerned, it appears to be adequate to emphasise that no study of intensifiers put forward so far has paid attention to the unique features inclusive AVS definitely has. Either it has been subsumed under adverbal intensifiers in general, cf. Edmondson and Plank (1978), Plank (1979a), Primus (1992), or it has been analysed as being equivalent in meaning to the additive particle *also*, cf. Browning (1993). According to the approach argued for here, by contrast, all three uses of intensifiers will need a different analysis, although they share the property of ordering sets into central and peripheral elements.

7.1 Adverbal inclusive versus adnominal SELF

What sets, semantically speaking, inclusive AVS most clearly apart from ANS is the inclusive effect. Sentence (7.1), for example, states that there is an individual who looks well and implies that there is another individual for which the same property holds, most likely the speaker in this case.

> (7.1)   You look well yourself.

(7.2a) gives the assertion for (7.1) and (7.2b) its implication or presupposition. We will discuss in due time whether it is justified to analyse the inclusive effect in terms of a presupposition.

> (7.2)   a $look\_well(x)$
>   b $\exists y\ (look\_well(y)\ \&\ x \neq y)$

Consider also (7.3a) which puts (7.1) into adequate context. Here, either interlocutor asserts of the other that he looks well and subsequently, when speaker B makes his statement, the presupposition is already fulfilled and hence inclusive AVS is grammatical. In (7.3b), by contrast, the presupposition cannot be fulfilled since a contradictory statement is made which, as one would expect, makes inclusive AVS unacceptable.

> (7.3)   a A: Good to see you Stephen; you look well. – B: You look
>   well yourself. [BNC]
>   b A: Good to see you Stephen; you don't look well. – B: *You
>   look well yourself.

That ANS does not impose comparable restrictions on its context is shown in (7.4). These examples are acceptable independently of whether the property in question, i.e. *look well* in the present case, holds for both referents or only for one of them.

(7.4)   a   A: Good to see you Stephen; you look well. – B: Thanks. You yourself look well too.

b   A: Good to see you Stephen; you look well. – B: Thanks. But you yourself don't look well. What's the matter?

Hence, there is no inclusive effect observable with ANS. One of the consequences is that ANS is compatible with both inclusive and exclusive particles, cf. (7.5).

(7.5)   a   Even the boss himself makes mistakes.

b   Only the president himself has the authority to veto a bill.

Inclusive AVS, by comparison, is compatible with neither. Inclusive or additive particles are incompatible because in this case the same contribution would be made twice whereas exclusive particles simply contradict what inclusive AVS contributes, cf. (7.6).

(7.6)   a   A: Good to see you Stephen; you look well. – B: ??Even you look well yourself.

b   A: Good to see you Stephen; you look well. – B: ??Only you look well yourself.

A further difference between ANS and inclusive AVS concerns the range of possible NPs they can be in association with. First, whereas ANS may interact with NPs denoting both human and non-human referents, inclusive AVS is restricted to human referents. Not even NPs denoting non-human animate referents will do. The current contrast is exemplified in (7.7) and (7.8).[1]

(7.7)   a   Before Rufus could reply Evan himself had come into the shop from a door at the back and was standing there spry and slightly smiling, looking not a day older than he had ten years before. [AFI: 220]

b   If people had to ask where a thing happened, it was a scientific certainty that the thing itself was not unique. [CS: 156]

(7.8)   a   It embarrassed him now to remember it, his pleadings, his promises. He had come close to tears himself. [AFI: 244]

b   *My goldfish already shows some grey scales itself$_{inclusive}$.

c   *My computer recently showed strange symptoms itself$_{inclusive}$.

Second, and this was already observed in section 4.3.4, inclusive AVS is by and large restricted to being in association with subject NPs whereas ANS can intensify any NP no matter what its grammatical function. Recall, however, that German and English differ in this respect, cf. example (4.111). And finally, third, the restriction on human referents can be translated into a restriction on the thematic role of the subject NP. On that account, inclusive AVS is tied to a role ranking above the one of a theme. Assuming a hierarchy of thematic roles as e.g. in (7.9), inclusive AVS defines a cut-off point between patient and theme.

(7.9)   agent > experiencer/beneficiary > patient > theme

(7.10)   I know what you mean.
         a I've given lectures myself. (agent)
         b I've seen the photograph myself. (experiencer)
         c I've been given a castle myself. (beneficiary)
         d I've been injured myself. (patient)

König and Siemund (1996a: 11) propose that inclusive AVS always interacts with the argument bearing the highest thematic role of those present in a predication. Note that this constraint can be overruled in passives where inclusive AVS can interact with a patient NP even in the presence of an agentive *by*-phrase. Still, the *by*-phrase can hardly count as a full argument (cf. Grimshaw 1992: 143ff.).

(7.11)   You don't have to tell me what it means to be hit by Paul because I've been hit by Paul myself.

Recall that in section 6.2, we drew attention to the fact that the restriction of ANS to NPs denoting human referents, which can be observed in certain languages, is a typological parameter of variation which can be accounted for in terms of the animacy hierarchy, cf. (6.30) and (6.31). This hierarchy is equivalent to an implicational scale predicting that if a language allows ANS with non-human NPs, it will also allow ANS with human NPs. A similar hierarchy, and by extension implicational scale, can be postulated for the different uses of intensifiers, cf. (7.12).

(7.12)   ANS > exclusive AVS > inclusive AVS

Viewed from a typological perspective, it turns out that if a language has a particular usage of the intensifier, it will also make available all the usages further to the left on that hierarchy, but not vice versa. The Romance languages (except French) are a case in point because they unanimously disallow inclusive AVS, but provide exclusive AVS as well as ANS, cf. (7.13) and (7.14). Note that in the examples given below, *also* is used instead of inclusive AVS.

(7.13)   Italian
Questo purtroppo   non lo so   nemmeno io.
that   unfortunately NEG it know.1P.SG also-not I
'Unfortunately, I don't know that myself.'

(7.14)   Spanish
No puedo   darte   dinero porque yo tampoco lo tengo.
NEG can.1P.SG give-you money because I also-not it have.1P.SG
'I can't give you money because I'm a little short myself.'

But let us return to the properties of the NPs inclusive AVS can interact with. In section 4.3 (example (4.44)), an attempt was made to settle the question whether it could be constructed with indefinite NPs, however, the subject evaded a final decision. Having looked at indefinite NPs in some detail in connection with ANS, let us briefly reexamine how inclusive AVS behaves in the relevant contexts.

That inclusive AVS is perfectly adequate with definite NPs has been sufficiently stated and needs no further exemplification. However, the mere fact that nearly all of the examples containing inclusive AVS so far considered featured definite NPs is indicative of the fact that it associates itself particularly well with these and that there might be some constraint to the effect that inclusive AVS needs an NP which uniquely identifies a referent. Hence, it might be conjectured that, as far as the properties of the relevant NPs are concerned, inclusive AVS behaves very much like ANS. The following points demonstrate that this is indeed so. In order to show that there are no differences between English and German, semantically equivalent examples of each language will be produced.

First, inclusive AVS can be constructed with intensional as well as extensional NPs, cf. (7.15), which is an example of an intensional NP. Examples of inclusive AVS together with extensional NPs have been produced in abundance and will not be exemplified separately.

(7.15)   a There is no point in asking a specialist because he would not
            know the answer himself.
         b Es hat keinen Sinn, einen Spezialisten zu konsultieren, denn
            er würde die Antwort selbst nicht wissen.

As far as indefinite NPs are concerned, we find that inclusive AVS is particularly adverse to those claiming the existence of more than one individual, i.e. when they function as true indefinite (i.e. non-specific and non-generic) descriptions, cf. (7.16) below, and this was exactly the same with ANS, recall (6.116).

(7.16)   a *A minister was surprised himself.
         b *Ein Minister war selbst überrascht.

As far as indefinite NPs in a specific interpretation are concerned, inclusive AVS also patterns along the lines of ANS. Inclusive AVS does not resist being constructed with such NPs. Consider (7.17) below which shows G. *man* and E. *one* respectively in their specific reading.

> (7.17) a It is disquieting to realise that one will sooner or later end up there oneself.
> b Es ist beunruhigend zu wissen, daß man eines Tages selbst dort enden wird. [Plank 1979a: 270]

Moreover, it turns out that generic NPs are adequate too. Consider first of all the generics based on plural NPs in (7.18) which are definitely acceptable. Generics produced from indefinite NPs are grammatical too, although they appear to require some accommodation, cf. (7.19). However, this is exactly the pattern we observed in the case of ANS.

> (7.18) a Professors know the needs of students because they once were students themselves.
> b Professoren kennen die Bedürfnisse der Studenten, denn sie waren selbst mal Studenten.

> (7.19) a As a professor one knows the needs of one's students because a professor once was a student himself.
> b Als Professor kennt man die Bedürfnisse seiner Studenten, denn ein Professor war schließlich selbst mal Student.

On the whole, then, it appears to be adequate to conclude that, with regard to its referential properties, inclusive AVS and ANS impose similar restrictions on the NP they interact with. Both of them need an NP which uniquely identifies a referent.

A point, however, which clearly distinguishes most occurrences of inclusive AVS from ANS is their strong context-dependence, cf. Edmondson and Plank (1978), König (1991). It is probably no exaggeration to say that most of the sentences listed so far to exemplify inclusive AVS which lacked explicit context needed a certain amount of accommodation. Occurrences of ANS, by contrast, contextualise easily – except for those examples containing NPs whose referents lack a natural periphery. (7.20) through (7.22) depict some representative examples where the b-sentences provide the necessary context to render the a-sentences impeccable. Note that in all of these examples, the clause containing inclusive AVS seems to give an explanation for why the proposition expressed in the matrix clause is plausible or not.

> (7.20) a ??Fred smells himself.
> b How can Fred complain about the odour of other people when he smells a little himself? [König 1991: 93]

(7.21) a ??Max is blind himself.
        b Max knows what it means to be blind because he is blind himself.

(7.22) a ??Ken snores himself.
        b Ken complains about my snoring although he snores himself.

Let us now come to the primary semantic contribution of ANS, namely to structure a set of individuals into a centre and a related periphery, and ask if a comparable structuring also takes place in the case of inclusive AVS. To put it bluntly, it does not. Although the constellation of a centre versus a related periphery, with inclusive AVS marking the centre, is by no means ruled out, it is not forced either and hence cannot be attributed to inclusive AVS if present. As a matter of fact, it is quite possible to find or construct examples in which inclusive AVS interacts with an NP whose referent would be judged as peripheral in comparison to another.

Consider the constellation of an organisational centre in (7.23a). Here, inclusive AVS readily interacts with the subject NP whose referent (secretary) is clearly peripheral in contrast to the referent denoted by the other NP present (the director). However, no decrease in acceptability is observable. Similarly (7.23b). Here, the speaker is not bound to any particular position within the hierarchy of the police force. The first person pronoun could either refer to the superior of the chief inspector or to one of his staff. Personally, I find the latter interpretation more likely than the former. Whichever constellation would finally turn out to be true, the important observation is that inclusive AVS does not comply with the distinction relevant for ANS.

(7.23) a The secretary was sympathetic to the director because she was beginning to feel uneasy herself.
        b I'm not sure some of the upright ones will hold you, Chief Inspector, I sit on them very gingerly myself. [BNC]

Exactly the same point can be made on the basis of situational centres. Here too, examples can be found with inclusive AVS intensifying a peripheral character. In the situation of an aircraft accident, as described in (7.24a), inclusive AVS interacts with the NP denoting the copilot and not the pilot. (7.24b) shows the same for the situation of a church service where the priest would be expected to be the central character.

(7.24) a In view of the oncoming plane, the pilot lost his consciousness. The copilot tried to stay in control of the aircraft, but couldn't help fainting himself.
        b The parish didn't mind that the old priest frequently forgot his lines. Most of them were fairly old themselves.

Although (7.23) and (7.24) in themselves generate sufficient evidence to prove the point, notice finally that inclusive AVS can also intensify the periphery of an identifying or defining centre, cf. (7.25), and that it need not be in association with the NP denoting the subject of consciousness in case one is present, cf. (7.26).

(7.25) a My brother told me that he would have failed himself.
        b John offered the olives to his daughter, but she did not want any herself.

(7.26) a Max wondered why Tom teased him for being poor. After all, he didn't own much money himself.
        b Sue noticed that Phil didn't feel well himself.

To sum up, this section has shown that there are a number of differences between inclusive AVS and ANS, but that they also share some properties. As for the differences, what sets inclusive AVS most prominently apart is the inclusive effect, the high context-dependence as well as the fact that it does not make the referent of the NP which it intensifies central in the same manner as ANS does. Moreover, inclusive AVS interacts only with NPs denoting human referents. With regard to the referential properties of the NPs concerned, however, adnominal and adverbal inclusive intensifiers do not seem to differ.

7.2 Repeatability and transferability

This section will mainly be concerned with the contextual factors influencing the interpretation of adverbal intensifiers, i.e. with those factors determining whether an occurrence of AVS is read in the inclusive or exclusive way. Since this study assumes two separate entries of AVS, the underlying question is which context selects which type of AVS. On the face of it, inclusive AVS and AVS in general have very specific operating conditions. They cannot occur in just any context, but rather impose strict demands on it. In the subsequent paragraphs, it will turn out to be important for the interpretation of AVS whether the VP it modifies denotes a repeatable or a transferable situation. Put in a nutshell, repeatability is a prerequisite for inclusive AVS whereas exclusive AVS is dependent on the transferability of a situation. If a situation possesses neither of these two features, AVS is blocked; if both are present, the relevant sentences are ambiguous between the two readings of AVS, i.e. either type of AVS is permitted. What repeatability and transferability exactly mean will be discussed shortly. We will also see that these two notions can partly be explicated in terms of the aktionsart of a verb or situation. Viewed from that perspective, definite aktionsarten pattern with exclusive AVS whereas indefinite ones trigger inclusive AVS. However, the relation between aktionsart and the reading of AVS is not unique. There is no direct mapping possible from the domain of aktionsarten into the domain of possible interpretations of AVS. Finally, the status of the object NP in transitive sentences matters to a certain degree. Again, definite object NPs correlate with exclusive AVS and indefinite ones with inclusive AVS, to a certain degree at least. Let us take these problems in order.

As far as repeatability is concerned, this is simply meant to capture the idea of whether a situation can be performed only once or more than once. Whether a situation can be repeated or not depends heavily on our assumptions about the world around us because in theory, every situation is repeatable. In practice, however, a number of situations are confined to happening one time only. Otherwise they would not be compatible with our world knowledge. Hence, the rescue of Eurydice as well as the christening of one particular girl can have been performed only once, cf. (7.27), whereas the situations of making a mistake or christening many little girls as shown in (7.28) can be repeated many times.

(7.27) a Orpheus rescued Eurydice.
        b The bishop christened the little girl.

(7.28) a Orpheus made a mistake.
        b The bishop has christened many little girls.

Inclusive AVS is only compatible with repeatable situations. Non-repeatable situations immediately trigger exclusive AVS. An explanation for this behaviour is not far to seek. Situations restricted to happening only once contradict the very idea of inclusion. Once one particular referent has been engaged in a non-repeatable situation, it is ruled out for another referent to do the same, hence inclusion is blocked. They are, however, compatible with the notion of exclusion. These considerations predict that adding AVS to (7.27) will not yield the inclusive interpretation. (7.29) shows that this prediction is indeed borne out; it is confined to the exclusive reading. (7.30), by contrast, allows for both the inclusive as well as the exclusive reading with varying degrees of imminence. In (7.30a) inclusive AVS seems to be the preferred interpretation, in (7.30b) exclusive AVS. (7.31) puts the above statements into a rule.

(7.29) exclusive
        a Orpheus rescued Eurydice himself.
        b The bishop christened the little girl himself.

(7.30) inclusive and exclusive
        a Orpheus made a mistake himself.
        b The bishop has christened many little girls himself.

(7.31) Non-repeatable situations correlate with exclusive AVS.

Whether a situation is singular, i.e. non-repeatable, or not depends on the kind of predicate involved. For reasons to become clear immediately, it is useful to distinguish between one-place and two-place predicates. Let us start with the latter. A two-place predicate or transitive verb denotes a relation holding between the referents of subject and object NP respectively. Non-repeatable relations are denoted by those predicates which describe the production of an irreversible change of state in the object referent. Since the object referent cannot be brought back into the original state and since this state is the prerequisite for the relation's being established in the first place, the relation can hold only once. If, on the other hand, the change of state can be reversed, the relevant relation may hold another time, in fact, an infinite number of times. Thus *kill* and *eat* in (7.32) denote non-repeatable relations whereas *clean* and *paint* in (7.33) represent repeatable ones. They can be performed several times on the same object referent simply because windows may become dirty again and sheds can be painted, say, every spring. As one would expect, the former examples are bound to exclusive AVS whereas the latter can receive an inclusive interpretation. Again, this is not necessarily so. The intensifiers in (7.33) do not have to be inclusive, the exclusive reading is possible too, but then, the repeatable relation is not used.

(7.32)   a   Macbeth killed Duncan himself. (exclusive)
         b   I have eaten the tomato myself. (exclusive)

(7.33)   a   I have cleaned the window myself. (inclusive, exclusive)
         b   I have painted the shed myself. (inclusive, exclusive)

As far as one-place predicates or intransitive verbs are concerned, it appears to be the case that there are none denoting non-repeatable situations. This is because it is hard to think of a property exclusively reserved for one referent. It appears that AVS can receive an inclusive interpretation in connection with all of them. However, not all one-place predicates provide suitable context for exclusive AVS, i.e. not all intransitive verbs denote transferable situations.

(7.34)   a   Paul has died/danced/sneezed himself. (inclusive)
         b   Paul came/drove/phoned himself. (inclusive, exclusive)

Examples like (7.34) take us to the issue of whether a situation is transferable or not. What transferability indicates is whether a situation is inalienably tied to one particular referent or whether it can be passed on to another referent. To be sure, a great variety of situations, states, activities, etc., cannot be relinquished and the examples in (7.34a) are clearly among them. Dying, dancing and sneezing cannot be done on behalf of someone else and neither can the situations exemplified in (7.35). The person referred to by the pronoun in (7.35a) cannot make somebody else have the experience of not feeling well instead of herself and if a situation is already transferred to another person as in (7.35b), it is hardly possible to transfer it another time. The situations in (7.36), by contrast, are not bound to one specific referent and hence they can be transferred to somebody else. The president in (7.36a) can pass on his attendance to his vice president and Rebecca in (7.36b) can go to the hairdresser's and have her hair cut there.

(7.35)   a   She does not feel well.
         b   She has had her hair cut.

(7.36)   a   The president is going to attend.
         b   Rebecca has cut her hair.

When adding adverbal intensifiers to the above examples, it becomes apparent that transferable situations allow for inclusive as well as exclusive AVS whereas situations that cannot be transferred to another referent universally trigger inclusive AVS, cf. (7.37) and (7.38). (7.39) formulates the relevant rule.

(7.37)   inclusive
         a   She does not feel well herself.
         b   She has had her hair cut herself.

(7.38)   inclusive and exclusive
         a   The president is going to attend himself.
         b   Rebecca has cut her hair herself.

(7.39)   Non-transferable situations correlate with inclusive AVS.

Note that it would also be possible to say that situations like attending and cutting one's hair in (7.38) can be delegated, instead of simply being transferred, and to postulate the impossibility to delegate a situation as the condition forcing inclusive AVS. By delegation we will understand the ability of one referent to place an activity he is interested to see done or supposed to perform on to the shoulders of another. This referent usually is in a lower position. Delegation, according to that view, is the intentional transfer of a situation, and indeed, most sentences containing exclusive AVS imply this more specific type of transfer. (7.40) gives some natural examples.

(7.40)   a   Now that her children are old enough to do without a
             nanny, Sheila refuses all help in the house, preferring to do
             all her shopping herself. [BNC]
         b   He always had some stomach complaint, even though the
             Nawab had undertaken the ordering of his meals himself
             and only the European-trained chef was allowed to prepare
             them. [BNC]

However, there are various situations of which it would be odd to claim that they can be delegated, but which, nevertheless, can be transferred. Consider (7.41). Here, the eating of the banana as well as the drinking of the beer are not tied to a specific referent, however, to describe the reason for their not being interpreted inclusively in terms of delegation seems to be besides the point. This would boil down to forcing the eating of the banana and the drinking of the beer respectively onto somebody else, which is conceptually odd. What is at stake in (7.41) is permission rather than delegation. Authentic examples can be found in (7.42).

> (7.41)   a I have eaten the banana myself.
> b He decided to drink the beer himself.

> (7.42)   a Elizabeth waited for a moment as though for someone else to open the door and then rose and went to do so herself. [BNC]
> b Promise me you'll let me have him, James. I must kill him myself. You understand that. [CS: 152]

Let us briefly go back to non-transferable situations, i.e. to those triggering inclusive AVS, and have a quick glance at the verb classes involved (cf. Levin 1993). We have already seen that verbs denoting bodily processes clearly belong to that list, cf. (7.43). It is extremely hard to imagine how to transfer processes like *sneezing, coughing* and *perspiring*, or situations described by hiccup, breathe and exhale verbs in general, to another referent. These verbs denote bodily activities tied to one individual.

> (7.43)   Paul sneezes/coughs/perspires himself.

Similarly, verbs denoting feelings and emotions as well as verbs of desire, i.e. psych verbs in general, pattern with inclusive AVS because feelings, emotions and desires are equally barred from being transferred:

> (7.44)   a John adores/loves/hates/despises Mary himself.
> b Dorothy wants/needs/craves/longs for new shoes herself.

But the group of verbs describing situations involving the human body is much larger. We find the same behaviour with verbs of non-verbal expression (7.45a), snooze verbs (7.45b), verbs denoting physical states of the body (7.45c) and, finally, verbs of change of bodily state (7.45d):

> (7.45)   a Paul laughed/grinned/yawned/jeered/whistled himself.
> b Gloria snoozed/dozed/slept herself.
> c Sharon shivered/quivered/shuddered/trembled herself.
> d Tessa fainted/sickened/swooned herself.

Besides verbs denoting bodily activities, there are also some verbs of motion in the list. Interestingly, verbs such as *run* and *walk* activate inclusive AVS so long as they are not understood as having a goal (i.e. as telic), cf. (7.46a). In case they have a goal, they can also be read in the exclusive sense, cf. (7.46b), however, these types of running and walking can be transferred or delegated.

(7.46)   a Paul runs/walks himself.
               b Paul ran/walked there himself.

When inclusive AVS is bound to repeatable situations and exclusive AVS to those that can be transferred, it seems reasonable to ask whether there are non-repeatable and non-transferable situations because these would have to be incompatible with either type of AVS. In fact, there are such situations, cf. (7.47) and (7.48) below.

(7.47)   a ??God has had the earth created himself.
               b ??She let the old man die herself.

(7.48)   a ?Mary gave birth to Jesus herself.
               b ?Bill divorced Kathy himself.

(7.47a) describes a unique event which has already been delegated or transferred. Therefore it cannot be repeated or transferred another time. Similarly in (7.47b). This is an interesting combination of the two verbs *let* and *die*. Whereas somebody's conversion from life to death is definitely non-repeatable, the authorisation of an event is bound to one referent in most of the cases, hence non-transferable. The combination of these two restrictions makes (7.47b) inadequate. The examples in (7.48) are slightly better because the giving of birth in (7.48a) can be somehow delegated to a midwife and Kathy in (7.48b) may have been divorced by several men. Note, finally, that the incompatibility of a situation with the notions of repeatability or transferability may be exploited to achieve stylistic effects:

(7.49)   Wo lassen Sie denken, Herr K.? – Herr K.: Ich denke selbst.
           [Plank 1979a: 274]
           'Who do you make think for you, Mr K.? – Mr K.: I think for myself.'

To sum up, what we have seen is that it matters a lot for the interpretation of adverbal intensifiers whether a situation is repeatable and whether it can be transferred. Repeatability is the prerequisite for inclusive AVS whereas transferability is a necessary condition for exclusive AVS. If a situation possesses only one of these two properties, the interpretation of adverbal intensifiers is fixed. If a situation can be both transferred and repeated, the

Table 7.1 Influence of the parameters 'repeatable' and 'transferable' on the interpretation of adverbal SELF

Repeatable	Transferable	AVS
no	no	no
yes	no	inclusive
no	yes	exclusive
yes	yes	inclusive/exclusive (ambiguous)

Table 7.2 Influence of the *aktionsart* on the interpretation of adverbal SELF

	States	Processes	Achievements	Accomplishments
Inclusive	yes	yes	no	no
Exclusive	no	no	yes	yes

relevant examples are ambiguous and if neither of the two features holds, AVS is ruled out. Table 7.1 summarises these dependencies.

Given that repeatability and transferability are parameters influencing the situation type, it should come as no surprise to find that the more conventional aktionsarten also pattern with adverbal intensifiers in a reasonably predictable manner. Atelic aktionsarten such as states (7.50a) and processes (7.50b) are in the majority of cases on a par with inclusive AVS whereas telic ones, such as events, i.e. achievements (7.51a) and accomplishments (7.51b) in the terminology of Vendler (1957), on the whole force an exclusive interpretation. The reason why this should be so is not difficult to see.

(7.50)   a I can speak Russian myself. (inclusive)
         b I cannot help you right now. I'm working myself. (inclusive)

(7.51)   a John cut through the wire himself. (exclusive)
         b Bill built the house himself. (exclusive)

Most of the cases of exclusive AVS involve the more particular notion of intentional transfer of a situation, i.e. delegation. Taken at face value, delegation means that e.g. referent A refers one of his tasks to referent B and that A expects a result. Since atelic situations lack a final state, the result as it were, they are difficult to delegate and hence block exclusive AVS to a certain extent. Moreover, many telic situations are non-repeatable in that their final state is irreversible and consequently inclusive AVS becomes the unlikely alternative. Looked at from the opposite angle, it is possible to say that atelic situations are usually repeatable and that telic ones can be transferred. This again accounts for the correlation proposed above, cf. Table 7.2.

Still, there is a great amount of overlap. AVS with either achievements (7.52a) and accomplishments (7.52b) can easily be inclusive, which shows that a classification of AVS on the basis of aktionsarten must be taken with a grain of salt. Moreover, exclusive AVS can coexist with activities as (7.53) makes clear. What seems to be the case, though, is that states always trigger inclusive, never exclusive AVS. One cannot transfer them to somebody else and they can always be repeated, i.e. several entities can be in the same state, at the same time or one after the other. This means, that apart from one cell, the correlation given in Table 7.2 can be no more than a rough guideline.

(7.52)   a Ken has lost 50 bucks himself. (inclusive)
         b Sue knows what it means to water these flowers because she has watered them herself. (inclusive)

(7.53)   a I will drive the car myself. (exclusive)
         b You must push the cart yourself. (exclusive)

Note that, besides aktionsart, even aspectual distinctions matter to a certain degree. The perfect of experience in (7.54a) characterises the situation of teaching one's daughter as repeatable because the relevant experience can have potentially been made by several referents. Hence, inclusive AVS is favoured. The same sentence in the simple present makes exclusive AVS more likely because only one referent will be assumed to take part in the now habitual teaching event, cf. (7.54b). A similar reasoning is possible in (7.55). The imperfective (7.55a) seems to force inclusive AVS whereas exclusive AVS is more probable in the perfective (7.55b). Note, however, that we are talking about preferences, not necessities.

(7.54)   a I have taught my daughter myself. (inclusive)
         b I teach my daughter myself. (exclusive)

(7.55)   a I was opening the document myself. (inclusive)
         b I opened the document myself. (exclusive)

The final factor influencing the interpretation of AVS which we will discuss is the type of object NP involved. What we find here is that definite NPs *grosso modo* correlate with exclusive AVS whereas indefinite NPs pattern with inclusive AVS, cf. (7.56) through (7.58), where the a-sentences prefer exclusive AVS, but the b-sentences make inclusive AVS more likely.

(7.56)   a I have felled the tree myself.
         b I have felled a tree myself.

(7.57)   a Fred has eaten the hamburgers himself.
         b Fred has eaten hamburgers himself.

Table 7.3 Influence of the object NP on the interpretation of adverbal SELF

	Reversible change of state	*Irreversible change of state*
Definite object NP	inclusive/exclusive	exclusive
Indefinite object NP	inclusive/exclusive	inclusive/exclusive

(7.58)   a   I have drunk the whisky myself.
        b   I have drunk whisky myself.

In the light of what was just said about repeatable and non-repeatable situations, an explanation is not difficult to find. A definite NP usually means that there is only one uniquely identifiable referent whereas an indefinite NP, generally speaking, implies that there are many, potentially infinitely many.

When definite object NPs occur together with predicates denoting an irreversible change of state in the referents of these NPs, the result is a non-repeatable situation which, according to the rules formulated here, selects exclusive AVS. The inclusive reading is ruled out in these cases. Indefinite NPs in combination with such predicates, however, still allow for the situation to be repeated since there are enough potential referents available with which the change of state can be performed. Hence, the preference for inclusive AVS, which is no must though.

Note that the behaviour described above is in no way particular to inclusive AVS. These are general requirements on inclusion which can be observed with all inclusive/additive particles. (7.59) is inadequate because one and the same tree cannot be felled twice.

(7.59)   a   ??I have also felled the tree.
        b   ??Even I have felled the tree.

Just as aktionsart cannot be regarded as a decisive criterion to determine the interpretation of adverbal intensifiers, the kind of object NP present cannot be accepted as a reliable gauge either. As soon as the range of predicates considered is extended to those denoting reversible changes of state, it becomes plain that definite NPs also allow inclusive AVS, cf. (7.60). Here, AVS freely oscillates between its two readings.

(7.60)   a   Fred has watered the flowers himself.
        b   Fred has watered flowers himself.

Table 7.3 summarises these relations.

Event verbs denoting no change of state in the referent of their object NP are always compatible with either type of adverbal intensifiers, no matter whether the NP is definite or indefinite, cf. (7.61). The inclusive effect in

(7.61a) is due to the fact that one and the same speech can be given several times by different people. In (7.61b), by contrast, more than one speech is under consideration.

(7.61)   a Sue has given the speech herself.
            b Sue has given a speech herself.

States always trigger inclusive AVS. No influence on the part of the object NP is discernible, cf. (7.62).

(7.62)   a Max adores the actress himself.
            b Max adores an actress himself.

Note that a partitive reading of a definite NP, as possible with e.g. substances, can also trigger inclusive AVS, cf. (7.63). Splitting up a definite quantity (of whisky) and spreading it over several drinkers is what permits the inclusive effect.

(7.63)   I have drunk of the whisky myself.

Note further that the definite object NP in (7.64) will invariably force inclusive AVS because it already achieves inclusion by itself.

(7.64)   I might have done the same myself.

Finally, as far as differences between English and German are concerned, there seems to be a tendency to translate G. inclusive *selbst* in the context of possessed object NPs as *x of my own* into English, cf. (7.65a,b). Translating the relevant sentences on a one-to-one basis leads to a decrease in acceptability, cf. (7.65c).

(7.65)   a A: Du kannst mein Auto nehmen. – B: Danke, ich habe selbst ein Auto.
            b A: You can use my car. – B: Thanks, I've got a car of my own.
            c A: You can use my car. – B: ?Thanks, I've got a car myself.

Note, however, that there are certain restrictions on the kind of possession involved (probably whether it is inalienable or not) which can align English with German:

(7.66)   a Ich weiß, was es heißt, Halsschmerzen zu haben, denn ich habe selbst Halsschmerzen.
            b I know what it means to have a sore throat because I have a sore throat myself.

     c ?I know what it means to have a sore throat because I have
       a sore throat of my own.

Let us now come to a summary of the major points. We have mainly
shown two things. First, the interpretation of adverbal intensifiers strictly
depends on two factors, namely whether the situation in the context of
which they occur is repeatable or whether it is transferable. The former factor
is necessary for inclusive AVS, the latter for exclusive AVS. If a situation is
non-repeatable and non-transferable, adverbal intensifiers are excluded, and
if it possesses both properties simultaneously, adverbal intensifiers become
ambiguous.

Second, the interpretation of adverbal intensifiers correlates to a certain
extent with the aktionsart of the verb and with the kind of object NP
present. Generally speaking, exclusive AVS prefers telic aktionsarten and
definite object NPs, inclusive AVS is more susceptible to atelic aktionsarten
and indefinite object NPs. This is plausible in so far as, ontologically speaking, telic verbs are akin to definite NPs whereas atelic verbs resemble indefinite NPs, cf. Mourelatos (1978). Telic situations or events can be identified
in the same manner as the referents of definite NPs can. Both are objects or
individuals. Atelic situations, i.e. states and processes, cannot be uniquely
identified since they are not bounded. They rather resemble masses or sets
containing infinitely many elements. But this is just what indefinite NPs
denote.

7.3 Contextual conditions

Recall from the beginning of this chapter that inclusive AVS – in contrast to
ANS and exclusive AVS – is highly context-dependent, cf. examples (7.20)
through (7.22). The aim of the following section, therefore, is to offer a
listing of the most dominant environments in which inclusive AVS can
occur. This section is meant to be an informal description rather than a
precise formal analysis.

    One kind of context that immediately springs to mind when surveying
larger sets of data are requests. These are prototypically declined or cannot
be answered. Consider (7.67a). Here, speaker A asks B to lend him some
money which B subsequently declines for lack of money. Similarly (7.67b),
where A asks B to make some coffee which B refuses since he does not have
the necessary time either. Inclusive AVS can be used, so it seems, to put
emphasis on utterances which decline a request. (7.68) gives an example
from a corpus.

    (7.67)   a A: I need some money. Could you lend me ten pounds? – B:
           I am sorry, but I am a bit short myself.
         b A: I'm up to my eyes in work. Could you make some coffee?
           – B: Believe it or not, I am very busy myself.

(7.68) A: So if you can try and explain to Sarah what you're doing, she'll know how to do it next time. – B: I don't know myself. [BNC]

Another prevalent type of context, which, in a way, can be regarded as the opposite to requests, are offers, cf. (7.69). If the significant characteristic of requests is that they are declined, then the important feature about the offers in the context of which inclusive AVS occurs is that they are turned down, or cannot be accepted or carried through. In (7.69a) speaker A wants to do speaker B a favour, namely show him the way, which B does not accept since he already knows the way. In (7.69b) Paul is prevented from putting his offer into action by his own illness. (7.70), again, provides material from the corpora.

(7.69) a A: Can I show you the way? – B: Thanks, I know the way myself.
b Mary had fallen ill. Paul wanted to look after her, but he had fallen ill himself.

(7.70) A: Would you like Chief Inspector Golding to call you when he returns? – B: No, thank you. I have to go out myself. [BNC]

The common denominator of the request contexts on the one hand and those involving offers on the other is that in either case two (or more) characters are about to enter a relation in which the one character would become a service provider for the other. However, the service relation is never established since either the service is not necessary or cannot be delivered.

In addition, inclusive AVS frequently occurs in the context of reproaches. More often than not, it is the case that one character criticises another and that the criticised character tries to reject the reproach, cf. (7.71). The relevant pattern is fairly obvious. Notice the parallel to requests and offers. Requests are declined, offers are turned down and reproaches refused or rejected. In every case, the declining, turning down and rejecting is done with the sentence containing inclusive AVS. As with requests and offers, interaction between two characters is intended, but never comes about because one character blocks it. The similarity becomes even more obvious when reproaches are regarded as negative services, as disservices so to speak. A corpus example is supplied in (7.72).

(7.71) a Jim is always finding fault with my way of dancing although he does not know how to dance himself.
b How can Liz complain about my snoring when she snores herself?

(7.72)   Let us talk instead about your hostess; what an extraordinary woman! You know, of course, that she will not let any of her daughters marry? But she has been married twice herself. [BNC]

A kind of context characteristic of inclusive AVS that is often exemplified in the literature, cf. Hall Partee (1965), Edmondson and Plank (1978), Plank (1979a), implicitly or explicitly characterises a referent as having gained particular experience in a certain event or as possessing special knowledge about some individual, object, state of affairs, etc., cf. (7.73). (7.73a) is almost self-explanatory because the phrase *knows what it means to* makes clear that experience is at stake and the focus of (7.73b) evidently lies on the shared knowledge of the two characters about Tokyo. Inclusive AVS can be found in the sentence describing the event leading to the subsequent knowledge or experience, or the state with which the relevant information is connected. Corresponding corpus examples are given in (7.74).

(7.73)   a   Scarlett knows what it means to be blown by the wind, for she was once blown by the wind herself. [Edmondson and Plank 1978: 385]
         b   Oh, you've been to Tokyo? I've been there myself. [Hall Partee 1965: 45–7]

(7.74)   a   But having been a player there myself you can still feel the buzz of the bloke 15 years on. [BNC]
         b   For several years we drove all the way down from Hertfordshire to Cornwall, very slowly, starting in the early hours of the morning and arriving about tea-time, if we were lucky. My father always used to say, 'The holiday begins the moment we set off on the way.' Nowadays, having myself experienced long car journeys with three young children, I appreciate what brave words those were. [BNC]
         c   Mary adds that even those who are successful in finding work and accommodation may suffer from loneliness and a sense of isolation in large cities like London. She adds, I used to live there myself. [BNC]
         d   Young girls are always squeamish and coy beforehand. I remember I was so myself. [BNC]

Based on experience is the notion of empathy which is the essential ingredient of the following type of context often to be found in the vicinity of inclusive AVS, cf. (7.75). What is at stake here is that two (or more) characters share a certain experience, i.e. have gone through comparable situations, and that, based on that experience, one character can make an expression of empathy towards the other. An overt expression of empathy is typically present in these contexts. Inclusive AVS, again, occurs in the sentence describing the event leading to the shared experience. Apart from the statement expressing empathy, this context is equivalent to the one involving experience or knowledge. (7.76) shows some corpus examples.

(7.75) a I can understand how you feel. I used to be lonely myself.
        b I can well imagine what you must have endured. I have lost a brother myself.

(7.76) a The professionals involved, the doctors and nurses, can find it deeply disturbing to tell the patients what they have to face. The most helpful sources of support are more likely to be the parents of other children who have experienced the same trauma. They understand because they have been there themselves. [BNC]
        b Jack felt the need to treat these outbursts by Warnie with firmness as well as with gentleness, not least because his brother was giving voice to feelings which he shared quite passionately himself. [BNC]

When inclusive AVS can be used to decline a request, turn down an offer and refuse a reproach, it appears reasonable to ask whether it can be used as a similar device, i.e. as a means to preempt the interaction between two characters, in the cases of experience and empathy. And indeed, one could argue that in those contexts describing the experience of two (or more) characters, the sentence containing inclusive AVS is used precisely to indicate that a body of shared knowledge exists and that therefore further information interchange about that topic is not necessary. In other words, the relevant sentences can be used to terminate the conversation or the current turn or prevent it from arising in the first place.

However, such a line of argument must appear premature in view of the following examples where the sentence containing inclusive AVS rather initiates a conversation and it remains to be inquired whether the declining, turning down or rejecting should be regarded as a contribution of inclusive AVS (unlikely) or merely as a pragmatic effect (likely).

(7.77) a Precisely because you have lost your brother yourself, we can talk about what it means to lose one.
        b We can talk about Tokyo because I've been to Tokyo myself.

The latter view gains some momentum from the fact that there are many examples which cannot be subsumed under any of the dominant groups discussed above and which do not show the related effects, cf. (7.78) below. Hence, as indicated at the beginning, the above classification can be regarded as no more than a convenient taxonomic aid.

(7.78)   a   At the beginning she had known clearly enough that he was an irrevocably solitary man, and it had seemed to her fortunate to live with him at all. He would say, 'People need air around them,' and she would pretend she agreed. Or perhaps she had felt it then herself. [BNC]

b   Ideally, she would love to become pregnant again herself but admits to another stumbling block, apart from age – there is no man in her life. [BNC]

c   Caro waited in the kitchen till she heard Bryony's heavy tread going from the bathroom to her bedroom. Then she went upstairs herself. [BNC]

When, in view of examples like (7.77) and (7.78), it is not possible to say that the common denominator of all the contexts in which inclusive AVS occurs is the termination of the interaction between two characters, it remains to be asked whether there is a common denominator at all and whether it can be spelt out precisely.

Notice that inclusive AVS frequently occurs in the context of conditional or causal connectives like *because, although, when, if, even if, since,* etc., cf. e.g. (7.76), and that if such a conjunction is present, inclusive AVS is usually contained in the sentence introduced by it. The noteworthy feature about the above conjunctions is that they characterise the subclause they introduce as the premise, reason or explanation, and sometimes even cause for the situation denoted by the main clause. This is why some of these conjunctions are also referred to as 'causal connectives'. Consider example (7.79) involving *because*. Obviously, the fact that Bill is a cook is the reason why he knows how to cook. (7.80) provides some authentic examples.

(7.79)   Bill knows how to cook because he is a cook himself.

(7.80)   a   'I think the course is a success partly because I am a farmer's wife myself,' admits Sue. [BNC]

b   Mr Gillis continued writing and when Alec turned to me I could see the strain on his face. I had no time to feel sorry for him though because I was under considerable strain myself. [BNC]

In (7.81) the relevant conjunction is the concessive connective *though/ although*, which indicates that there is a conditional relation between two propositions under standard assumptions, but that the consequent holds without the truth of the antecedent. Poor people are unlikely to donate money.

(7.81)   He told me that it would hurt his self-respect that any other man should find the money for such an object, and that though he was a poor man himself he would devote his last penny to removing the obstacles which divided us. [LLC]

The connective *so* in (7.82) is equivalent to *therefore*. Again, there is a link between two propositions with inclusive AVS being part of the statement describing the reason.

> (7.82)   I could not have put it better myself, so perhaps I should not try. [BNC]

Notice further that sentences containing inclusive AVS can establish a relation to another proposition in the absence of such conjunctions too. Consider the examples in (7.83) taken from the contexts of requests, offers and reproaches respectively. Speaker B's lack of money in (7.83a) is the reason why he cannot lend speaker A any; that speaker B in (7.83b) already knows the way explains why speaker A does not have to show him the way and the fact that Liz snores in (7.83c) makes it inappropriate for her to complain about the snoring of others. As a matter of fact, in all of the examples discussed so far, some sort of connection between the sentence containing inclusive AVS and some proposition relevant in the surrounding discourse can be discovered.

> (7.83)   a   A: I need some money. Could you lend me ten pounds? – B: I am sorry, but I am a bit short myself.
> b   A: Shall I show you the way? – B: Thanks, I know the way myself.
> c   How can Liz complain about my snoring when she snores herself?

In addition to that, there appears to be a conditional implication observable in sentences which are taken completely out of context. Consider the examples in (7.84). Each of these sentences taken as such appears deficient, however, they are far from being ungrammatical. This simply means that they need accommodation which in turn means that they have implications beyond what can be made sense of on the basis of the information provided by the sentences themselves.

> (7.84)   a   ?I've got a headache myself.
> b   ?You drive a Jag yourself.
> c   ?She is single herself.

As soon as context is supplied which allows them to be interpreted as a premise, reason or explanation for another proposition, they become impeccable:

(7.85)   a I've got a headache myself. Therefore, I cannot read to you.
         b You drive a Jag yourself. Therefore, you should know how
            expensive it is.
         c She is single herself. Therefore, she cannot tease me for not
            being married.

What the previous discussion has shown is that inclusive AVS frequently
occurs in subclauses introduced by a conditional connective, but that the
conditional implication is present even if an overt marker of conditionality
is missing. Moreover, and most important, detached sentences appear to give
rise to a conditional implication too. This seems to point in the direction
that the premise, reason or explanation implied is related to or even due to
the intensifier and cannot be attributed to some other element in the
surrounding context. Put differently, it could be argued that inclusive AVS
determines or selects the conditional context. On the basis of these observations, we can tentatively formulate the following condition for the well-
formedness of inclusive AVS:

(7.86)   Contextual condition of inclusive AVS:
         Inclusive AVS prototypically occurs in a sentence which gives
         the premise for a conclusion. The conclusion may either be
         inferred or stated in the context.

It may be worth mentioning that inclusive AVS in no way influences the
range of propositions for which the sentence it is contained in can be used
as an explanation or reason. The introductory sentence *I've got a headache
myself* in (7.87) is a possible reason for (7.87a–d) in the same way as *I've got
a headache* is. That the one proposition can be considered a reason for the
other is due to general world knowledge. Hence, we would be unlikely to say
I've got a headache. Therefore, I cannot close my eyes, although such a statement
is always possible within adequate context. That a proposition is characterised as a reason for another, by contrast, is probably related to inclusive
AVS because a sentence like *I've got a headache* as such is not necessarily
understood as a reason or explanation for something.

(7.87)   I've got a headache myself.
         a Therefore, I cannot drive the car either.
         b Therefore, I cannot proofread the article either.
         c Therefore, I cannot look after the children either.
         d Therefore, ...

Against the background that conditionality is a dominant feature of the
contexts in which inclusive AVS is to be found, it becomes understandable
why declined requests, turned-down offers and refused reproaches form such
a stable pattern in the data. Certainly, these are definitely pragmatic effects

following from the conditional component involved because, usually, a reason is necessary to decline a request, turn down an offer and refuse a reproach. For the very same reason, it becomes clear why in those contexts in which two characters exchange their experience about some state of affairs or where one character expresses empathy towards another, we often have the impression that the conversation or the current turn is explicitly terminated with the statement containing inclusive AVS. In order to do so, again, it is necessary by convention to give a reason.

Note, though, that it would be premature to regard conditionality as a direct or even the central contribution of inclusive AVS. An analysis of inclusive AVS as a conditional operator is probably not justified because it may well be the case that the conditional implication must be put down to an even more central meaning component of the intensifier. The most obvious property that argues against such a view is that inclusive AVS is always in association with an NP. This rather seems to indicate that it modifies an NP and not that it connects two propositions marking one as the premise, reason or explanation for the other. For the time being, however, we will not pursue this issue any further and simply note that conditionality is at some level involved.

7.4 Comparison: inclusive AVS versus *also*

There are obvious similarities between *also* and inclusive AVS. They are, as a matter of fact, so striking that they provided incentive enough for Browning (1993) to label this use of intensifiers '*also*-reflexives'. To start with, it appears to achieve simple inclusion in much the same manner as *also*. The shared meaning of *also* and inclusive AVS could then be described as follows: i) both *also* and inclusive AVS claim that there is a referent in addition to the one denoted by their focus NP (existential claim); and ii) the predication *also* or inclusive AVS has scope over, i.e. the background, is said to hold for both of these referents. Put differently, the two expressions evoke alternatives to their focus value and characterise focus and alternatives as identical with regard to some predication. As far as these two criteria are concerned, (7.88a) and (7.88b) are equivalent. Note that *too* in (7.88c) is an alternative expression to *also*, however, it is restricted to postfocal positions.

(7.88)   a   Betty has been unemployed herself.
         b   Betty has also been unemployed.
         c   Betty has been unemployed too.

Normally, *also* is classified as a focus particle which structures a proposition into a focused and a backgrounded part. Hence, it can be regarded as a binary operator which accepts an individual and a property as input, cf. e.g. König (1991: 62). (7.89a) below gives a possible formalisation saying that there is a predication p containing a variable position x – the focus of the particle – and that α is an adequate value for that variable. Inclusive particles and focus particles in general entail the corresponding sentence without the particle as shown in (7.89b). The presupposition in (7.89c) states that there is another entity besides α for which the predicate ρ is true. This reflects the evoking of alternatives to the focus.

(7.89) a assertion: *also* $[\lambda x\ (\rho(x)),\ \alpha]$
        b entailment: $\rho(\alpha)$
        c presupposition: $\exists y\ (\rho(y)\ \&\ y \neq \alpha)$

According to (7.89), example (7.88b) can be translated in the following way:

(7.90) a assertion: *also* $[\lambda x\ (x\ \text{has been unemployed}),\ \text{Betty}]$
        b entailment: Betty has been unemployed.
        c presupposition: $\exists y\ ((y\ \text{has been unemployed})\ \&\ y \neq \text{Betty})$

The question is whether inclusive AVS satisfies entailment and presupposition in the same manner as *also*. As far as the entailment relation is concerned between a sentence containing inclusive AVS and the parallel sentence without it, we find that inclusive AVS passes this test without problems. (7.91a) below implies (7.91b), and exactly the same observation can be made with inclusive AVS in general. Since this is a property all focus particles share, it can be counted as another point in favour of analysing inclusive AVS as a focus particle.

(7.91) a Betty has been unemployed herself. $\Rightarrow$
        b Betty has been unemployed.

Concerning the presupposition that there has to be an alternative referent to the one denoted by the focus, we also find that under this criterion inclusive AVS behaves alike to *also*. The relevant test for a presupposition is to check whether it is stable under negation. As the two sentences in (7.92) make clear, this is indeed the case. The positive as well as the negative sentence imply the existence of an additional referent.

(7.92) a Betty has been unemployed herself.
        b Betty has not been unemployed herself.

Questions are another test for presuppositions. Under this test too, inclusive AVS turns out to presuppose an alternative referent in the same manner as *also*, cf.:

(7.93) Why does Betty know how difficult it is to find a job? Has she been unemployed herself?

On the face of it, then, it seems to be possible to analyse inclusive AVS in the same spirit as *also*, i.e. according to (7.89). And indeed, Browning (1993) claims that inclusive AVS makes exactly the same contribution as *also*, cf. (7.94), which gives the semantic analysis of (7.88a) according to her proposal. This is nicely reflected in her terminology because, as we have mentioned, she names this use of AVS '*also*-reflexives'.

(7.94)   Betty has been unemployed & there is someone ≠ Betty who has the attribute 'has been unemployed'.

The two questions that will be pursued in the following are: i) in how far do the two expressions differ in terms of their functionality; and ii) do the specifications given in (7.89) exhaustively capture the semantic contribution of inclusive AVS. Let us discuss these questions in order.

Inclusive AVS is bound to a position behind its focus. It can never occur in prefocal position. *Also*, by contrast, may be placed in prefocal as well as in postfocal position. If it occurs before its focus, the focus is invariably stressed. If it occurs behind its focus, the stress falls on *also* itself, cf. (7.95). Notice that postfocal *also* triggers the same stress pattern as (postfocal) inclusive AVS.

(7.95)   a Bill also met LIZ.
         b Bill ALSO met Liz.

Since *also* lacks agreement features, it is potentially more prone to focus ambiguities. In (7.96) either *I* or *London* may be the focus of *also*. To be sure, prosody resolves such ambiguities in many cases. Inclusive AVS, by contrast, can often clearly identify the focus via its ϕ-features, cf. (7.97).

(7.96)   a I have ALSO been to London.
         b I have also been to LONdon.

(7.97)   I have been to London mySELF.

Moreover, the range of possible foci is different with the two expressions. Whereas inclusive AVS is bound to nominal foci, *also* shows more variability and interacts freely with verbs, prepositions, adjectives and adverbs, cf. (7.98). What (7.98) in connection with (7.95) also shows is that *also* imposes no restrictions onto the grammatical function of its focus. It readily interacts with subjects, objects, predicates, etc. Inclusive AVS, by contrast, is mainly restricted to interacting with subject NPs (at least in English).

(7.98)   a I also TYPED it.
         b Max also kissed MY girlfriend.
         c It is also HOT in here.
         d He came also YESterday.

The restriction on [+human] focus referents does not apply either, cf. (7.99) below.

(7.99)   a My dog ALSO suffers from rheumatism.
         b *My dog suffers from rheumatism itSELF.

Also is entirely insensitive to the aktionsart of the verb present. Whereas event verbs *grosso modo* select exclusive and state verbs inclusive AVS, *also* does not show comparable restrictions. In point of fact, its contribution to the meaning of a sentence remains exactly the same, namely (7.89). Consider the (non-) contrast in (7.100). Note, though, that it is not impossible to evoke the inclusive reading of AVS in (7.100a). It just needs adequate context.

(7.100) a I have (also) washed my car (myself). (exclusive)
         b I (also) used to adore movie stars (myself). (inclusive)

Besides being applicable as a focus particle, *also* can be put to use as a conjunction too, cf. (7.101). Its basic meaning, i.e. inclusion, is clearly visible in these examples. Obviously, intensifiers in general are inadequate for any such purposes.

(7.101) a Also, many people fail to see that immediate action is required. [König 1991: 65]
         b Also, I had trouble with the gearbox, the lever became spongy and I wasn't sure what was happening. [BNC]

Finally, notice an interesting parallel between German *auch* and *selbst*. Both particles can occur either before or after their respective focus. In prefocal as well as in postfocal position both particles allow for an inclusive interpretation. However, in prefocal position inclusion is always accompanied by a scalar effect. The focus value is placed at the bottom of a scale of likelihood interpreted against the background of the remaining open sentence. Prefocal scalar *auch* and *selbst* would invariably translate into Englishas *even*.

(7.102) a Riesen haben AUCH/SELBST mal klein angefangen.
            'Giants once started from small beginnings too/themselves.'
         b Auch/selbst RIEsen haben klein angefangen. [cf. König 1991: 63]
            'Even giants started from small beginnings.'

In sum, it seems to be no exaggeration to say that, as far as functionality is concerned, *also* outranks inclusive AVS by several margins. It associates with a wider range of foci in terms of lexical category, grammatical function and semantic properties of the focus referent. Moreover, E. *also* has developed into a sentence connector and G. *auch* into a scalar additive particle.

Let us now come to the second point, i.e. to the question whether (7.89) exhaustively captures the semantic contribution of inclusive adverbal intensifiers. This boils down to asking if *also* and inclusive AVS are equivalent in meaning or if inclusive AVS possibly contributes a little more. Here, a number of pros and cons can be brought forward.

As for the pros, notice first of all that *also* and inclusive AVS hardly ever co-occur when they are in association with the same focus. This cannot be due to the fact that they take the same focus since multiple occurrences of focus particles interacting with one focus are a common phenomenon, cf. *only Max alone, not only Lucy*, etc., so that it appears reasonable to conclude that the strong or even complete meaning overlap of the two particles impedes their co-occurrence, cf.:

(7.103)   a   ??I know what it means to suffer from rheumatism because I also suffer from rheumatism myself.
          b   ??How can she be angry about his jealousy when she is terribly jealous herself too?

Moreover, *also* readily co-occurs with adnominal intensifiers and exclusive AVS which shows that its incompatibility with inclusive AVS cannot be due to an incompatibility with intensifiers in general:

(7.104)   a   Bill himself also lit a cigarette.
          b   I have also washed my car myself.

Recall that adnominal intensifiers can occur behind the finite verb. This is a property that makes them hard to distinguish from inclusive AVS and AVS in general on purely structural grounds. Therefore, *selbst* in (7.105), which can co-occur with *auch* (*also*), might be mistaken for inclusive AVS. However, (7.105) is only grammatical under double focus which makes clear that it is an example of ANS.

(7.105)   a   Ich habe SELBST // AUCH Kinder.
          b   *Ich habe selbst auch Kinder.
              'I've got children of my own.'

Recall furthermore that for inclusive AVS to function properly, the situation in the context of which it occurs must be repeatable. (7.89) predicts that *also* shares this constraint, otherwise one and the same predication could not hold of two referents. (7.89) reflects this state of affairs by giving p both in the assertion as well as in the presupposition. (7.106) shows that this prediction is indeed borne out.

(7.106)   a   *She let the old man die herself.
          b   *She also let the old man die.

As far as the cons are concerned, it seems reasonable to ask why a language should provide two expressions with exactly the same meaning in the first place. After all, no true synonyms exist according to a widely accepted view. Where then do *also* and inclusive AVS differ?

The most remarkable fact about *also* in comparison with inclusive AVS is that it is by far less dependent on adequate context. It has already been mentioned that *also* readily occurs in contexts where inclusive AVS leads to a considerable amount of accommodation or where it appears to be barred altogether. (7.107) repeats the odd sentences given in (7.20a) through (7.22a), but replaces *also* for inclusive AVS. The need for accommodation thereby disappears.

(7.107) a Fred ALSO smells.
         b Max is ALSO blind.
         c Ken ALSO snores.

(7.108) provides explicit context to satisfy all clauses of (7.89) above. Nevertheless, inclusive AVS is much less acceptable than *also*. The inevitable conclusion seems to be that *also* and inclusive AVS are different, and since the latter demands more extensive context, its semantic contribution must be the more complex of the two.

(7.108) a Paul owns a house and Max owns a house too.
         b ?Paul owns a house and Max owns a house himself.

Edmondson and Plank (1978: 384ff.) were probably the first to point to the fact that certain occurrences of intensifiers are unacceptable unless well-tailored context is provided. However, since they do not regard these examples as involving a separate type of intensifier similar in meaning to *also*, they do not ask what this type of intensifier contributes in addition to it. Here are two of their prominent examples.

(7.109) a *John was taller than Mary himself.
         b John knows what it means to be taller than Mary, for he is taller than Mary himself.

(7.110) a *Scarlett was blown by the wind herself.
         b Scarlett knows what it means to be blown by the wind, for she was once blown by the wind herself.

Browning (1993: 85) shares the intuitions on the context-dependence of inclusive AVS and points out that the following short text (7.111) becomes much more propitious if the NP *John* has been mentioned in the previous discourse. This limitation does not hold for *also*, cf. (7.112).

(7.111) A: Bill is always whining about that class. Yesterday he was just furious at the professor. – B: Well, John was pretty angry at the professor himself, and he doesn't usually complain.

(7.112) A: Bill is always whining about that class. Yesterday he was just furious at the professor. – B: Well, John was also pretty angry at the professor, and he doesn't usually complain.

The necessity for adequate context makes clear that the description of *also* according to (7.89) does not exhaustively capture the semantic contribution inclusive AVS makes. The question that remains to be asked is whether the additional contribution of inclusive AVS can be made more precise.

Recall from the previous section that inclusive AVS prototypically occurs in sentences giving the premise, reason or explanation for another proposition present in the current universe of discourse. Apparently, this is related to the fact that inclusive AVS does not contextualise easily. A disconnected sentence which tries to give an explanation for something must seem odd in the absence of context justifying the expression of such an explanation. Since sentences containing *also* do not express an explanation or reason in a similar manner, they are less particular about the context around them which accounts for the differences in acceptability observed, cf. the examples below.

(7.113) a Fred (also) snores/laughs/smells (?himself).
         b I am (also) a parent (?myself).

As a matter of fact, it turns out that the property of inclusive AVS, namely to characterise the sentence it occurs in as providing a reason or explanation for something, can be analysed as an additional presupposition of it. The reason implied remains stable under negation and does not disappear in questions either, cf. (7.114) and (7.115) respectively. Note that the negative sentence containing inclusive AVS in (7.114) gives an explanation for the negative counterpart of the proposition the corresponding positive sentence gives an explanation for.

(7.114) a I know what London looks like because I've been to London myself.
         b I don't know what London looks like because I haven't been to London myself.

(7.115) How can you know that raising children is expensive? Are you a parent yourself?

Given that the reason or explanation implied by inclusive AVS can be analysed as a presupposition, there now is a clear difference in meaning between inclusive AVS and *also*: it consists in an additional presupposition.

Subsequently, the semantic contribution of *also* as described in (7.89) can be extended to yield the contribution of inclusive AVS as specified in (7.116). Note, though, that it cannot be ruled out entirely that the additional presupposition has a deeper cause.

(7.116) a assertion: x-*self* [λx (ρ(x)), α]
         b entailment: ρ(α)
         c presupposition₁: ∃y y (ρ(y) & y≠α)
         d presupposition₂: there is a proposition σ in the surrounding context for which ρ(α) can be interpreted as a premise, reason or explanation

This additional presupposition is the reason why inclusive AVS is preferred over *also* in contexts where some sort of explanation is expected. Consider (7.117).

(7.117) a As a child, I used to watch tennis on television. Today, I play tennis myself.
         b As a child, I used to watch tennis on television. Today, I also play tennis.

Here, (7.117a) is slightly more natural than (7.117b) because the context suggests that the watching of tennis on television is not necessary any longer. (7.118) strikes a similar chord. Only (7.118a) characterises the referent referred to by *I* as being fully aware of the implications of losing one's father.

(7.118) a I had often heard that people lose their parents sooner or later, but only realised the full implications after I had lost my father myself.
         b I had often heard that people lose their parents sooner or later, but only realised the full implications after I had also lost my father.

Similar effects can be observed in (7.119) and (7.120). In the former case, the sentence containing inclusive AVS explains why Sue had no reason to be impressed and in the latter, it gives the reason why the friend from California does not have to send a horse.

(7.119) a Back from Kuwait, Bill told Sue how struck he was at the prosperity found there. She was only a little impressed because in Bahrain she had encountered comparable wealth herself.
         b Back from Kuwait, Bill told Sue how struck he was at the prosperity found there. She was only a little impressed because in Bahrain she had encountered comparable wealth too.

(7.120) a My friend breeds horses in California. He wants to send me one although I breed horses here in Berlin myself.
b My friend breeds horses in California. He wants to send me one although I breed horses here in Berlin too.

Against the background that the common denominator of inclusive AVS and *also* can be seen as an identity statement of the form 'x and y are identical with respect to their involvement in a situation', Plank (1979a: 280ff.) hypothesises that *also* imposes stricter identity conditions than inclusive AVS on the referents concerned. However, strict identity of two (or more) referents with respect to a situation is not responsible for the difference in interpretation which inclusive AVS and *also* achieve in the following example.

(7.121) a Müllers können nicht auf Meyers Kinder aufpassen. Sie gehen am Sonntag selbst ins Theater.
'The Müllers cannot look after the Meyers's children. They plan to go to the theatre on Sunday themselves.'
b Müllers können nicht auf Meyers Kinder aufpassen. Sie gehen am Sonntag auch ins Theater.
'The Müllers cannot look after the Meyers's children. They plan to go to the theatre on Sunday too.'

The difference between (7.121a) and (7.121b) consists in the fact that in the sentence containing inclusive AVS, the Müllers and the Meyers are the only characters for whom identity with respect to going to the theatre is claimed. In (7.121b), by contrast, a third party could be implied. Imagine the following scenario. In a block of flats, family A asks family B to look after their children because they want to go to the theatre. B declines because they want to go to the theatre too. Here, inclusive AVS is the most natural option. When B, however, in an attempt to help A, asks family C if they could look after A's children, and C wants to go to the theatre too, C will be most likely to decline the request with the statement containing *also*, i.e. (7.121b). Families A, B and C are strictly identical with regard to going to the theatre, but still, there is a difference between inclusive AVS and *also*. The reason rather seems to lie in the fact that C is asked only indirectly via B and does not have to justify the declining to B in the same manner as B has to A. When C says to B that they will go to the theatre, this statement does not give a relevant explanation from B's point of view because it is A's children that are under discussion and not B's. As far as the exchange of information between B and C is concerned, the implications of going to the theatre do not matter in the context given and therefore *also* seems to be preferred.

We can summarise that (7.89) does not exhaustively capture the contribution that inclusive AVS makes to the meaning of an utterance and that *also* and inclusive AVS are far from being synonymous. It follows that accounts which try to reduce the meaning of inclusive AVS to the one of *also*, such as Browning (1993) and Kibrik and Bogdanova (1995), cannot be regarded as adequate analyses of it. Inclusive AVS appears to carry the additional presupposition specified in (7.116). Since, apart from this presupposition, the meaning profiles of *also* and inclusive AVS are the same, the relation between the two particles is such that inclusive AVS implies *also*, but not vice versa. This conclusion is also arrived at in König and Siemund (1996a: 12).

> (7.122)   a   Max has served in the forces himself. $\Rightarrow$
> b   Max has served in the forces too.

As far as differences between English and German are concerned, it may be interesting to note that there are English sentences containing inclusive x-*self* which, when translated into German, do not permit *selbst*, but rather require *auch* in combination with the adnominal intensifier, cf. the contrast between (7.123a,b). Neither *auch* nor *selbst* produces an adequate translation as (7.123c) makes clear (although *auch* is slightly better than *selbst* in the present context). What we see here is that ANS and inclusive AVS fuse into one occurrence of x-*self*. Note, though, that *selbst* appears to be sufficient on its own if the subject pronoun is stressed.

> (7.123)   a   I know people are looking for another upset here because Sutton are a decent team, but we're not bad ourselves. [BNC]
> b   Ich weiß, daß man hier auf einen weiteren Überraschungssieg hofft. Sutton ist in der Tat eine gute Mannschaft, aber wir selbst sind auch nicht schlecht.
> c   Ich weiß, daß man hier auf einen weiteren Überraschungssieg hofft. Sutton ist in der Tat eine gute Mannschaft, aber wir sind ?auch/??selbst nicht schlecht.

7.5 Inclusive AVS as ANS plus *also*

Let us now come to a discussion of the proposals to analyse inclusive AVS and start with the one advanced in König and Siemund (1996a: 18ff.). There, it is assumed that inclusive AVS is the product of a fusion process of two particles, the adnominal intensifier on the one hand and *also* on the other. Inclusive AVS is believed to unite the separate semantic contributions of these two particles in one expression. This process is shown in (7.124).

> (7.124) $\text{SELF}_{adnominal} + also \Rightarrow \text{SELF}_{inclusive}$

To assume a fusion of the two particles appears reasonable for several reasons.

First of all, note that the separate meanings are compatible. The ranking of focus and alternatives in terms of centre and periphery is compatible with their inclusion into one set with respect to a certain property or state of affairs and vice versa. Indeed, some occurrences of ANS even show inclusive effects on their own:

(7.125) God himself might not know about the origins of the universe.

Second, ANS and *also* can occur in the same sentence and be in association with the same NP. They share one and the same focus, however, their scope is not co-extensive. Whereas the scope of ANS is restricted to its focus, *also* takes wide scope over the entire predication, cf. (7.126), (7.127).

(7.126) a Elisabeth herself lives in New Jersey.
         b Elisabeth also lives in New Jersey.

(7.127) a *herself* [λx (x), Elisabeth]
         b *also* [λx (x lives in New Jersey), Elisabeth]

Third, and here the argument must be restricted to German, ANS and G. *auch* can occur adjacent and, what is more, in a position which is extremely indicative of inclusive AVS, namely behind the finite verb, cf. (7.128a). Recall, however, that this becomes possible under double focus only. And finally, fourth, this structure appears to be equivalent in meaning to the one containing inclusive AVS alone, cf. (7.128b).

(7.128) a Ich habe SELBST // AUCH Kinder.
            'I myself have children too.'
         b Ich habe SELBST Kinder.
            'I have children of my own.'

On the basis of the above observations, König and Siemund conjecture that it would be justified to assume that *auch* transfers its meaning to ANS, which yields inclusive AVS, and subsequently gets deleted. (7.129) shows this derivation.

(7.129) a Ich SELBST$_{adnominal}$ habe AUCH Kinder. ⇒
         b Ich habe SELBST$_{adnominal}$ AUCH Kinder. ⇒
         c Ich habe SELBST$_{inclusive}$ Kinder.

Although this analysis seems to be well-motivated, it must meet some serious objections. The first problem arises from the observation that inclusive AVS imposes restrictions on the NP it interacts with different than ANS. Recall that inclusive AVS requires [+human] NPs whereas ANS is unspecified in this respect, cf. (7.8). Moreover, ANS marks its focus as central in a way which is not typical of inclusive AVS. The latter easily interacts with NPs whose referents would count as peripheral in terms of the adnominal intensifier, cf. (7.23). If, however, inclusive AVS contained the meaning of ANS as a proper part of it, it should also impose equivalent or at least similar restrictions on its focus referent.

Another problem, and probably the main one, results from the fact that ANS followed by *also* and inclusive AVS simply do not make the same contribution. Although there seem to be contexts where the former can be exchanged for the latter, in the majority of cases such a replacement entails a clear change in meaning. In the following mini-dialogue, the answer containing ANS + *also* is felt as rather unnatural and gives the impression that a third party, apart from speaker and hearer, is involved. (7.131) is the English counterpart of (7.130).

(7.130)   Kannst du mir Geld leihen?
    a   Ich bin selbst etwas knapp.
    b   ?Ich selbst bin auch etwas knapp.

(7.131)   Could you lend me some money?
    a   I'm a little short myself.
    b   ?I myself am a little short too.

(7.132) and (7.133) give another mini-dialogue which shows the same effect. Here too, it is felt that there is a third party who does not have a watch.

(7.132)   Kannst du mir sagen, wie spät es ist?
    a   Tut mir leid. Ich habe selbst keine Uhr.
    b   ?Tut mir leid. Ich selbst habe auch keine Uhr.

(7.133)   Do you know what time it is?
    a   Sorry, I'm in need of a watch myself.
    b   ?Sorry, I myself am in need of a watch too.

Moreover, the implicatures inclusive AVS typically generates are lost after the substitution. Only the *myself* in (7.134a) characterises the referent of its focus as knowing all about raising children.

(7.134)   a   I have raised ten children myself.
    b   I myself have raised ten children too.

Since these implicatures appear to be the basis for why statements containing inclusive AVS are usually interpreted as the reason or explanation for some other proposition, this loss renders ANS + *also* inappropriate in contexts requiring such an explanation, cf. (7.135) and (7.136) below.

(7.135) a I know what it means to raise ten children because I have raised ten children myself.

b ?I know what it means to raise ten children because I myself have raised ten children too.

(7.136) a 'I hate to cut you short,' said Richard from the hatch, 'it's only that I can hardly expect my staff to be in time if I'm late myself.' [LLC]

b ?'I hate to cut you short,' said Richard from the hatch, 'it's only that I can hardly expect my staff to be in time if I myself am late too.'

In sum, the cons against analysing inclusive AVS as a synthesis of ANS and *also* seem to outweigh the pros by a wide margin. The fact that there is a difference in meaning is particularly problematic.

7.6 Scalar analyses

An analysis of adverbal intensifiers which is dominant in the existing literature on the topic regards them as scalar adverbs. According to this view, intensifiers rank the denotation of the constituent they interact with on a scale, cf. Edmondson and Plank (1978), Plank (1979a), Primus (1992). These approaches typically regard the scalar contribution as the common denominator underlying all uses of intensifiers. Where they differ is on the properties of the scales involved as well as on the assumptions they make concerning the constituent the intensifier interacts with. This leads to disagreement as to which denotation is ranked on the scale. Edmondson and Plank, for instance, state the difference between adnominal and adverbal intensifiers in terms of the scale involved (expectancy versus involvement) whereas Primus leaves the scale constant (likelihood), but claims that ANS and AVS interact with different constituents (NP versus VP).

Another common feature of these scalar approaches is that they do not distinguish between inclusive and exclusive AVS, but rather try to explain all occurrences of adverbal intensifiers on one and the same basis. Since it does not really matter whether we discuss these analyses here or postpone their treatment to the chapter on exclusive AVS, we will deal with them here. Nevertheless, they are less convincing for inclusive than for exclusive AVS.

Edmondson and Plank (1978: 406) claim that adverbal intensifiers, or *himself*$_2$ in their terminology, characterise the subject referent as the most directly involved referent in the situation denoted by the predication. Depending on the thematic role of the subject NP present, they distinguish between most directly involved agents or experiencers. Figure 7.1 shows the relevant scale.

The underlying assumption of Edmondson and Plank is that 'many predicates are simply vague about the degree of agency, involvement or

indirect involvement   direct involvement

Figure 7.1 A scale of involvement.

independent causation expressed by their subjects' (p. 406) and that AVS clarifies which of the referents under discussion is most intensely involved. Thus, AVS in examples like (7.137) makes clear that Ironside was not rolled by a third party and that the president was not acquainted with the news via a messenger. The characterisation of the subject referent as most directly involved seems to explain why this referent is interpreted as the one ultimately responsible for the situation.

(7.137)   a Ironside rolled over the edge himself.
          b The president heard the news himself.

Generally speaking, what adverbal intensifiers do, according to Edmondson and Plank, is to associate a propositional schema with a scale of involvement and place the denotation of the subject at the extreme of this scale labelled 'most directly involved'. (7.138) gives the relevant schema for (7.137a), however, note that this is equivalent to viewing AVS as an operator which structures propositions, cf. (7.139). From here, it is only a small step to saying that *Ironside* is the focus and *rolled over the edge* the background or remaining open sentence. We will basically analyse inclusive AVS in the spirit of (7.139).

(7.138)   x rolled over the edge

(7.139)   *himself* [λx (x rolled over the edge), Ironside]

Since pragmatic scales associated with a propositional schema, such as the one shown in Figure 7.1, are usually assumed to invert in negative polarity contexts, cf. the analysis of E. *even* or G. prefocal *selbst* in section 6.1, Edmondson and Plank seem to correctly predict that the negative counterparts to (7.137) mark the subject denotation as least directly involved in the relevant situations, cf. (7.140).

(7.140)   a Ironside did not roll over the edge himself.
          b The president did not hear the news himself.

In Plank (1979a), a more determined step towards an analysis of inclusive AVS is made. Still, adverbal intensifiers are not considered polysemous and the final goal of this paper is to subsume AVS in the meaning of *also* under the analysis of Edmondson and Plank (1978) where many of his ideas originate. Plank pursues three lines of investigation. First, he discusses what the semantic contribution of AVS in the sense of *also* is, second, he tries to single out the meaning component in AVS, or rather SELF in general, which allows for the drift towards *also*, and third, he suggests a common denominator underlying all uses of AVS, which, according to him, consists in the expression of identity.

As indicated above, Plank wants to show that inclusive AVS can be analysed in terms of scales that grade involvement, i.e. as an intensifier which characterises the subject referent as the one who is most directly involved in the situation under consideration. Since inclusive AVS, however, mostly occurs with predicates denoting situations which cannot be transferred, i.e. passed on to another referent, he faces the problem of how to convincingly justify the idea of graded involvement. It is indeed not easy to see how the subject referent can be more or less involved in the following examples:

(7.141)   a   The Pope died himself.
            b   John snores himself.

Moreover, the discussion in section 7.2 has shown that inclusive AVS has a strong affinity for stative predicates, and here it becomes hard to defend the idea of involvement in the first place.

(7.142)   a   I am terribly frightened myself.
            b   I used to have such a car myself.

The solution Plank offers (p. 275) is based on the assumption that referents participating in non-transferable situations (prototypically states) always derive a certain amount of knowledge or experience from these situations and that there usually are alternative means to acquire this knowledge. In the case of dying, for instance, one can see or experience how people die around oneself and a similar statement is possible in the case of being frightened. What, according to Plank, AVS in the meaning of *also* does in these cases is to underline the involvement of the subject referent in the *gathering* of this knowledge or experience.

As for the second point, recall that Plank assumes that the scalar contribution is the common denominator underlying all uses of SELF. In other words, intensifiers are supposed to always show a scalar effect of some sort. *Also*, by contrast, always quantifies over a set, recall (7.89). However, under certain conditions, intensifiers can show a quantifying and *also* a scalar effect. It is in precisely these contexts that the intensifier is interpreted as similar in meaning to *also*, cf. (7.143) below.

(7.143)   Selbst/auch Riesen haben klein angefangen.
            'Even giants started from small beginnings.'

Concerning the common denominator relevant to both inclusive and exclusive AVS, Plank suggests that the main function of adverbal intensifiers consists in reducing a statement to a specific expression of identity. For cases of exclusive AVS like (7.144a) below, the relevant identity relation is supposed to hold between the agent and the beneficiary of the situation. Both roles are taken up by Max in this case. This reflects the intuition that such sentences typically imply that the subject referent benefits most from the relevant situation. The role apart from the agent may vary from predicate to predicate. The identity relation established by inclusive AVS holds between focus and alternatives with respect to the predication, cf. (7.144b).

(7.144) a Max configured his computer himself. (exclusive)
        b Max has worked with a computer himself. (inclusive)

Before discussing the validity of the above approaches, let us also briefly sketch how Primus (1992) analyses adverbal intensifiers. As already indicated, she too favours a scalar account, however, the relevant scale, according to her view, is not one of involvement, but of likelihood. This scale can be derived from the one given in Figure 7.1 by replacing 'indirect involvement' by 'most likely' and 'direct involvement' by 'least likely'. Adverbal intensifiers place a value at the extreme labelled 'least likely'. Note that this is not a Horn scale, cf. Horn (1972). Since Primus assumes the same scale for the analysis of adnominal intensifiers, there is no difference between ANS and AVS as far as the pragmatic scale is concerned. Hence, both (7.145) and (7.146) are supposed to claim that something is unlikely.

(7.145) The dean himself came.

(7.146) The dean came himself.

On the account Primus offers, the difference between the two examples given above is the following. Recall from section 6.1 that Primus views ANS as a focus particle which takes as its focus the NP it is adjoined to and which has the remaining open sentence in its scope, thereby making the latter the background for the interpretation of the focus value. This is shown in (7.147) for (7.145). The focus (the NP-denotation) is ranked as unlikely against the background (the VP-denotation). According to Primus, the difference between ANS on the one hand and AVS on the other simply consists in that the latter focuses the VP and not an NP, and characterises the VP-denotation as unlikely for the subject referent, which now serves as the relevant background. (7.148) depicts this analysis for (7.146). In comparison with G. prefocal *selbst* in the meaning of 'even', ANS as well as AVS are considered to be non-quantifying.

(7.147) *himself* [λx (x came), the dean]

(7.148) *himself* [λx (the dean x), came]

Expressed informally, the difference between (7.147) and (7.148) boils down to saying that ANS characterises the dean as unlikely to have come whereas AVS says that his past coming was unlikely for the dean. The alternatives evoked by ANS are referents who were more likely to come than the dean; in the case of AVS, more likely past situations for the dean are evoked. Concerning (7.146), plausible alternatives include the ones given in (7.149) below.

(7.149) The dean came himself.
    a He sent a substitute.
    b He rather wanted to rely on the minutes.
    c ...

As Edmondson and Plank do, Primus mostly deals with instances of exclusive AVS, as e.g. (7.146), however, her analysis is also meant to cover inclusive AVS. The explanation she offers for a typically inclusive example like (7.150) below is that being a witch is an unlikely property under common assumptions. Therefore, using the intensifier is appropriate.

(7.150) She is herself a witch.

She also tries to account for why many examples containing inclusive AVS are extremely context-dependent and hardly make sense on their own. In her view, (7.151a) and (7.152a) are odd because 'without further stipulations, it is not unlikely to die or to be taller than somebody else' (p. 83). Therefore, the intensifier is assumed to be inadequate.

(7.151) a. ??The Pope died himself.
       b How could the Pope speak of immortality when he knew he would die himself.

(7.152) a. ??John is taller than Mary himself.
       b John knows what it means to be taller than Mary, for he is taller than Mary himself.

Each of the two approaches outlined above must raise serious objections. As far as Primus is concerned, her suggestion that the intensifier takes the VP as focus is not compatible with the fact that inclusive AVS, and AVS in general, is always in association with an NP which, at least in English, is marked by overt agreement (person, number, gender) on the intensifier. But also in German we have clear intuitions about the intensifier interacting with an NP. If this were not so, we could not explain why sentences containing inclusive AVS require at least one [+human] NP.

In addition to that, inclusive AVS clearly evokes alternatives to the NP it interacts with. Therefore, this NP should be regarded as its focus, not the VP. Moreover, if inclusive AVS focused the VP, it would be difficult to motivate the inclusive effect which, since it is stable under negation and in questions, has the status of a presupposition in the same way as the one observed with *also*. It may also be pointed out that it is not adequate to use inclusive AVS in a universe of discourse containing just one character. A statement about Adam like (7.153) before the creation of Eve is evidently unacceptable.

(7.153)   ???Adam felt hungry himself.

These few points are in fact sufficient to show that Primus is not correct in assuming that inclusive AVS focuses the VP. However, even if it were the case, it would not be justified to say that the VP-denotation is graded as an unlikely property of the subject referent. In the following example, it is precisely because the addressee has the desired or established, but definitely not unexpected property, that marking by inclusive AVS is possible and indeed necessary.

(7.154)   I know you've been to the Arctic yourself, so may I ask you whether you too felt quite fatigued after about two months?

Finally, and this leads over to a criticism of Edmondson and Plank (1978) and Plank (1979a), Primus is unable to explain why inclusive AVS characterises the sentence it occurs in as a premise, reason or explanation for another proposition. This, so it seems, is the reason why these sentences have to be embedded into larger context. Neither Edmondson and Plank nor Plank explain this, and simply ranking the subject referent as the one who is most directly involved in the current situation will not achieve that. Moreover, the idea of direct involvement is problematic in itself because involvement, let alone involvement to a higher or lower degree, in a stative situation is, intuitively speaking, not plausible. Recall from the outline of the analyses given above how laborious an explanation has to be. More or less direct involvement has to be translated into 'varying degrees of directness' (Edmondson and Plank 1978: 385) in the acquisition of the knowledge or experience associated with the relevant state.

Note further that due to the inclusive effect, the idea of gradation also is in need of additional stipulations because focus and alternatives should be equivalent with respect to the VP-denotation. However, here it would be feasible to talk of differing degrees of knowledge or experience associated with a property. Nevertheless, where Edmondson and Plank as well as Plank's view totally breaks down is in the context of negation. Recall that inclusive AVS has scope over negation although, at least in English, this is not reflected in the order of the constituents on the surface. Subsequently, inclusive AVS in negative polarity contexts should characterise its focus as most directly involved in the state of not having a certain property or, since involvement in a state is impossible, in the activity leading to that non-state. However, the examples in (7.155) do not characterise the subject referent as knowing everything about not having a girlfriend and children respectively as a consequence of losing them, but as relevant properties *per se*.

(7.155) a I know what it means to be single because I don't have a girl-friend myself.

b I know what it means to be childless because I don't have children myself.

Plank's analysis of adverbal intensifiers as operators which reduce state-ments to expressions of identity, by contrast, is fairly plausible, even more so because it makes correct predictions for negative sentences. (7.156) shows the negative counterparts of (7.144) above and, given that exclusive AVS is in the scope of negation whereas inclusive AVS has scope over it, this analy-sis explains why (7.156a) does not state identity between the actual agent – which is not the referent denoted by the subject NP, but the alternative evoked – and the beneficiary whereas (7.156b) does, namely between Max and somebody else with respect to not having worked with a computer. However, note that this approach reduces inclusive AVS to *also* which, as was pointed out in section 7.4, cannot be correct.

(7.156) a Max did not configure his computer himself. (exclusive)

b Max has not worked with a computer himself. (inclusive)

To conclude this discussion, note that neither of the above analyses is able to explain why adverbal intensifiers can, in certain contexts, be ambiguous between an inclusive reading on the one hand and an exclusive reading on the other. Moreover, both types of adverbal intensifiers can co-occur in one and the same sentence.

(7.157) a I have tried it myself. (inclusive, exclusive)

b I have myself~inclusive~ once flown a Jumbo myself~exclusive~.

7.7 Presupposition: negative proposition

Somewhat related to the scalar account put forward by Primus (1992) is the following idea, which usually takes shape in the mind of the analyst after considering the following representative examples of inclusive AVS:

(7.158) a A: Could you lend me some money? – B: I'm a little short myself.

b A: I can tell you, life in Berlin can be tough. – B: I know because I live in Berlin myself.

The relevant intuition is that sentences containing inclusive AVS seem to imply that for the focus, or the denotation of the subject NP, the negative value of the proposition expressed by the sentence must have been true in the previous discourse and that the felicity of inclusive AVS depends on this condition being satisfied. Consider (7.158a). Here, character A makes a request to character B. In order for the request to be adequate, A must assume that it can be fulfilled, i.e. that the relevant property (have money) holds of B. Character B then declines the request by asserting that the opposite of the property assumed to be true for him is in fact the case, namely to have no money. Similarly (7.158b). Here, character A wants to relate a personal experience to B, again, on the assumption that B does not have that experience. Otherwise, one could argue, the statement would not be relevant for B in the sense of Sperber and Wilson (1986). B then states that he does, thereby ending the current turn.

Since this negative implication appears to be stable under negation and in questions, it can be regarded as a presupposition, and hence, the difference in meaning between inclusive AVS and *also* could be put down to that additional presupposition, cf. (7.159). The similarity of this approach to the one proposed by Primus is due to the fact that requiring the opposite property to be true of a referent in the previous discourse is more or less equivalent to characterising the asserted property as unlikely.

(7.159)   a   assertion: $x\text{-}self\,[\lambda x\;(\rho(x)),\;\alpha]$
           b   entailment: $\rho(\alpha)$
           c   presupposition₁: $\exists y\;(\rho(y)\;\&\;y \neq \alpha)$
           d   presupposition₂: $\neg\rho(\alpha)$

The idea delineated above forms the basis of Kibrik and Bogdanova's (1995) analysis of intensifiers. They universally regard SELF, or rather Russian *sam*, as an operator which the discourse partners can make use of in order to correct their mutual assumptions, cf.:

> SELF directs the attention of the addressee to the fact that the speaker knows that the information contained in the present utterance about referent X contradicts the expectations of the addressee and that therefore the knowledge about referent X must be corrected. [p. 35; my translation]

On that account, the contribution inclusive AVS makes to the meaning of an utterance turns out to be nothing but a special instantiation of that general case:

> Expectations of addressee: There are potential participants for situation R. The addressee follows from his knowledge about the properties of referent X that X does not participate in R.

Instruction to addressee to correct his expectations: X also participates in R. [p. 30; my translation]

Given the proximity of this approach to the one offered by Primus, we can basically raise the same objections to it. Most obvious, however, is that there are numerous examples contradicting the idea that the negative counterpart to the proposition expressed by the sentence containing inclusive AVS must hold in the preceding discourse. More often than not it is the case that the discourse partners present have the same background assumptions, recall (7.154) and cf. the authentic examples below.

> (7.160) a He was particularly pleased to be patron of Great Ormond Street, he said, because he had been there himself as a child. [BNC]
>
> b She understood his grief and his sense of loss and loneliness – she had been there herself, after the King's death – and she knew about the feelings of despair and the long, long time the scars would take to heal, but she also knew about the importance of carrying on. [BNC]

7.8 Central representative of property

The preceding sections have documented that sentences containing inclusive AVS possess a number of peculiar properties. Since the relevant sentences without inclusive AVS lack characteristic features of comparable proportion, they must be due to the presence of the intensifier. An analysis of adverbal inclusive intensifiers must at least be able to explain the following effects.

1 Inclusive AVS makes a sentence extremely context-dependent.
2 Inclusive AVS turns a sentence into a premise, reason or explanation for a proposition given in the previous or following discourse.
3 Sentences containing inclusive AVS are often used to decline an offer/request or to reject criticism.
4 The referent of the NP inclusive AVS interacts with is often characterised as possessing particular knowledge about the situation denoted by the actual sentence.
5 Inclusive AVS often appears to make the sentence it is contained in particularly adequate as an expression of empathy.
6 Inclusive AVS has a presupposition similar to *also*.
7 Inclusive AVS is not equivalent to *also*.

None of the analyses proposed so far offers an explanation for these effects, apart from maybe 6. The essence of the proposal argued for here can be summarised as follows. Inclusive AVS evokes alternatives to the referent of the NP it is in association with. Hence, it can be analysed as a focus particle (for a more careful discussion, cf. section 2.2). The focus value and the alternatives evoked are characterised against the background of the actual sentence which inclusive AVS can be regarded as having in its scope. Inclusive AVS characterises the focus referent as central and the alternatives as peripheral with regard to the property denoted by the predication. Modification of an NP by inclusive AVS marks the relevant referent as the central representative of this property. In addition, inclusive AVS has specialised in contexts where two referents are identified with respect to a conditional schema. This ability is closely connected to its primary semantic contribution.

Before discussing this analysis in greater detail, however, let us take a look at a suggestion made in König and Siemund (1996a,b), which already points in the present direction. König and Siemund (1996a) hypothesise that, within the boundaries of a certain context, inclusive AVS indicates that the focus referent is as central as the alternatives evoked. It requires a context which already contains a central character and can then be used to state the centrality of another character. In the context of borrowing money as in (7.161), character A is central because he does not have money. Similarly, in the context of giving money away (7.162), Max is central precisely because he has money. What, according to König and Siemund, the sentences containing inclusive AVS assert is that character B and Bill are as central as character A and Max with regard to having no money and having money respectively.

(7.161) A: Could you lend me some money? – B: I'm a little short myself.

(7.162) Max does not have to give Bill money. Bill's got enough money himself.

(7.163) and (7.164) schematise the above examples.

(7.163) Y wants to borrow money from X
       precondition: Y has no money
       assertion: X has no money
                       (X is as central as Y)

(7.164) Y wants to give money to X
       precondition: Y has money
       assertion: X has money
                       (X is as central as Y)

The above analysis primarily wants to capture what inclusive AVS contributes to the meaning of an utterance in addition to *also*. What it obviously fails to account for is why sentences containing inclusive AVS are often felt as giving an explanation or reason for some proposition in the surrounding context. Character B's utterance in (7.161) is felt as a justification for why he cannot lend money to A and so is the statement in (7.162) about Bill in the context of giving money to Bill.

Departing from the analysis sketched above, König and Siemund (1996b) suggest that the main contribution of inclusive AVS lies precisely in converting a given sentence into such an explanation or reason. However, no answer is given for why that should happen in the first place. Apart from that, they adhere to their previous account.

Another problem with König and Siemund's analysis is the idea of one character being as central as another. This is not convincing because, by definition, being central requires a related periphery. Another centre should nullify the contrast. Note that this idea also is at variance with the analysis of adnominal intensifiers. What König and Siemund certainly capture with their analysis is the context-dependence of inclusive AVS, which is due to the fact that the relevant sentences always give an explanation.

However, given that the ability to structure sets into a central element and related peripheral elements is a reasonably precise approximation of the semantic contribution adnominal intensifiers make, trying to transfer this idea to the analysis of inclusive AVS appears to be a sensible move. The context-dependence of the relevant sentences is probably the key to uncovering this contrast in the correct location. Consider the sentence in (7.165).

(7.165) Liz wears glasses herself.

Presented as such, this sentence is certainly not felicitous. It requires additional context. In other words, sentences containing inclusive AVS require the accommodation of implicatures which are relevant beyond the boundaries of the actual sentence. The common property of all sentences containing inclusive AVS seems to be that they massively generate contextually relevant implicatures. (7.166) shows some possible implicatures of (7.165).

(7.166) a Liz often has a headache.
         b Liz knows how expensive good glasses are.
         c Liz does not like driving in the dark.
         d ...

The implicatures generated can be integrated into the semantic analysis of inclusive AVS. According to (7.167), then, inclusive AVS has the same presupposition as *also*, however, unlike *also*, generates a set of implicatures derived from the current sentence. There is some special kind of connection between the implicatures and the proposition producing them.

(7.167) a assertion: x-*self* [λx (x wears glasses), Liz]
         b entailment: Liz wears glasses.

    c. presupposition: $\exists y \, ((y \text{ wears glasses}) \, \& \, y \neq Liz)$
    d. implicatures: {Liz often has a headache, Liz knows how expensive good glasses are, Liz does not like driving in the dark, ...}

(7.168) depicts the above analysis of inclusive AVS abstracted away from the current example with $\{\sigma_1 \ldots \sigma_n\}$ being potential contextually relevant implicatures.

(7.168) a assertion: $x\text{-}self\,[\lambda x \, (\rho(x)), \, \alpha]$
         b entailment: $\rho(\alpha)$
         c presupposition: $\exists y \, (\rho(y) \, \& \, y \neq \alpha)$
         d implicatures: $\{\sigma_1(\alpha), \, \sigma_2(\alpha), \, \sigma_3(\alpha), \, \ldots, \, \sigma_n(\alpha)\}$

The present analysis already accounts for a number of the effects listed at the beginning. If it is a crucial property of adverbal inclusive intensifiers massively to generate contextually relevant implicatures to the sentence they are contained in, then the extreme context-dependence of these sentences can no longer be surprising. Appropriate context is necessary to accommodate these implicatures. Second, it becomes understandable why the sentences in question are felt to give a reason or explanation for another proposition in the surrounding discourse. To see why this should be so, let us take a look at two prototypical examples of this effect again:

(7.169) a A: Could you help me today? – B: Sorry, I'm terribly busy myself.
         b Sarah knows what it means to have a boyfriend for she has a boyfriend herself.

In example (7.169a), the fact that character B is terribly busy serves as an explanation for why he cannot help character A. Also, that Sarah in (7.169b) has a boyfriend helps to explain why she knows what it means to have a boyfriend. Note, now, that in both cases, the proposition that is given a reason for by the sentence containing the intensifier is also an implicature, one could say the contextually relevant implicature, that can be derived from this sentence. Being terribly busy can imply that one cannot help somebody else, and from having a boyfriend it may be inferred that one knows about the implications of this state. However, given that an implicature is deduced from a sentence by pragmatic inference, there is a certain chance for there to be some kind of conditional relation between the two underlying propositions so that the effect under discussion loses some of its mystery.

To be sure, this is a slightly simplified picture. As far as conditional implicatures are concerned, a sentence such as (7.170) below appears to be able to produce at least two different kinds.

(7.170) Liz wears glasses.

On the one hand, it is possible to infer a reason for the underlying proposition. A realistic example is given in (7.171a). On the other hand, a consequence of the relevant situation may be deduced, cf. (7.171b).

(7.171) a Liz suffers from bad eyesight. (reason for (7.170))
         b Liz often has a headache. (consequence of (7.170))

The following pair of sentences exemplifies this state of affairs in more detail.

(7.172) a The reason why Liz wears glasses is because she suffers from bad eyesight.
         b The reason why Liz often has a headache is because she wears glasses.

It is noteworthy that a sentence containing inclusive AVS only produces implicatures corresponding to (7.171b), i.e. those which can be interpreted as consequences of the situation denoted by this sentence. Only for these does this sentence serve as a premise, reason, or explanation. Therefore, (7.173a) is less expected than (7.173b).

(7.173) a Liz suffers from bad eyesight. She wears glasses herself.
         b Liz often has a headache. She wears glasses herself.

As a kind of spin-off, the present analysis also explains why inclusive AVS is frequently found in sentences used to decline an offer/request or to reject criticism. These are prototypical contexts for which some sort of explanation is required. To be sure, we here deal with pragmatic effects which do not belong to the basic semantic contribution of inclusive AVS.

Since sentences without inclusive AVS do not generate implicatures to a similar degree as the relevant sentences containing the intensifier, it appears reasonable to assume that this is a contribution of inclusive AVS. However, whereas the source of these implicatures is relatively easy to detect, it is by far less clear why inclusive AVS should generate implicatures to its host sentence in the first place. Moreover, it is not easy to understand why precisely those implicatures are produced which can be interpreted as a consequence. Another question that has neither been posed yet nor answered relates to the factor determining which implicature is finally selected. A sentence carrying inclusive AVS potentially generates a set of implicatures, but only one of these is selected, i.e. becomes relevant in the current context.

As for the implicature selected, this problem is intimately connected with the surrounding context. In the examples (7.174) through (7.176) below, the implicature triggered by the sentence *I'm tired myself* obviously depends on the preceding context, i.e. the statements made by character A. The relevant implicature is given in brackets.

(7.174) A: Could you mow the lawn? I'm tired.
B: I'm tired myself. (Therefore, I cannot mow the lawn either.)

(7.175) A: Could you clean the carpet? I'm tired.
B: I'm tired myself. (Therefore, I cannot clean the carpet either.)

(7.176) A: Could you repair the car? I'm tired.
B: I'm tired myself. (Therefore, I cannot repair the car either.)

It appears that the implicature selected must match some proposition present in the current universe of discourse, either explicitly stated or inferred. All the statements made by character A above imply that he cannot perform the activity in question, and this is precisely what character B implies.

Another interesting observation about the utterances of character A above is that from all of them, a conditional schema of the form *if p, then q* can be derived, cf. (7.177) below. Their common denominator is the antecedent or premise *if you are tired.* They differ in the relevant consequent.

(7.177) a If you are tired, you cannot mow the lawn.
b If you are tired, you cannot clean the carpet.
c If you are tired, you cannot repair the car.

The answers character B gives in (7.174) to (7.176) as well as the corresponding implicatures can also be reduced to the conditional schema *if p, then q*. The answers match the antecedents in (7.177), the implicatures equal the relevant consequents. These parallels suggest an analysis of inclusive AVS in terms of an operator which identifies two referents with regard to a contextually relevant conditional schema. (7.178) depicts this analysis.

(7.178) a assertion: $x\text{-}self\,[\lambda x\,(\rho(x)),\,\alpha]$
b entailment: $\rho(\alpha) \Rightarrow \sigma(\alpha)$
c presupposition: $\exists y\,(\rho(y) \Rightarrow \sigma(y)\;\&\;y\neq\alpha)$

At this point, a brief comparison with the additive particle *also* might be in order, cf. (7.179). Here, entailment and presupposition involve simple propositions. In the case of inclusive AVS, however, it is a conditional schema. Nevertheless, focus value and alternatives evoked are attributed with the same property – ρ – in either analysis, which explains why inclusive AVS is felt as being similar to *also*, but not equivalent to it.

(7.179) a assertion: $also\,[\lambda x\,(\rho(x)),\alpha]$
b entailment: $\rho(\alpha)$
c presupposition: $\exists y\,(\rho(y)\;\&\;y\neq\alpha)$

Let us in the following discuss a few more examples and draw attention to the relevant conditional schemata. Consider (7.180), which gives a mini-dialogue between a driver and a passenger.

(7.180)   D: Could you fill up the car? I am wearing light trousers.
          P: I am wearing light trousers myself.

In this example, the driver establishes the conditional schema depicted in (7.181). He also makes clear that it is relevant to him and that he therefore cannot fill up the car. The passenger, in turn, states that he satisfies the antecedent or premise of this conditional schema. The presence of the intensifier makes the necessary inference possible because it generates a set of implicatures of which one matches the consequent. The passenger is identified with the driver before the background of the conditional schema.

(7.181)   If you wear light trousers, you cannot fill up the car.

Another example of a common context in which inclusive AVS occurs is provided in (7.182). (7.183) shows the underlying conditional schema on the basis of which it operates. This type of context is so widespread because being aware of a certain property is tantamount to knowing all the implications associated with that property.

(7.182)   I know what it means to be a parent because I'm a parent myself.

(7.183)   If you are a parent, you know what it means to be a parent.

(7.184) displays the abstract version of the conditional schema presently under discussion. Notice that inclusive AVS can identify referents with respect to relatively specific schemata (7.181) and to those which can be reduced to more general ones (7.183). As a rule, specific schemata are more explicitly introduced in the context than those depending on general assumptions.

(7.184)   If you possess property x, you know about the implications of possessing property x.

Other examples operate on the basis of even more implicit conditional schemata, cf. (7.185). This statement relies on the condition that if somebody does a certain thing, he is not allowed to complain about others doing the same thing, cf. (7.186).

(7.185)   Ken complains about my snoring although he snores himself.

(7.186) Only do what you expect others to do./Only do to others what you would do to yourself./etc.

Sometimes, the negative counterpart of a conditional schema is made use of rather than the conditional schema itself. The schema implicitly evoked by character A in (7.187) is (7.188a). However, the answer character B formulates to decline the request operates on the basis of (7.188b).

(7.187) A: Could you lend me some money? – B: I'm a little short myself.

(7.188) a If you have money, you can lend money.
          b If you do not have money, you cannot lend money.

It should also be pointed out that the present analysis can easily be transferred to negative sentences containing inclusive AVS, cf. (7.189). What we find in these examples, though, is an underlying conditional schema with a negative antecedent, as shown in (7.190).

(7.189) A: Could you prepare dinner? I don't feel well. – B: I don't feel well myself.

(7.190) If you do not feel well, you cannot prepare dinner.

Although the analysis argued for here, namely that adverbal inclusive intensifiers identify two referents with regard to a contextually relevant conditional schema, appears to capture the basic mechanism on which this type of intensifier operates, it, nevertheless, gives rise to a number of additional questions. There are mainly three questions, the first two of which have been briefly mentioned above. First, an explanation has to be given for why inclusive AVS can produce implicatures to its host sentence. Second, it is quite surprising that of all the propositions that could possibly be inferred from a certain sentence, inclusive AVS focuses precisely on those which can be interpreted as a consequence thereof. And third, the specialisation to conditional schemata requires clarification.

The third question appears to be the easiest to answer because once a proposition is characterised as a premise or reason for another, the extension to a conditional schema can be regarded as a natural next step.

There is also an answer imaginable to the first question. This problem can be reduced to the centralising function of intensifiers. Recall that adnominal intensifiers characterise a referent as central on the basis of its inherent properties. Adverbal inclusive intensifiers, by contrast, make a referent central against the background of the property denoted by the sentence they are contained in. To give an example, a sentence such as *Liz wears glasses herself* characterises *Liz* as the central representative of the property *wear glasses*. The centrality for the property in question gives rise to the implicatures observed because a central representative of a certain property can be thought of as being associated with all related properties. Thus, the basic semantic contribution of adverbal inclusive intensifiers can be summarised as follows:

(7.191) Adverbal inclusive intensifiers structure a set of elements with a common property P into a central representative X of P and peripheral representatives Y of P.

The same state of affairs can also be stated the other way round. The centrality of the focus referent in comparison with the alternatives evoked lies precisely in these associations which can be regarded as additional attributes. This also explains two further problems posed at the beginning of this section, namely that inclusive AVS often characterises the focus referent as possessing particular knowledge associated with the property under discussion and that sentences containing inclusive AVS can be used as expressions of empathy. Knowledge can be regarded as the possession and awareness of attributes and expressions of empathy must be based on a certain amount of experience or knowledge.

The tough nut to crack is the second question. It is not easy to comprehend why inclusive AVS characterises its host sentence as a premise, or, viewed from the opposite angle, why it produces implicatures to be interpreted as consequences thereof. As so often, it turns out to be easier to understand how a certain system functions than to explain what sets it into motion. Further research will have to unearth the answer to that question.

Notes

1 Of course, when animals are assigned human properties, inclusive AVS can interact with the relevant NPs too:

(i) A worker bee also uses the sun in a similar way. Having found a group of flowers bearing nectar, it is able, taking its cue from the sun, to fly straight back along a reverse bearing to its hive. What is more, it is able to tell others what direction they must fly in order to get food themselves. [BNC]

8 Adverbal exclusive intensifiers

Having discussed inclusive AVS in great detail, we will now turn to a description and analysis of the semantics of exclusive AVS, which is the remaining subtype of adverbal intensifiers. This subtype of SELF is an exclusive particle in that it semantically separates its focus from the set of alternatives. Essentially, what is true for the focus does not hold for the alternatives evoked and vice versa. This is to be understood in direct opposition to inclusive AVS, which asserts that what is true for the focus is also true for the relevant alternatives. The property of excluding alternatives necessarily also separates it from adnominal intensifiers. Still, much more than simple exclusion is at stake. In this respect, it is similar to inclusive AVS because inclusion in itself does not account for the entire semantic contribution of inclusive AVS either. As with inclusive AVS, the focus and the set of alternatives must have particular properties and stand in a special relation to one another to make things work.

As has already been mentioned, exclusive AVS is semantically related to expressions like *alone, on x's own, without anyone's help*. Therefore, we can use these expressions as rough glosses for it, cf. (8.1a). Like exclusive AVS, they also say that something happens or is achieved without the intervention or assistance of somebody else. Moreover, in certain contexts *personally*, which one can also substitute for ANS, seems to be the most adequate paraphrase, cf. (8.1b).

(8.1)   a   I made this wardrobe myself/on my own/alone/without anyone's help.
        b   The managing director appeared himself/personally.

However, this superficial similarity is misleading and should not tempt us into equating these expressions. They are not always mutually interchangeable.

(8.2)   a   I live alone/on my own/*myself.
        b   He wrote the article himself/alone/on his own/without anyone's help.

(8.2a) shows that exclusive AVS as such cannot have the meaning 'without any other people' which *alone* and *on x's own* have as a further possible interpretation. *Myself* in (8.2a) is not acceptable. To allow for this reading, x-*self* has to be an argument of the preposition *by*, cf. *I live by myself*. Conversely, the glosses cannot cover the whole meaning range available to exclusive AVS as (8.2b) makes clear. *Himself* in (8.2b) seems to make a contribution different from its paraphrases.

The above statements already indicate that we will analyse exclusive AVS as a focus particle too. Although it shares many features with manner adverbs, recall section 4.2, the fact that there is always a set of alternatives evoked to the referent of the NP with which it interacts clearly points in this direction.

As for previous accounts of exclusive AVS, it has first of all to be borne in mind that not all studies on the subject distinguish between two types of adverbal intensifiers, but analyse AVS *en bloc* so that it is not entirely clear whether it is justified to discuss and criticise them in the present context. However, studies acknowledging only one adverbial intensifier usually discuss those occurrences of SELF which by and large resemble what is here referred to as exclusive AVS so that they may be included.

Due to the fact that exclusive AVS possesses properties which make it look like a focus particle on the one hand and like a manner adverb on the other, we find that most of the analyses proposed in the literature are divided on precisely that line. Apart from that, there are also some singular analyses which cannot be subsumed under this dichotomy. Kibrik and Bogdanova (1995), for instance, analyse all occurrences of the Russian intensifier *sam* as NPs and markers to guide the expectations of the discourse partners present. Moreover, Girke (1993) sees the decisive criterion in the fact that those NPs interacting with the adverbial exclusive use of Russian *sam* appear to undergo a change in their thematic role relative to the preceding context. Edmondson and Plank (1978) and Browning (1993) belong to the group who consider exclusive AVS a manner adverb, although Edmondson and Plank do not assign this label explicitly. Edmondson and Plank claim that the contribution of exclusive AVS and AVS in general consists in characterising a referent as most directly involved in a situation in contrast to less directly involved referents. Browning holds that it emphasises the agent role of the subject NP. Primus (1992) as well as König and Siemund (1996a,b) hold that exclusive AVS is best regarded as a focus particle, but whereas Primus favours a scalar account and analyses the contribution exclusive AVS makes in terms of likelihood, König and Siemund try to subsume it under the notion of centrality, which is an idea we will spell out in more detail here. In particular, we will pursue the idea that exclusive AVS characterises its focus referent as the one who is central in a situation (and who can be so for a number of different reasons) and opposes it to referents which may participate, but, nevertheless, are not central in the relevant situation. Here, again, we find the contrast between central and peripheral referents.

The present chapter is structured as follows. We will start with a listing of the most dominant properties of exclusive AVS. This section will also serve the purpose of properly separating exclusive AVS from ANS and inclusive AVS, although most of the facts concerning the latter have already been dealt with in the previous chapter, cf. section 7.2. Next, we will attempt a rather informal description of the dominant contexts exclusive AVS occurs in, state the meaning components involved and delineate the pragmatic effects a proper analysis would have to capture. The remainder of the chapter is devoted to a discussion of the proposals advanced so far followed by our own analysis.

8.1 Basic properties

Exclusive AVS, just as adnominal and inclusive AVS, is a true intensifier in that, at first sight, it does not seem to semantically contribute anything significant. Whether it is left out or not, the subsequent modification of the sentence containing it is, in terms of truth-conditional semantics, hard to describe. And indeed, sentences with exclusive AVS seem to universally entail those without it in exactly the same manner as those with adnominal and inclusive AVS do:

>(8.3)   a The gardener has watered the roses himself. $\Rightarrow$ (8.3c)
>   b The gardener himself has watered the roses. $\Rightarrow$ (8.3c)
>   c The gardener has watered the roses.

As far as the NP is concerned with which exclusive AVS is in association, it has already been observed that exclusive AVS differs from ANS and inclusive AVS in so far as it allows interaction with indefinite NPs. However, we have also tried to draw attention to the fact that many indefinite NPs which occur with exclusive AVS appear to require either a generic or a specific interpretation. (8.4a) is a statement concerning all teachers and in (8.4b) a particular general seems to be under discussion, the desired interpretation being *One of the generals has commanded the army himself*.

>(8.4)   a A teacher should clean the blackboard himself.
>   b A general has commanded the army himself.

Hence, it appears to be the case that, after all, exclusive AVS is not that much different from inclusive AVS and ANS, and indeed, non-generic, non-specific indefinites are not as easy to make sense of.

>(8.5)   a ??A prince kissed Sleeping Beauty awake himself.
>   b ??A woman was driving the car herself.

Similarly, the indefinite pronoun *someone* seems to yield inadequate results as long as it is not read specifically. This also seems to point in the direction that exclusive AVS preferably interacts with NPs denoting uniquely identifiable referents:

(8.6) a ??Suddenly, someone opened the door himself.
       b ??Someone wrote me a letter himself.

On the other hand, the related indefinite pronoun *anyone*, which is always non-specific, is acceptable with exclusive AVS, cf. (8.7).

(8.7) a Would anyone like to try that himself?
       b I wonder if anyone would find the answer to such a question himself.

It is also possible to construct exclusive AVS with the negative indefinite pronoun *nobody*. Here, an interesting contrast arises to the sentence without the intensifier. A sentence like (8.8a) means that (disregarding tense) it is not the case that there is an x such that x comes, i.e. (8.9a). The same sentence with the intensifier (8.8b), however, does imply that somebody came, cf. (8.9b). This, however, does not mean that exclusive AVS always claims the physical existence of a referent, as the generic example in (8.4a) makes clear.

Note that given the existence of an example like (8.8), there is at least one exception to the rule stated initially that sentences containing exclusive AVS entail the relevant sentences without it.

(8.8) a Nobody came.
       b Nobody came himself.

(8.9) a $\neg \exists x \, (\text{come}(x))$
       b $\exists x \, (\text{come}(x))$

In addition to that, quantified NPs do not block exclusive AVS, cf. (8.10). After all, the referents of these NPs cannot be uniquely identified. Moreover, and as already mentioned, exclusive AVS is possible with interrogative pronouns too.

(8.10) a Some/many/all presidents came themselves.
        b Some/many/all people wash their cars themselves.

(8.11) Who/which president came himself?

Hence, it seems to be the case that the referential properties of the NP exclusive AVS interacts with do not matter at all. The question, however, that remains to be answered is why certain sentences involving indefinite NPs are odd. An answer may be linked to the fact that exclusive AVS, just as the two other uses of intensifiers, evokes alternatives to the referent of the NP it interacts with (its focus, as it were) and that certain NPs do not easily allow the evoking of alternatives. Recall that precisely this constraint explained a number of odd cases in connection with ANS.

This takes us immediately to some remarks concerning the semantic properties of the NPs which exclusive AVS is constructed with as well as to a discussion about the relation between focus and alternatives. Recall that inclusive AVS imposes a restriction on its focus NP to the effect that the relevant referent has to be human. ANS is unrestricted and allows [±human] head NPs. Exclusive AVS lies somewhere in the middle. Its focus NP must have the feature [+animate], i.e. humans as well as (higher) animals are possible referents, cf. (8.12):

(8.12)   a You must decode the message yourself.
         b My dog managed to open the kitchen door himself.
         c *The vase broke itself.

An additional constraint is that the referent in question must be able to perform an activity on an intentional basis. This is why we only find NPs denoting agentive referents in association with exclusive AVS. In other words, it is sensitive to the thematic role of an agent and blocks every other role apart from it, cf. (8.13). On a thematic role hierarchy like agent > experiencer > patient > theme, exclusive AVS defines a cut-off point between agent and experiencer.

(8.13)   a Paul opened the window himself. (agent, exclusive)
         b I have heard Pavarotti myself.[1] (experiencer, only inclusive)
         c He has been sentenced to three years in prison himself. (patient, only inclusive)

Exclusive AVS is also adequate with NPs whose referents are animate and agentive only by extension. Therefore, NPs denoting forms of organisation are possible too:

(8.14)   a The authority exercises the power itself.
         b The WHO is used to doing such things itself.

To conclude from the above observations that exclusive AVS merely requires agentive NPs would not be correct, though, as the following examples make clear. Note that *itself* in (8.15) is possible under the adnominal interpretation.

(8.15)   a *The wind opened the kitchen door itself$_{exclusive}$.
         b *The lightning set fire to the belltower itself$_{exclusive}$.

Moreover, double agentives show that exclusive AVS cannot interact with just any agentive, animate NP, but that it must be in association with the subject (except for the German *by*-phrase). In other words, agentivity and animacy as such are not sufficient and another feature is necessary which may, as indicated at the beginning, be captured with the notion of centrality.

(8.16)   a The scientist ran the rat through the maze himself/*itself.
          b He galloped the horse through the forest himself/*itself.
          c I burped the baby myself/*himself/*herself.

Another point where exclusive AVS is different from ANS, however, on a par with inclusive AVS, is in the relation between focus referent and alternatives evoked. Apparently, exclusive AVS does not follow ANS in building up a relation of centre versus periphery between them based on the inherent properties of the referents concerned. If centrality is at stake, it will have to be interpreted in a different manner. By and large, referents of low rank interact with exclusive AVS, cf. (8.17). We will return to that point in section 8.2.

(8.17)   Our caretaker still waters the roses himself.

What all the points so far discussed have shown is that exclusive AVS imposes different restrictions on its environment than ANS. A comparable statement can be made with regard to the relation between exclusive and inclusive AVS. Recall that nearly all sentences containing inclusive AVS as such do not easily contextualise and have to be embedded into larger context in order to become fully acceptable. We could show that this context-dependence is due to the fact that sentences containing inclusive AVS always give a premise, reason or explanation for some proposition contained in the surrounding discourse. Exclusive AVS is free from such a presupposition and is always perfectly acceptable within the context of the current predication.

The only constraint which has to be satisfied, and which once again shows that exclusive AVS can be counted as a member of the class of focus particles, is that it must be possible to evoke alternatives to the referent of the NP it interacts with. In a universe containing one element only, as e.g. the world before the creation of Eve (disregarding animals), it is clearly unacceptable to use exclusive AVS, and in fact, all types of intensifiers.

(8.18)   ???Adam ploughed the fields himself.

Concerning the semantic differences between exclusive AVS as well as ANS and inclusive AVS, the former brings in a contrast which can roughly be described as one between transfer and non-transfer of the situation under consideration. By transfer of a situation we will understand that e.g. an activity can be passed on to another referent who performs it in somebody's stead. In specific contexts, this contrast may materialise as one between delegation and non-delegation. Exclusive AVS marks the non-transfer of a situation. Although the set of characters involved is the same in (8.19a) and (8.19b) – president versus, say, his minister – only the former implies that the president did not delegate the signing of the treaty to his minister.

> (8.19)   a   The president signed the treaty himself. (exclusive)
>   b   The president himself signed the treaty. (adnominal)

That delegation is at stake becomes clearer as soon as more context is supplied. Consider (8.20a). The second sentence is inadequate because the first suggests that the signing of the treaty was not or could not be delegated. In other words, the president was the only one to sign the treaty. Subsequently, it is unexpected to find the minister sign the treaty too. (8.20a) disregards that x-*self* here is an exclusive particle. (8.20b), by contrast, is well formed because now the second sentence supports the non-transfer of the signing, in fact, it even gives a reason why the transfer did not happen. Finally, (8.20c) shows that ANS does not evoke a contrast between transfer and non-transfer.

> (8.20)   a   The president signed the treaty himself. ?His minister signed it too.
>   b   The president signed the treaty himself. His minister was not allowed to.
>   c   First, the president himself signed the treaty. Then, his minister signed it too.

Nor does inclusive AVS. However hard we try, it is impossible to read the relevant contrast into (8.21). Moreover, it would be inconsistent with the presupposition of inclusive AVS discussed in section 7.4, namely that what is true of the focus must also hold for the relevant alternative values.

> (8.21)   The president could understand his minister's indignation about signing the treaty because he had to sign it himself.

That (non-) transfer or (non-) delegation is at stake in sentences containing exclusive AVS becomes particularly clear under negation. Consider (8.22). The b-sentence is the negative counterpart of the a-sentence, however, both sentences say that a meal was eaten, i.e. that the situation in question took place. What sentences like (8.22) show is that negation does not deny the completion of a situation, but only its execution by a particular agent. Moreover, (8.22b) seems to imply that the eating of the meal by the alternative agent was an authorised process.

> (8.22)   a   Mark ate his meal himself.
>   b   Mark did not eat his meal himself.

The contrast between (8.23a,b) below shows that the execution by an alternative agent is more than merely an implicature because the event of the meal-eating cannot be cancelled. This means that exclusive AVS does indeed influence the truth-conditions of a sentence. (8.22b) is true only in case that somebody apart from Mark ate Mark's meal. The actual reason for the difference in truth conditions between a negative sentence with exclusive AVS and the relevant sentence without it lies in the fact that in case of the latter, the negation interacts with the predication whereas it interacts with exclusive AVS and by extension with the subject NP in the former. Put differently, exclusive AVS shifts the focus of negation, in fact, it attracts it. This is another point in favour of analysing exclusive AVS as a focus particle because focus particles always interact with the descriptive negation, cf. Moser (1992), Löbner (1995).

(8.23)　　a　Mark did not eat his meal, in fact, he threw it away.
　　　　　b　?Mark did not eat his meal himself, in fact, he threw it away.

(8.24a,b) again show that ANS does not arouse the idea of delegation or transfer. Here, we only find a contrast between two people, but not necessarily the authorisation of the meal-eating to somebody else under negation, although, of course, something like that may be read into it. But if we do so, we can easily cancel any effect of delegation implied, cf. (8.25).

(8.24)　　a　He himself ate his meal.
　　　　　b　He himself did not eat his meal.

(8.25)　　He himself did not eat his meal, in fact, he threw it away.

Another point to show that the (non-) transfer of a situation is an effect bound to exclusive AVS can be made on the basis of examples involving VP ellipsis, cf. (8.26). Under a sloppy reading of *his lawn,* (8.26a) means that both Max's lawn and Bill's lawn get mown. However, whereas Max is not involved in the mowing of his lawn (he delegates it), Bill mows his lawn with his own hands and two lawns are mown in the end. The same sentence with ANS does not show a similar effect, cf. (8.26b). Here, only Bill's lawn gets mown. (8.27) makes the meaning of (8.26) more precise and shows that in the case of exclusive AVS, but not with ANS, negation interacts with the subject NP.

(8.26)　　a　Max didn't mow his lawn himself, but Bill did. (both lawns mown)
　　　　　b　Max himself didn't mow his lawn, but Bill did. (only Bill's lawn mown)

(8.27)　　a　not x mows x's lawn and y mows y's lawn
　　　　　b　x not mows x's lawn and y mows y's lawn

Another interesting effect arises under a strict reading of the anaphoric object NP. In order to facilitate this interpretation, we will make the point with a definite NP, which is equivalent to a variable in a strict reading. Consider (8.28). Due to the definite object NP, there is only one lawn under consideration. Since exclusive AVS shifts the focus of negation from predication to subject NP, the only escape hatch in (8.28a) is to interpret the lawn as having been affected twice. The lawn in (8.28b) under ANS ends up less well tended. (8.29) gives this in a slightly more formal representation.

> (8.28)   a   Max didn't mow the lawn himself, but Bill did. (lawn mown twice)
>   b   Max himself didn't mow the lawn, but Bill did. (lawn mown once)

> (8.29)   a   not x mows lawn and y mows lawn
>   b   x not mows lawn and y mows lawn

Exclusive AVS, in contrast to its close paraphrase *alone*, indicates total (non-) transfer of a situation. Whereas (8.30a) appears to say that the entire writing of the autobiography was delegated to a ghostwriter, (8.30b) rather describes an event of collaboration. Note also that *alone* does not imply an intentional act of delegating the situation.

> (8.30)   a   She did not write her autobiography herself.
>   b   She did not write her autobiography alone.

A partial interpretation becomes possible with exclusive AVS too when quantified NPs enter its scope. The writing of the text in (8.31a) and the picking of the apples in (8.31b) are distributed over focus referent and alternatives.

> (8.31)   a   Most of the text I have written myself.
>   b   Some of these apples I picked myself.

Again, it is important not to understand the (non-) delegation of a situation as the essential semantic contribution of exclusive AVS. Talking of non-transfer would be much more adequate. The idea of delegation emerges only in connection with particular foci and predications. (8.32a) easily allows for it since the activities in question may be delegated to a specialist. The drinking of wine in (8.32b), by contrast, is impossible to delegate, but it is an activity that can be transferred to another character.

> (8.32)   a   We put the kitchen and bathroom in ourselves because we couldn't afford anyone to do it. [BNC]
>   b   'Dear Ma'am,' replied Elinor, smiling at the difference of the complaints for which it was recommended, 'how good you

are! But I have just left Marianne in bed, and, I hope, almost asleep; and as I think nothing will be of so much service to her as rest, if you will give me leave, I will drink the wine myself.' [S&S: 167]

Another way of looking at the examples in (8.32) is to say that they show a contrast between obligation and permission similar to G. *lassen*, which is ambiguous between these two interpretations. Hence, we can assign to these examples the canonical form given in (8.33), in which G. *lassen* is represented by the semantic primitive LET. This captures the intuition that the situation is transferred in the negative sentence, but not in the affirmative one.

(8.33) a [x DO[...]] & NOT [x LET[y DO[...]]]
        b NOT [x DO[...]] & [x LET[y DO[...]]]

However, (8.33) does not cover all examples. The transfer of a situation can also materialise as an alternative activity by the focus referent as (8.34a) makes clear. Figuratively speaking, the activity of *going there* is transferred to a letter. Finally, note the option that things may happen by themselves and that this is a valid alternative to the predication containing exclusive AVS, cf. (8.34b). In examples like these, additional assumptions are necessary to recover the alternative agent.

(8.34) a It's quicker to go there yourself (you'll get a copy within about three days) but you can also apply by post, which takes about four months. [BNC]
        b In my experience that sort of shake-up comes along of its own accord when the time is ripe. No need to do anything about it yourself. [CS: 15]

8.2 Responsibility, benefit and suffering

In the same way as we proceeded in the case of inclusive AVS, we will, before discussing possible analyses of exclusive AVS, give an informal and rather indirect account of its semantic contribution as well as of the contexts in which it typically occurs. This will be the aim of the present section.

It has already been mentioned that exclusive AVS, and intensifiers in general, are always in association with an NP and that they evoke alternatives to the referent of that NP. This mainly is the reason why exclusive AVS can be analysed as a focus particle. According to the semantic characteristics of its focus, we can single out three dominant contexts of exclusive AVS. First, the focus referent can be interpreted as the person who is responsible for the actual situation, second, it can be read as its beneficiary and third, the focus

referent can be seen as the one who suffers from the situation, is its maleficiary, so to speak. All these effects appear to depend on or are at least underlined by the presence of the intensifier. Any semantic analysis of exclusive
AVS would have to capture at least these three cases.

As for the first type of context, we can note down as another dominant
characteristic that the focus referent usually possesses a somewhat elevated
status in comparison with the alternatives evoked. We here often find referents of high rank within a hierarchy, referents of importance or significance,
in brief, those who are treated with esteem for whatever reason or simply
enjoy prestige. Consider the examples in (8.35) below.

(8.35)   a   The president signed the treaty himself/personally.
         b   The director came to open the meeting himself/personally.

(8.35a) says that the treaty was signed by the president and not delegated to
some proxy of his. In (8.35b) we find a contrast between the director
and e.g. his deputy for the event of opening the meeting. This in itself
is extremely reminiscent of the contrast between centre and periphery found
to be at the heart of adnominal intensifiers. More so, because NPs denoting
people of low rank would appear inadequate in these positions. For a
possible counterexample, however, cf. (8.17). The alternatives evoked are
always lower in the hierarchy than the focus referent itself, provided that
the referents under consideration belong to a hierarchy. Only this usage of
exclusive AVS can be reasonably well paraphrased by *personally*, and given
that *personally* by and large is restricted to foci of somewhat higher positions,
this is certainly not entirely unexpected. Moreover, it should seem feasible to
relate the observation that the relevant referents are responsible or in charge
of the situation directly to the fact that they are of high rank or, generally
speaking, central, provided that responsibility or centrality is judged with
respect to the situation. As usual, we also provide some authentic material,
cf. (8.36).

(8.36)   a   At first relations were kept quite close by sending a monk
             from Cluny herself or one of her elder daughters to super-
             vise the new foundation and be its first prior; and the abbot
             of Cluny received the professions of all new monks and
             appointed many of the priors himself. [BNC]
         b   'At present Sir David is out of the country', replied his assis-
             tant Rafe Bullock, 'and therefore unable to reply himself.'
             [BNC]

That the notion of responsibility is involved in these cases becomes particularly clear under negation. Although neither the president nor the director
any longer directly participates in the actual situations or events, the examples in (8.37) still characterise the two chiefs as being in charge of them.

Otherwise, they could not delegate them. Note again that the situations are described as taking place, in spite of the negation. These examples typically give the impression that there is a reason why personal involvement of the chief is not the case (lack of time, inclination, etc.).

(8.37) a The president did not sign the treaty himself/personally.
        b The director did not open the meeting himself/personally.

In addition, the idea of responsibility is also often to be found in connection with first person subjects. Again, this must be due to the special status the speaker has in discourse, recall the discussion in section 6.2.

(8.38) a Her aunt lives there and gave her a room, so as to avoid the strife here. But for now she lives over the border in the Dominican Republic. I took her there myself while off duty after being injured by a faulty grenade. [BNC]
        b 'I have had enough of this', he said. 'I am thinking of going there myself to try to sort this out.' [BNC]

With regard to the second dominant context mentioned above, it is noteworthy that the characterisation of the subject referent as the beneficiary of the situation patterns to a high degree with object NPs denoting an entity possessed by the subject referent, cf. (8.39). In contexts like these, exclusive AVS is best paraphrased by *on one's own*. *Personally*, by comparison, is a little misplaced as a gloss here, mainly because it makes the subject referent too pompous for the situation or, by virtue of characterising the subject referent as important, ascribes a status to the situation which it does not deserve.

(8.39) a I make my bed myself/on my own.
        b John polishes his shoes himself/on his own.

(8.40) a In Home Economics, which really means cooking and sewing, I've learned how to install a zipper and make a flat-fell seam, and now I make a lot of my clothes myself because it's cheaper, although they don't always turn out exactly like the picture on the front of the pattern. [LLC]
        b She's now a fully fledged clock 'doc' and can repair her treasures herself. [BNC]

Given that every activity a possessor or owner executes on an item he possesses, which, in addition, affects that item in a positive way, will by default be interpreted to his benefit, it would be reasonable to argue that the interpretation of the subject as a beneficiary is not due to exclusive AVS, but to the surrounding context. Under negation, however, this interpretation persists and since negation destroys it in sentences lacking exclusive AVS, it must be due to the intensifier or at least related to it. Note once again that the situation is described as being completed despite the negation.

(8.41)   a   I do not make my bed myself.
         b   John does not polish his shoes himself.

The above explications are not meant to imply that possessive object NPs always entail a beneficiary reading of the subject NP. Among this group too we find cases in which the subject referent is characterised as being responsible for the actual situation, in particular for the referent of the object NP. In the following authentic examples, cf. (8.42), this reading is strengthened by the fact that the latter is animate and the offspring of the former. A positive effect on a close relative, who can be viewed as an extension of one's own self, is likely to be interpreted as beneficial to the agent.

(8.42)   a   Archibald Geikie somehow learnt the manual alphabet, and
             there being no school for the deaf in Edinburgh at that time
             (Braidwood's Academy had moved to Hackney in 1783),
             undertook the teaching of his son himself. [BNC]
         b   Frantic mother Ashleigh Gaunt had dialled 999 after trying
             in vain to free her baby herself. [BNC]

What the above examples strongly suggest is that there is a certain connection between responsibility on the one hand and benefit on the other. This is probably so because nobody will assume responsibility without there being some benefit. Example (8.43) contains both notions at the same time.

(8.43)   If I had been able to run my own theatre, like Alan Ayckbourn
         or Neil Simon, I would definitely have directed all my plays
         myself. [BNC]

The interpretation of these vague examples narrows as soon as the intensifier is replaced by the two possible glosses *personally* and *on one's own*. Take the additional example in (8.44). Only under the first paraphrase does John become an authority for the preparation of the meal, under the second, he will rather be one of its consumers, its beneficiaries as it were.

(8.44)   John prepared the meal himself/personally/on his own.

Closely related to the idea of benefit is the notion of interest because any situation one benefits from will usually also be in one's interest. The characterisation of the subject referent as the interested party is most clearly perceptible in those situations in which this referent does not gain an immediate material benefit, but only a less tangible one, cf. (8.45) and (8.46). Again, under negation, this effect does not go away.

(8.45)   a   She wrote her autobiography herself.
             b   He always opens his letters himself.

(8.46)   a   She did not write her autobiography herself.
             b   He does not open his letters himself.

When a semantic analysis of exclusive AVS has to be general enough to explain how the intuitions of responsibility and benefit come about, it will, in addition to that, be required to account for the opposite case of a beneficiary, namely a maleficiary. In examples like (8.47), exclusive AVS interacts with an NP the referent of which is the cause as well as the victim of a negative event, i.e. the one who is negatively affected. Naturally, one can find possessive object NPs here too. These examples also seem to say that the responsibility for the hardship caused lies with the subject referent, however, this is a different sense of 'being responsible' than the one under consideration above. One can hardly be in charge of one's hardship.

(8.47)   a   He has ruined his career himself.
             b   She felt that he had caused his hardship himself.

Nevertheless, when all the examples discussed so far appear to indicate that characterising the referent of the subject NP as being responsible for the situation is the common property all contexts exclusive AVS occurs in share, such an assumption must immediately be given up in view of the fact that the negative counterparts of (8.47) do not show a comparable effect any longer, cf. (8.48).

(8.48)   a   He has not ruined his career himself.
             b   She felt that he had not caused his hardship himself.

This is plausible in so far as people are unlikely to take charge of inflicting hardship on themselves, only on others. As a consequence, the effect of (non-) delegation is entirely missing in the maleficiary contexts (which again underlines that it is more adequate to regard (non-) transfer as the essential concept) and hence, an adversative statement based on the semantic primitive LET is ruled out, recall (8.33). Instead, a continuation with a statement in the passive is likely. (8.49) and (8.50) show examples which, depending on the larger context, are open to a beneficiary or maleficiary interpretation. In what respect the subject referent of (8.50a) is supposed to be a beneficiary is, of course, a little difficult to understand, but the example can be made sense of in the context of e.g. unwanted conscription.

(8.49)   a   He did not delete the files himself. He asked Paul to delete them. (beneficiary)
             b   He did not delete the files himself. They were deleted by Paul/a virus. (maleficiary)

(8.50)   a   He did not mutilate his legs himself. He had a doctor do it. (beneficiary)

            b   He did not mutilate his legs himself. It was done (against his will) by a doctor. (maleficiary)

When the beneficiary/maleficiary interpretation of examples containing exclusive AVS is particularly obvious in the presence of a possessive object NP, it should also be possible to find it in reflexive sentences. This is indeed so, however, recall from section 3.2 that English does not formally differentiate between intensifier and reflexive anaphor, but that it, nevertheless, makes sense to regard stressed occurrences of x-*SELF* as in (8.51) as intensifiers. Still, it is not easy to read them as exclusive AVS. ANS here clearly is the preferred interpretation.

(8.51)   a   Bill is tickling himSELF.
            b   Paul killed himSELF.

This is much easier in the corresponding German examples, cf. (8.52), which are also ambiguous between ANS and exclusive AVS.

(8.52)   a   Bill kitzelt sich selbst.
            b   Paul hat sich selbst umgebracht.

That these sentences have two interpretations becomes clear in disambiguating contexts.

(8.53)   a   Who did Paul tickle? – Paul tickled himself. (adnominal)
            b   Who tickled Paul? – Paul tickled himself. (exclusive)

(8.54)   a   Who did Paul kill? – Paul killed himself. (adnominal)
            b   Who killed Paul? – Paul killed himself. (exclusive)

A more indirect way to elicit the exclusive interpretation in reflexive contexts is to use an NP denoting the body or a part thereof instead of the reflexive:

(8.55)   Paul is tickling his body himself.

In German sentences containing exclusive AVS, we often find a dative pronoun in the function of the so-called '*dativus commodi/incommodi*', cf. (8.56) and (8.57). These dative pronouns precisely indicate beneficiary and maleficiary respectively.

(8.56)   Ich backe mir mein Brot selbst. (*dativus commodi* = beneficiary)
          'I bake my own bread.'

(8.57)   Diese Suppe hast du dir selbst eingebrockt. (*dativus incommodi*
         = maleficiary)
         'You've got yourself into a fine mess.'

In English, the PP *for* x-*self* can be used in the meaning of exclusive AVS,
cf. (8.58). Given that *for* generally assigns a goal or beneficiary role, this is a
welcome observation.

(8.58)   a They are well able to collect their food for themselves.
            [BNC]
         b Most hole dwellers have to excavate their homes for them-
            selves and that can be hard work. [BNC]

For a brief summary, let us now take a slightly different perspective. The
above discussion centred around object NPs whose referents are possessed by
the relevant subject referents. Depending on whether the predicate denotes
a positive or a negative effect on the object referent, the subject referent
is characterised either as the beneficiary or the maleficiary of the relevant
situation. We do not have to consider predicates with effected objects
separately because they behave in a comparable manner. In case the object
referent is animate, this characterisation is better described in terms of
responsibility. If there is no possessive object NP, the resulting effect is also
one of responsibility. What we have not discussed yet are intransitive verbs,
but here, *grosso modo*, the subject referent is characterised as being responsible for the situation too, cf.:

(8.59)   a He came/participated/drove himself.
         b He did not come/participate/drive himself.

In all probability, it would not be correct to regard the characterisation of the
subject referent as responsible, as a beneficiary or maleficiary an immediate
semantic contribution of exclusive AVS. For this to be true, these effects
would have to be less heterogeneous and context-dependent. Notice that
beneficiary and maleficiary pattern with verbs expressing positive and negative effect on a one-to-one basis. There must be a more general common
denominator. However, before we dive into a detailed semantic analysis as
well as an appraisal of the proposals made so far in the literature, let us take
a look at some more particular contextual effects.

Recall that we suggested that exclusive AVS is a focus particle because it is
always associated with an NP and evokes alternatives to this NP. Due to the
fact that exclusive AVS always interacts with agentive NPs, focusing and the
subsequent evoking of alternatives result in a set of agents, one of which
possesses a special status in so far as it is the one who is either responsible for
the actual situation or affected by it, be it in a positive or negative way. We
here disregard that only one of these agents participates in the situation.

Generally speaking, one of these agents is different from the rest of the set and a substantial part of the current investigation is devoted to making this difference precise.

Since some of the examples above characterising the subject referent as responsible involve referents of high rank and oppose them to less important alternatives, a reasonable conjecture would be to say that exclusive AVS orders focus and alternatives in the same manner as adnominal intensifiers, namely in terms of centre and periphery according to the properties of the referents. This view is supported by the pair of sentences below taken from Edmondson and Plank (1978: 406).

> (8.60)   a The King plowed the Royal fields himself.
>   b ?The serfs plowed the Royal fields themselves.

Let us also look at (8.61) in this context. Here, the focus is unspecified with respect to rank or position in a hierarchy. Still, Richard is easily understood as being the head or centre of a business or organisation.

> (8.61)   Richard deals with selected clients himself.

That such a conclusion is premature, however, is made clear by the following minimal pair where exclusive AVS readily interacts with a peripheral referent, but ANS in the same context yields less acceptable results, cf. the contrast between (8.62a) and (8.62b).

> (8.62)   a The director wants his secretary to make the coffee herself.
>   b ?The director wants his secretary herself to make the coffee.

Neither does exclusive AVS show aversion to the remaining contexts where adnominal intensifiers turned out to be clearly unacceptable, recall the discussion of ANS in section 6.2. In (8.63a) exclusive AVS interacts with a referent which is defined via another; it is not restricted to the defining one as ANS is, cf. (8.63b). In (8.64a) it is not bound to the subject of consciousness although there clearly is one present. Again, ANS sounds odd in the same context, cf. (8.64b).[2]

> (8.63)   a Bill knows that his brother would feed the dog himself.
>   b ?Bill knows that his brother himself would feed the dog.

> (8.64)   a John wondered whether Mary would be able to solve the problem herself.
>   b ?John wondered whether Mary herself would be able to solve the problem.

Also, note that it poses no problem for multiple cases of exclusive AVS to be represented in one and the same sentence. Such a constellation is clearly ruled out for ANS on the grounds that there can be only one central character within a certain discourse domain. (8.65) exemplifies this contrast. Examples like (8.65) indicate that the idea of centrality can only be maintained if its scope is restricted to the predication exclusive AVS is part of. This, however, calls for an explanation for why (8.60b) is odd.

(8.65)   a   I mow my lawn myself and you mow yours yourself.
         b   ??I myself mow my lawn and you yourself mow yours.

What the above discussion has shown is that exclusive AVS does not obey the constraint demanding interaction with a central referent, if this interaction is interpreted in the same manner as in the case of ANS. However, although exclusive AVS seems less restricted in this respect, this does not mean that it did not impose such requirements on its context. Consider the following stereotypical situation.

A woman, say Ms Jones, takes her car to the garage one morning and hands it over for repair to one of the mechanics. Then she leaves. She is followed by several other customers who also leave their cars at the garage for repair. As soon as a sufficient number of cars has arrived, the mechanics start distributing the work of the day. Now suppose one of the mechanics states (8.66):

(8.66)   Smith is going to take care of Ms Jones's car himself.

As one might expect, this statement characterises Smith as responsible for the repairing of Ms Jones's car. The question to be asked here is after the status of Smith in the garage. As far as I can see, in the present context he can only be the head mechanic. Otherwise, he could not assume responsibility for a particular car or, alternatively, would not be free to decide which car to repair. In other words, exclusive AVS in (8.66) does indeed characterise Smith as central with respect to the remaining mechanics. Note again that this interpretation is stable under negation:

(8.67)   Smith is not going to take care of Ms Jones's car himself.

But now note what happens when we replace Ms Jones's car by one owned by the subject referent, i.e. Smith. Consider (8.68). Now, Smith is not necessarily read as the head mechanic of the garage any longer. Here, he can be any of the mechanics and it is immediately plausible that nobody other than Smith should look after Smith's car. In brief, Smith in the context of repairing Ms Jones's car is interpreted as the head mechanic, in the context of repairing his own car, Smith can be an ordinary mechanic, in fact, he could be anybody. Again, a semantic analysis of exclusive AVS would have to be able to explain why this should be so.

(8.68)   Smith is going to take care of his car himself.

Consider another, in a way stereotypical situation. A man named Bob invites a couple of friends for dinner at his home. After the meal, one of the guests rises from his chair and utters (8.69), much to the surprise of the remaining guests and particularly Bob himself. What is wrong in this example? Notice that there is only one person at the party who could felicitously utter (8.69), and this is Bob, i.e. the host. He could do so after one of the guests had offered to do the washing up.

(8.69)   I will do the washing up myself.

Before we come to a summary of these effects, let us briefly look at one final situation. Imagine, for the purpose of illustration, an informal get-together of some friends who end up discussing personal habits. Suddenly, somebody states (8.70). This should yield more than the raising of an eyebrow and the question once again is why.

(8.70)   I don't brush my teeth myself.

What the examples in the three situations above again underline is that the subject referent, by virtue of the relevant NP being in association with exclusive AVS, receives a special status in and with respect to the situation. This special status can manifest itself in his relation to the referent of the object NP. If the subject referent is not the owner of the object referent, exclusive AVS characterises him as being in an elevated position. Otherwise, he would not be allowed to affect an entity he does not possess. If, by contrast, the subject referent does own the object referent, he has a special status with regard to the object referent almost by definition because everybody is responsible for one's own belongings. Therefore, he is not interpreted as being of high rank which accounts for the contrast between (8.66) and (8.68). Note that such sentences are the preferred context for the exemplification of exclusive AVS.

A similar explanation offers itself for (8.69). This statement in the context described is odd because a guest at a party does not have the authority to touch the property of his host without permission. Neither does he own the dishes nor is he above his host in rank before the background of their being washed up.

Finally, (8.70) is not likely to occur in this context because here authority is transferred for an activity which is restricted to one's own responsibility. Note that we are now in a position to explain why (8.60b) appears inadequate. There, the serfs do not own the fields they plough, i.e. they have no authority over them, and they are in too low a position to assume authority by themselves. (8.71) is, by comparison, a well-formed sentence.

(8.71)   The serfs plowed their fields themselves.

The discussion above has shown that exclusive AVS does indeed characterise its focus referent in a certain way and assigns it a special status in comparison with the alternatives evoked. However, it has also become clear that this special status depends on the predication exclusive AVS occurs in. Otherwise, modifying the object NP should not matter. In this respect, exclusive AVS is different from ANS which characterises its focus referent as central on the basis of its inherent properties. In terms of information structure, this means that the scope of ANS is co-extensive with its focus, but that exclusive AVS has scope over the entire predication.

8.3 Agentivity

There are two studies pertaining to the analysis of exclusive AVS which explicitly draw on the observation that it is always in association with an agentive NP. Edmondson and Plank (1978) propose that exclusive AVS characterises the referent of that NP as the most directly involved agent, whereas Browning (1993) sees its main contribution in reemphasising the assignment of the agent role to that NP. (8.73) gives Browning's analysis of a prototypical example like (8.72). Here, *her* is assumed to be identical with Mary.

(8.72)   Mary wrote this memo herself.

(8.73)   Mary(agent) wrote this memo(patient) & her=(agent)

The following remarks apply to Edmondson and Plank as well as Browning because most direct agentivity and reemphasis of agentivity are, from the present perspective, comparable concepts. Both try to capture the idea of a high degree of agentivity. Where the two approaches differ is in the assumption of alternative, less agentive values for the agent NP.

From my point of view, either approach over-estimates the importance of agentivity while neglecting other crucial factors. Edmondson and Plank claim that exclusive AVS interacts with an NP bearing an agent role the referent of which is more agentive than other alternative referents (this is what most direct involvement of an agent boils down to), whereas Browning says that the relevant agent is more agentive than an agent normally is. Either analysis holds that an agentive NP differs in the degree of its agentivity in a sentence with and without exclusive AVS. But when we once again look at prototypical examples of exclusive AVS, it cannot go unnoticed that Adam in either sentence of (8.74) below does exactly the same job, no more and no less. Therefore, the degree of his agentivity must be exactly the same. As for the alternatives evoked, these are not involved at all and can at most be regarded as alternative agents. Under such a strict interpretation, the semantic contribution of exclusive AVS according to Edmondson and Plank as well as Browning is in fact zero. Agent reemphasis and most direct involvement of an agent are notions which are difficult to motivate.

(8.74) a Adam took his daughter and carried her back to bed.
        b Adam took his daughter and carried her back to bed himself.

Notice that under negation, most examples do indeed seem to say that the focus of the intensifier is least involved, i.e. is still a little involved, because by delegating it, the relevant referent still controls the situation. However, malefactive contexts such as (8.75) below clearly contradict such a view.

(8.75) She did not cause her death herself.

Although it can hardly be denied that exclusive AVS requires an agentive NP to interact with and imposes a constraint on that NP to this effect, viewing agentivity as its essential semantic contribution fails to account for all the phenomena discussed in section 8.2. Recall that exclusive AVS always characterises its focus as somehow special with respect to the alternatives evoked and that the way in which this special status materialises heavily depends on the predication. We mainly discussed three cases: i) the focus referent is responsible for the situation; ii) he is its beneficiary; and iii) he is its maleficiary. The first case occurs with foci of high rank, the second with predicates denoting a positive effect and the third with those denoting a negative effect. Combinations of these are to a certain extent possible. They are not supposed to represent an exhaustive classification. (8.76) shows some additional examples.

(8.76) a The Lord Yahweh says this: 'I am going to look after my
           flock myself and keep it in my view ...' [LLC]
        b When cooking with the children we want to finish with
           something eatable, so we are likely to add the liquid care-
           fully ourselves. [BNC]
        c She felt that he had caused his hardship himself.

The important feature of these interpretations is that they are stable under negation and that they therefore have the status of presuppositions. In the following, we will regard these presuppositions as the primary semantic contribution of exclusive AVS and will try to find their common denominator.

8.4 Centrality in situation

In comparison with adverbal inclusive intensifiers, whose semantic analysis poses intricate problems, the semantic contribution of exclusive AVS is, relatively speaking, less difficult to specify. For the reasons given in section 2.2, exclusive AVS can be regarded as a focus particle in the same manner as ANS and inclusive AVS. Essential to the understanding of exclusive AVS is that it also structures sets of referents into a central element (the referent of the focus) and peripheral elements (the alternatives evoked). Similarly to inclusive AVS, adverbal exclusive intensifiers have scope over the sentence in which they are contained. This means that the focus referent is characterised as central only against the background of the remaining open sentence. A valid generalisation is to say that the focus is marked as central *in* the situation denoted by the predication.

An important property of sentences containing exclusive AVS, in contrast to those lacking it, is that under negation, they still assert and do not deny that the situations described by these sentences take place, cf. the contrast between (8.77) and (8.78). What the negative counterpart to a sentence like (8.78a) states is that the relevant activity was performed by a referent, more precisely an agent, other than the one denoted by the subject NP.

(8.77) a Max repaired his bike.
    b Max did not repair his bike.

(8.78) a Max repaired his bike himself.
    b Max did not repair his bike himself.

This points in the direction of analysing the contribution that exclusive AVS makes to the meaning of a sentence in terms of a presupposition and a step in this direction is indeed made in König and Siemund (1996a). They depart from the observation that sentences which express a possessive relation between two arguments represent an unproportionally high share of the cases used to exemplify exclusive AVS and suggest that this is so because the presupposition of exclusive AVS is particularly well accommodated in these examples, cf.:

(8.79) a Paul washes his car himself.
    b WASH SELF (a, b)
    c POSS(a, b)

Such an analysis, however, fails to account for examples like the ones given below. Here, the subject referent does not own the object referent.

(8.80) a The prime minister is going to talk to the strikers himself.
    b The chancellor is going to make the statement himself.

Therefore, König and Siemund proceed to hypothesise that the presupposition of exclusive AVS is a condition on the relevant sentences to the effect that they must always express a relation between the two arguments apart from the one expressed by the main predication, cf.:

(8.81)   a P SELF (a, b)
        b R(a, b) & R≠P

The problem with a formulation according to (8.81), as the authors themselves note, is that the relation specified is not precise enough. Moreover, (8.81) does not cover exclusive AVS in intransitive sentences.

(8.82)   a I heard that Nasser intended to come himself, but in the end he appointed a substitute. [CS, p. 117]
        b So Mrs Thatcher, demonstrating hitherto unsuspected social graces, decided to step into the breach herself. [BNC]

Examples such as (8.80) and (8.82) rather seem to express that the subject referent is responsible for or interested in the situation described by the sentence. Therefore, König and Siemund propose to analyse the presupposition of exclusive AVS as an obligation of the subject referent with regard to putting into existence the relevant situation. (8.83) and (8.84) depict this analysis for intransitive and transitive predicates respectively.

(8.83)   a P SELF (a)
        b □ CAUSE(a, P(x))

(8.84)   a P SELF (a, b)
        b □ CAUSE(a, P(x, b))

The fact that the focus referent is characterised as responsible for the situation in question, whereas the alternatives evoked are not, allows for a generalisation of the semantic contribution of exclusive AVS in terms of centre and periphery. The set of referents under consideration is divided precisely along that line and the parallel to adnominal intensifiers lies in this ability to structure sets. The structure imposed on the relevant set remains stable under negation with both ANS and exclusive AVS.

However, there are a few cases which are not covered by the above analysis. Although examples like (8.85) at first sight give the impression that they could be subsumed under this analysis, because they too seem to state that the subject referent is to be held responsible for the calamity described, a closer look reveals that this effect is not stable under negation, cf. (8.86). Therefore, it cannot belong to the presupposition of exclusive AVS. Moreover, the sense of responsibility under consideration here cannot be equated with an obligation to bring about a certain event.

(8.85)   a John has ruined his career himself.
        b She has brought about her hardship herself.

(8.86)   a John has not ruined his career himself.
        b She has not brought about her hardship herself.

In order to be able to cover such cases too, König and Siemund (1996b) relax the formulations in (8.83) and (8.84) even further. They now suggest to describe the presupposition of exclusive AVS as follows:

> Sentences containing exclusive adverbal intensifiers presuppose that of all the referents under consideration in a certain situation, the one denoted by the focus constituent is maximally affected by the activity described in the sentence and hence central. [p. 292; my translation]

On the basis of what has been said so far, the semantic contribution of exclusive AVS can be summarised as shown in (8.87). It structures a proposition into a focused part and a backgrounded part, cf. (8.87a), and evokes alternatives to the focus. (8.87b) states that a sentence containing exclusive AVS entails the corresponding sentence without it. The interesting part is the presupposition (8.87c), which captures the intuition that the focus referent is always the affected entity in the situation denoted by the relevant sentence.

(8.87) a assertion: $x\text{-}self\,[\lambda x\,(\rho(x)),\,\alpha]$
        b entailment: $\rho(\alpha)$
        c presupposition: $\text{AFFECT}(\rho,\,\alpha)$

The major problem with the formulation given in (8.87) is that the predicate AFFECT cannot be made more precise. However, even this rather indeterminate definition accounts for a number of conspicuous effects. It can explain, for instance, that negating a sentence containing exclusive AVS never denies that the corresponding situation takes place. This follows from the fact that the focus referent is always characterised as affected. And where there is an effect, there must be a cause, i.e. some event. Moreover, it makes clear why intensified sentences often imply that the focus referent does not delegate the activity in question to somebody else and, conversely, that negated intensified sentences precisely seem to claim that a situation is delegated. This is so because it is implausible for someone to do a job for somebody else, i.e. to affect him, without there being some sort of incentive or compensation. Finally, it becomes apparent why delegation is not at issue in situations affecting the focus referent in a negative way. Here, the resulting effect is not desired.

What is not so adequately captured in (8.87) is the intuition that, in a wide variety of examples, the focus referent is characterised as responsible for, or in a, situation. As pointed out in section 8.2, this effect is often accompanied by an elevated position of the focus referent in comparison with the alternatives evoked, always judged against the background of the actual situation, recall (8.80). In view of examples like these, it appears to be necessary to move a step back and to formulate the presupposition of exclusive AVS in even more general terms. The structuring of sets into a central and related peripheral elements certainly is the generalisation of choice, not least because it allows an analysis of adverbal exclusive intensifiers in the same spirit as adnominal intensifiers, cf. (8.88) below.

> (8.88)   Adverbal exclusive intensifiers structure a set of possible agents in a situation S into a central agent X and oppose it to peripheral agents Y.

Under such a general formulation, then, mainly three subcases can be distinguished, cf. (8.89). The relevant factors these subcases depend on are the properties of the focus referent, the predicate type and whether there is a possessive relation between subject and object referent. As indicated above, (8.89a) is mainly found with foci higher in rank than the alternatives evoked. The lion's share of (8.89b,c) is made up of examples with the aforementioned possessive relation. Whether the focus referent is characterised as beneficiary or maleficiary, by contrast, clearly depends on the type of predicate involved.

> (8.89)   a   X is responsible for S.
> b   X is the beneficiary of S.
> c   X is the maleficiary of S.

The following examples illustrate these subcases:

> (8.90)   a   The director led the negotiations himself.
> b   She weaves her hair herself and she cuts it herself.
> c   Paul has ruined his career himself.

Examples that do not at first reading correspond to the above criteria require accommodation. (8.91a) is not appropriate because the task of picking ministers lies with the chancellor and not the state-secretaries. In (8.91b) the focus referent is, contrary to what exclusive AVS indicates, not the beneficiary, and the target of the negative effect described in (8.91c) is not the focus referent himself, but somebody else.

> (8.91)   a   The state-secretary picked the ministers himself.
> b   I prefer to make your tea myself.
> c   Paul has ruined Kathy's career himself.

Notice, finally, the following way of looking at the contrast between exclusive and inclusive AVS. The two types of adverbal intensifiers are equivalent with respect to: i) the status of being focus particles; ii) the evoking of alternatives to their focus; and iii) the characterisation of the focus as central and the alternatives as peripheral. Where they differ is in the fact that the kind of centrality involved is stable under negation with exclusive AVS whereas it changes in the case of inclusive AVS. Consider the examples of exclusive AVS in (8.92) and those of inclusive AVS in (8.93).

(8.92)   a I handle all my cases myself.
          b I don't handle all my cases myself.

(8.93)   a I like it that way myself.
          b I don't like it that way myself.

Either sentence in (8.92) characterises the subject referent as being responsible or the beneficiary of the situation. This is what makes him central. (8.93) is different. Whereas (8.93a) makes the subject referent central with respect to the property 'like it that way', (8.93b) does so against the background of 'not like it that way'. One possible way to capture this difference is to say that exclusive AVS marks a character as central on a presuppositional level whereas inclusive AVS does so on the level of assertion.

Notes

1 Note that in certain contexts the exclusive interpretation of AVS appears also to be possible with experiencer subjects, but verbs of perception such as *see, hear, feel,* etc. are known to allow agentive experiencer subjects besides 'pure' experiencer subjects:

    (i) I've only been told about the accident. I didn't see it myself.

2 The oddity of these examples disappears if the alternatives evoked by the intensified NPs are sought in the wider context rather than within the relevant sentences (e.g. the children of Bill's brother/of Mary instead of Bill/John).

9 Summary

The present study has aimed at dealing with a number of issues pertaining to the analysis of intensifiers. The major results can be summarised thus:

1   It is necessary to distinguish three uses of intensifiers: adnominal intensifiers, adverbal inclusive intensifiers and adverbal exclusive intensifiers. Each type of usage possesses particular syntactic and semantic properties. The most persuasive argument for this differentiation comes from the fact that all three types can occur in one and the same sentence while being in association with the same NP, cf. *Bill himself has himself not found the answer himself.* Although being a laboratory sentence, such examples indicate that the three uses of intensifiers make different contributions to the meaning of an utterance and represent a clear case of polysemy and not of vagueness.

2   It is reasonable to regard intensifiers as expressions interacting with the focus structure of a sentence. Intensifiers structure a sentence into a focused or highlighted part and a backgrounded part. The major point in favour of such a view is that they are prosodically prominent and always evoke alternatives to the NP they are in association with. Moreover, intensifiers show a high degree of positional variability. Nevertheless, this view is not entirely uncontroversial. Intensifiers differ from established members of the group of focus particles in that they are restricted to nominal foci. Also, that English intensifiers show agreement with their focus in person, number and gender deviates from standard assumptions.

3   Adnominal intensifiers are adjuncts and can be analysed as endocentric expansions of the NP they interact with. They are adjoined to maximal projections and always occur at the right periphery of a phrase. Adverbal intensifiers, by contrast, are adjuncts of the VP, which they expand endocentrically. In spite of being part of the VP, adverbal intensifiers interact with an NP. The clear difference in meaning between the two major types makes it impossible to analyse adverbal intensifiers as occurrences of adnominal intensifiers which have been moved into the VP.

4 The syntactic distribution of intensifiers is regulated by well-defined constraints. Adnominal intensifiers modifying subjects can be dislocated to a position before the NP they interact with as well as behind the finite verb. A necessary prerequisite is a double focus on the sentences concerned. In English, dislocation behind the finite verb is only possible if the intensifier cannot be mistaken for the reflexive anaphor, with which it is formally alike. Adnominal intensifiers cannot be dislocated from within object positions or adverbials.

There is an asymmetry observable between English and German concerning the intensification of pronouns. Whereas there are no restrictions in German, English imposes a constraint to the effect that only pronouns in subject position can be intensified. This constraint can be motivated on grounds of language economy. Sequences like *himself himself* and *him himself* are reduced to *himself* due to over-specification.

5 As for adverbal intensifiers, these can be topicalised in German, but not in English. Moreover, topicalisation is restricted to adverbal exclusive intensifiers and it is necessary that the relevant sentences possess a double focus. Passivisation of adverbal intensifiers is only possible in German. The reason appears to be the more relaxed word order in German in comparison with English. Adnominal intensifiers, by contrast, pose no problems.

Adverbal intensifiers show interesting properties in the presence of additional scope bearing elements. As it turns out, inclusive intensifiers always have scope over such elements (they take wide scope) whereas exclusive intensifiers are always within their scope (they have narrow scope). This distribution is clearly connected to the semantics of the two adverbal intensifiers. In German, these scope relations are reflected in the relative order of the relevant expressions. In English, by contrast, semantic scope is not discernible on the surface which, again, is due to its relatively fixed word order. We are here confronted with the effects of a fairly general phenomenon.

English and German adverbal inclusive intensifiers differ with regard to the range of possible foci. Whereas English inclusive intensifiers are confined to interacting with subjects, German also allows direct and indirect objects. Nevertheless, there appears to be a constraint which requires the argument ranking highest in terms of case hierarchy and thematic hierarchy to be selected.

The differentiation between inclusive and exclusive adverbal intensifiers goes hand in hand with a number of more subtle phenomena. Inclusive intensifiers show a preference for indefinite object NPs, exclusive intensifiers for definite object NPs. Moreover, verb alternations can influence the interpretation of adverbal intensifiers. Finally, tense and aspect appear to have a certain bearing.

6 Although the final word on the distribution of reflexive anaphors in English has yet to be spoken, it could be shown that the analysis of

intensifiers can provide valuable insights for our understanding of the underlying processes. Locally free or untriggered reflexives have a lot in common with adnominal intensifiers in terms of their semantic contribution as well as their prosodic features. They are always stressed and make the referent of the NP they interact with (their antecedent) central. The conclusion arrived at in this study is that it is reasonable to analyse the majority of occurrences of x-*self* violating the Binding Conditions as adnominal intensifiers, however, as those lacking an overt head NP. Sequences like [*him himself*] and [*her herself*] are reduced to [e *himself*] and [e *herself*] respectively for reasons of language economy.

7   It could be shown that it is not necessary to assume a separate use type of intensifiers for role reversal structures. Intensifiers in sentences like *Lucrezia poisoned Lorenzo, and was herself poisoned by Cesare* can be subsumed under the adnominal variety because these coordinations can be split up into two separate sentences which are equivalent in meaning to the original formulation, cf. *Lucrezia poisoned Lorenzo. She herself was poisoned by Cesare.* The role reversal observed has a cause outside the semantic contribution that the intensifier makes.

Let us now come to a summary of the main points concerning the semantic analysis of intensifiers.

1   Although intensifiers appear to make a scalar contribution in terms of likelihood, expectancy or remarkability in certain cases, this is not the common denominator underlying all the data available. Intensifiers do not characterise individuals as least likely/expected or most remarkable participants in a situation, and if such effects creep in, they can be attributed to the context. Hence, it would be entirely misplaced to draw parallels to German *sogar* or English *even.*

It could be demonstrated that it is much more reasonable to regard intensifiers as operators which structure sets of entities into a central element (the focus value) and peripheral elements related to it (the alternative values). The differentiation into centre and periphery is to be understood in the sense of König (1991). The semantic contribution in terms of centre and periphery is most obvious in the case of adnominal intensifiers. Nevertheless, this concept is also applicable to the adverbal uses.

Within the realms of focus structure, it is possible to say that focus and scope are co-extensive in the case of adnominal intensifiers. They are restricted to the relevant NP. Adverbal intensifiers, by contrast, have scope over the sentence they are contained in. This leads to different interpretations of centrality. In the case of adnominal intensifiers, centrality is established on the basis of the inherent properties the focus referent has. Adverbal intensifiers, by contrast, make the referent of the focus central against the background of the property/situation denoted by the relevant sentence.

2 Concerning the range of NPs which intensifiers can modify, there is much more diversity than previously assumed. Large amounts of data drawn both from the corpora available as well as from casual reading can leave no doubt about that. However, it is necessary to deal with the three uses of intensifiers separately since each of them has different requirements.

Adnominal intensifiers show hardly any constraints. They can intensify NPs denoting human as well as non-human referents. Human referents can be of high or low rank as long as it is possible to interpret them as central with respect to alternative referents. The majority of non-human referents is made up of material objects, but we also find times, locations and abstract concepts. Note that the human/non-human distinction is a typological parameter of variation. Nevertheless, adnominal intensifiers can only modify NPs which are definite descriptions in the sense of Russell (1905). Since this constraint is purely semantic in nature, there is no perfect correlation with respect to definite and indefinite NPs. Intensifiers can interact with indefinite NPs if these NPs allow a specific or generic interpretation. This constraint appears to be intimately connected to the semantic contribution of adnominal intensifiers, namely to characterise the relevant referents as central.

By comparison, the distribution of NPs which adverbal intensifiers can modify is governed by more specific rules. Adverbal inclusive intensifiers are most rigid in this respect because they require NPs denoting human referents. The exclusive use of adverbal intensifiers is slightly less restricted. Here, it is sufficient for the relevant referents to be animate. Nevertheless, they must be agentive. The referential properties of the NPs in question have turned out to be somewhat difficult to judge. Although it would not be justified to assume a constraint on definiteness in the same manner as with adnominal intensifiers, pure indefinite descriptions are far from being compatible with adverbal intensifiers. If indefinite NPs are involved, they tend to receive a specific or generic interpretation, as is the case with adnominal intensifiers.

3 Role reversal structures can be analysed as S-topics or cases of '*I-Topikalisierung*' (I-topicalisation) in the sense of Büring (1997) and Jacobs (1996). This analogy is possible because these structures possess the necessary prosodic features, have an adversative implicature, etc. It can be shown that the role reversal observed is not a contribution of the intensifier, but that it can be accounted for on the basis of the properties this particular type of topicalisation has. The specific contribution of the intensifier consists in marking a topic. In terms of information structure, the topic can be regarded as the central piece of information.

4 Going over the semantic properties of adverbal intensifiers with a fine-tooth comb yields the following results. There are two criteria which

determine whether a given sentence permits the inclusive or the exclusive intensifier. If the situation denoted by the sentence is repeatable, but not transferable (i.e. possible to execute by a referent other than the one denoted by the focus), the inclusive variety is selected. If it can be transferred, but not repeated, then the exclusive intensifier is invariably chosen. If the situation is both repeatable and transferable, the interpretation of the intensifier is ambiguous, i.e. either variety is permitted. In other words, a repeatable situation is a necessary condition for inclusive intensifiers, and so is a transferable situation for exclusive intensifiers. Sentences describing non-repeatable, non-transferable situations block adverbal intensifiers.

Whether a situation is repeatable or transferable correlates with its aktionsart, at least to a certain extent. Moreover, the properties of the object NP matter, if present. Indefinite object NPs are more likely to co-occur with inclusive intensifiers whereas definite object NPs roughly correlate with exclusive intensifiers. However, all these effects can be explained on the basis of the two criteria discussed above.

Concerning adverbal inclusive intensifiers proper, it has become apparent that there are a number of prototypical contexts in which they occur. Most prominent are requests, offers and reproaches, but also those contexts in which the referent of the NP modified by the intensifier is characterised as possessing particular knowledge or experience about the current situation, or makes an expression of empathy towards another character. A noteworthy property of these requests, offers and reproaches is that they are usually declined, turned down and rejected. Another important context of inclusive intensifiers are conditional or causal subclauses introduced by connectives such as *if, since, because, although*, etc. This observation leads to the generalisation that adverbal inclusive intensifiers typically occur in sentences which give the premise, reason or explanation for another proposition in the previous or following discourse. This is why they are so useful for statements of refusal.

As for adverbal exclusive intensifiers, these are most frequently found in sentences against the background of which the referent of their focus NP has a somewhat distinguished position. This special status may either rest on the fact that the focus referent is responsible for the relevant situation, that he is its beneficiary or its maleficiary. That these characterisations are related to the intensifier becomes apparent under negation, where the effects observed persist.

5   Adverbal inclusive intensifiers appear to share their core meaning with the additive focus particle *also*. Either expression identifies focus value and alternatives evoked with respect to the property denoted by the predication in their scope. However, the two expressions differ both in terms of their functionality and the contribution they make to the meaning of a sentence. Inclusive intensifiers take only nominal foci denoting human referents. In English, they interact only with subjects.

Also shows no restrictions in this respect. Moreover, English *also* can be used as a sentence connector and German *auch* as a scalar additive particle. Although inclusive intensifiers and *also* share their core meaning, which can be analysed in terms of a presupposition, intensifiers contribute something in addition to that, so that it becomes possible to say that sentences containing inclusive intensifiers imply the corresponding sentences containing *also*, but not vice versa. This additional contribution can be analysed as a further presupposition to the effect that there has to be a proposition in the surrounding discourse for which the sentences containing inclusive AVS can be interpreted as a premise, reason or explanation.

6 An analysis of adverbal inclusive intensifiers should depart from the observation that these expressions make the sentence they are contained in extremely context-dependent. The requirement on adequate context is strong enough to render many sentences given as such unacceptable, cf. *Max snores himself.* What this high context-dependence boils down to is the massive generation of implicatures. Additional context is necessary to accommodate them. Another relevant observation is that inclusive intensifiers turn their host sentence into a premise, reason or explanation for another proposition. This proposition can be identified with one of the implicatures produced, namely the one that is contextually relevant. In other words, sentences containing adverbal inclusive intensifiers generate precisely those implicatures which can be understood as consequences of the situations described by them. To give an example, a statement like *Liz wears glasses herself* can imply that *Liz cannot drive in the dark*, and here, the latter proposition can be understood as a consequence of the former.

The conditional relation between the implicature and the sentence producing it is the prerequisite for the most remarkable semantic contribution of inclusive intensifiers. As it turns out, adverbal inclusive intensifiers can be analysed as operators which identify two referents with respect to a conditional schema of the form *if p, then q.* The felicity conditions of inclusive intensifiers require that there is such a conditional schema salient in discourse. The sentence containing the intensifier takes up the antecedent or premise, the implicature derived matches the consequent. The presence of the intensifier allows to draw the conclusion on the basis of the premise given. In the context of the example given above, the relevant conditional schema would be *if you wear glasses, you cannot drive in the dark.*

Although it appears plausible, in view of the implicatures generated, that inclusive intensifiers have specialised themselves to fit into such a conditional schemata, an explanation has to be given for why these implicatures can be produced in the first place. This can be linked to the fact that inclusive intensifiers characterise the referent of their focus as central with regard to the property denoted by the actual sentence. The

262 Intensifiers in English and German

characterisation as central for a property can be understood as an attribution with associated properties which, in turn, form the basis of the implicatures derived. Nevertheless, further research will have to find an answer to the question why adverbal inclusive intensifiers produce precisely those implicatures which can be interpreted as consequences of the situations described by their host sentences.

7   In contrast to adverbal inclusive intensifiers, the contribution that adverbal exclusive intensifiers make to the meaning of a sentence is relatively easy to describe. These intensifiers characterise the referent of their focus as central in the situation denoted by the sentence they are contained in. The centrality of this referent in comparison with the alternatives evoked can be due to basically three properties. First, it may be the responsible or interested party in the actual situation. Second, it is possible that the focus referent is the beneficiary and third, the maleficiary of the situation. These individual characterisations are heavily context-dependent so that it is reasonable to assume the more general contribution in terms of centrality as basic. One could also say that the focus referent is characterised as the focal point in the situation. Since this semantic contribution is stable under negation, it has the status of a presupposition.

Bibliography

Abney, S. (1987) 'The English Noun Phrase in its Sentential Aspects', unpublished PhD dissertation, MIT, Cambridge, MA.

Abraham, W. (1997) 'Sundry paradigms of reflexives and anaphora: their semantic and DT-semantic representations', *Conference on Reflexives and Reciprocals*, Boulder, CO, handout.

Altmann, H. (1976) *Die Gradpartikeln im Deutschen*, Tübingen: Niemeyer.

—— (1978) *Gradpartikelprobleme*, Tübingen: Gunter Narr.

—— (1981) *Formen der 'Herausstellung' im Deutschen*, Tübingen: Niemeyer.

Anderson, S.R. (1972) 'How to get *even*', *Language* 48, 893–906.

Baker, C.L. (1978) *Introduction to Generative-Transformational Syntax*, Englewood Cliffs, NJ: Prentice Hall.

—— (1995) 'Contrast, discourse prominence, and intensification, with special reference to locally free reflexives in British English', *Language* 71, 63–101.

Barnhart, R.K. (ed.) (1988) *The Barnhart Dictionary of Etymology*, The H.W. Wilson Company.

Bickerton, D. (1987) '*He himself*: anaphor, pronoun, or ... ?', *Linguistic Inquiry* 18, 345–8.

Bolinger, D. (1965) *Forms of English: Accent, Morpheme, Order*, edited by I. Abe and T. Kanekiyo, Cambridge, MA: Harvard University Press.

Brinton, L. (1995) 'Non-anaphoric reflexives in free indirect style: expressing the subjectivity of the non-speaker', in D. Stein and S. Wright (eds), *Subjectivity and Subjectivization in Language*, Cambridge: Cambridge University Press, 173–94.

Browning, M.A. (1993) 'Adverbial reflexives', *NELS* 23, Vol. I, 83–94.

Büring, D. (1997) *The Meaning of Topic and Focus: The 59th Street Bridge Accent*. London: Routledge.

Büring, D. and Hartmann, K. (1995) 'All Right', in U. Lutz and J. Pafel (eds), *On Extraction and Extraposition in German*, published as vol. 11 of the series *Linguistik Aktuell/Linguistics Today*, Amsterdam: Benjamins.

Burzio, L. (1991) 'The morphological basis of anaphora', *Journal of Linguistics* 27, 81–105.

—— (1996a) 'The role of the antecedent in anaphoric relations', in R. Freidin (ed.), *Current Issues in Comparative Grammar*, Dordrecht: Kluwer, 1–45.

—— (1996b) 'Anaphora and soft constraints', *Proceedings of the Workshop on Optimality in Syntax 'Is the Best Good Enough?'*, MIT Working Papers in Linguistics.

Cantrall, W.R. (1969) 'On the Nature of the Reflexive in English', PhD dissertation, University of Illinois, Urbana.

—— (1973a) 'Reflexive pronouns and viewpoint', *Linguistische Berichte* 28, 42–50.

—— (1973b) 'Why I would relate *own*, emphatic reflexives, and intensive pronouns, my own self', *CLS* 9, 57–67.

—— (1974) *Viewpoint, Reflexives, and the Nature of Noun Phrases*, The Hague: Mouton.

Chesterman, A. (1991) *On Definiteness. A Study with Special Reference to English and Finnish*, Cambridge: Cambridge University Press.

Chomsky, N. (1957) *Syntactic Structures*, The Hague: Mouton.

—— (1970) 'Remarks on nominalization', in R.A. Jacobs and P.S. Rosenbaum (eds), *Readings in English Transformational Grammar*, Waltham, MA: Ginn and Co, 184–221.

—— (1981) *Lectures on Government and Binding*, Dordrecht: Foris.

—— (1982) *Some Concepts and Consequences of the Theory of Government and Binding*, Cambridge, MA: The MIT Press.

—— (1986a) *Barriers*, Cambridge, MA: The MIT Press.

—— (1986b) *Knowledge of Language: Its Nature, Origin and Use*, New York: Praeger.

—— (1995) *The Minimalist Program*, Cambridge, MA: The MIT Press.

Christophersen, P. and Sanved, A.O. (1969) *An Advanced English Grammar*, London: Macmillan.

Collins (1990) *Collins Cobuild English Grammar*, London: Longman.

Comrie, B. (1981) *Language Universals and Linguistic Typology. Syntax and Morphology*, Oxford: Blackwell.

Curme, G.O. (1931) *A Grammar of the English Language, Volume II*, Essex, CT: Verbatim.

Declerck, R. (1991) *A Comprehensive Descriptive Grammar of English*, Tokyo: Kaitakusha.

Dirven, R. (1973) 'Emphatic and reflexive in English and Dutch', *Leuvense Bijdragen* 63, 285–99.

—— (ed.) (1989) *A User's Grammar of English: Word, Sentence, Text, Interaction*, Frankfurt/M.: Peter Lang.

Di Sciullo, A.-M. (1996) 'Word-internal pronouns and reflexives', *Belgian Journal of Linguistics* 10, 103–21.

Donnellan, K.S. (1966) 'Reference and definite descriptions', *The Philosophical Review* 75, 281–304.

Dowty, D. (1979) *Word Meaning and Montague Grammar. The Semantics of Verbs and Times in Generative Semantics and in Montague's PTQ*, Dordrecht: Reidel.

Dowty, D., Wall, R.E. and Peters, S. (1981) *Introduction to Montague Semantics*, Dordrecht: Reidel.

Duden (1989) *Der große Duden, Etymologie, Herkunftswörterbuch der deutschen Sprache*, Mannheim: Dudenverlag, Band 7.

Edmondson, J.A. (1978) 'Ergative languages, accessibility hierarchies governing reflexives and questions of formal analysis', *Studies in Language Companion Series* 1, 633–58.

Edmondson, J.A. and Plank, F. (1978) 'Great expectations: An intensive self analysis', *Linguistics and Philosophy* 2, 373–413.

Everaert, M. (1986) *The Syntax of Reflexivisation*, Dordrecht: Foris.

Faiß, K. (1977) *Aspekte der englischen Sprachgeschichte*, Tübingen: Narr.

—— (1989) *Englische Sprachgeschichte*, Tübingen: Francke.

Faltz, L.M. (1985) Reflexivization: A Study in Universal Syntax, New York: Garland.

Farmer, A. and Harnish, M. (1987) 'Communicative reference with pronouns', in M. Papi and J. Verschueren (eds), *The Pragmatic Perspective*, Amsterdam: Benjamins, 547–65.

Farr, J.M. (1905) 'Intensives and Reflexives in Anglo-Saxon and Early Middle-English', dissertation, Baltimore: Furst.

Fasold, R.W. (1996) 'Form versus Function in the Distribution of *Self*-Forms', Georgetown University, ms.

Fauconnier, G. (1975a) 'Pragmatic scales and logical structure', *Linguistic Inquiry* 5, 353–75.

—— (1975b) 'Polarity and the scale principle', *CLS* 11, 188–99.

Ferro, L. (1993) 'On "self" as a focus marker', *ESCOL '92: Proceedings of the Ninth Eastern States Conference on Linguistics*, Ithaca, NY: Cornell University, 68-79.

Frajzyngier, Z. (1985) 'Logophoric systems in Chadic', *Journal of African Languages and Linguistics* 7, 23–37.

—— (1989) 'Three kinds of anaphors', in I. Haik and L. Tuller (eds), *Current Progress in African Linguistics*, Amsterdam: Foris, 194–216.

Francescotti, R.M. (1995) 'Even: the conventional implicature approach reconsidered', *Linguistics and Philosophy* 18, 153–73.

Freeman, M.H. (1996) 'Grounded Spaces: Deictic -*Self* Anaphors in the Poetry of Emily Dickinson', Los Angeles Valley College, ms.

Fukoda, K. (1989) 'On emphatic reflexives', *English Linguistics* 6, 36–51.

Gelderen, E. van (1996a) 'Case to the object in the history of English', *Linguistic Analysis* 26, 117–33.

—— (1996b) '*Self* in the History of English', *Germanic Linguistics Annual Conference* 2, Arizona State University, handout.

—— (1996c) 'The emphatic origin of reflexives', *Berkeley Linguistics Society* 22, 106–15.

—— (1996d) 'Historical binding domains', Paper presented at Linguist on-line conference *Geometric and Thematic Structure in Binding*, WWW.

Geniušienė, E. (1987) *The Typology of Reflexives*, Berlin: de Gruyter.

Girke, W. (1993) 'Rollenwechsel und konservierte Spur: Eine funktionale Beschreibung von *sam*', in H.R. Mehlig (ed.), *Slavistische Linguistik 1993, Referate des XIX. Konstanzer Slavistischen Arbeitstreffens Kiel 21.-23.9.1993*, München: Verlag Otto Sagner, 81-100.

Givón, T. (1993) *English Grammar. A Function-Based Introduction*, Volume II, Amsterdam: Benjamins.

Grimm, J. (1967) *Deutsche Grammatik*, Hildesheim: Georg Olms Verlagsbuchhandlung (reprint).

Grimm, J. and Grimm, W. (1905) *Deutsches Wörterbuch*, Leipzig: Verlag von S. Hirzel, 10. Band.

Grimshaw, J. (1992) *Argument Structure*, Cambridge, MA: The MIT Press.

Haegeman, L. (1991) *Introduction to Government & Binding*, Oxford: Blackwell.

Hagège, C. (1974) 'Les pronoms logophoriques', *Bulletin de la Societé de Linguistique de Paris* 69, 287–310.

Haiman, J. (1995) 'Grammatical signs of the divided self', in W. Abraham, T. Givón and S. Thompson (eds), *Discourse Grammar and Typology*, Amsterdam: Benjamins, 213–34.

Hall Partee, B. (1965) 'Subject and object in modern English', MIT doctoral dissertation, Trier: LAUT.

Halliday, M.A.K. (1966) 'Intonation systems in English', in A. McIntosh and M.A.K. Halliday (eds), *Patterns of Language*, London: Longman, 111–33.

—— (1967) *Intonation and Grammar in British English*, The Hague: Mouton.

Hawkins, J. (1978) *Definiteness and Indefiniteness*, London: Croom Helm.

—— (1986) *A Comparative Typology of English and German. Unifying the Contrasts*, London: Croom Helm.

—— (1991) 'On (in)definite articles: implicatures and (un)grammaticality prediction', *Journal of Linguistics* 27, 405–42.

Heim, I. (1982) 'The Semantics of Definite and Indefinite Noun Phrases', PhD dissertation, University of Massachusetts.

Helke, M. (1970) 'The Grammar of English Reflexives', doctoral dissertation, Cambridge, MA: The MIT Press.

Hermodsson, L. (1952) *Reflexive und Intransitive Verba*, Uppsala: Almqvist & Wiksells Boktryckeri.

Heyse, J.C.A. (1968) *Handwörterbuch der deutschen Sprache (Reprographischer Nachdruck der Ausgabe Magdeburg 1849)*, Hildesheim: Georg Olms Verlagsbuchhandlung.

Higginbotham, J. (1983) 'Logical form, binding and nominals', *Linguistic Inquiry* 14, 395–420.

—— (1985) 'On semantics', *Linguistic Inquiry* 16, 547–93.

—— (1989) 'Elucidations of meaning', *Linguistics and Philosophy* 12, 465–517.

Hintikka, J. and Kulas, J. (1985) *Anaphora and Definite Descriptions*, Dordrecht: Reidel.

Hirschberg, J. (1991) *A Theory of Scalar Implicature*, Cambridge: Cambridge University Press.

Holthausen, F. (1974) *Altenglisches etymologisches Wörterbuch*, Heidelberg: Winter.

Horn, L.R. (1969) 'A presuppositional analysis of *only* and *even*', *CLS* 5, 98–107.

—— (1972) *On the Semantic Properties of Logical Operators in English*, Indiana University Linguistics Club, mimeo.

—— (1985a) 'Metalinguistic negation and pragmatic ambiguity', *Language* 61, 121–74.

—— (1985b) 'Towards a new taxonomy for pragmatic inference: Q-based and R-based implicatures', in D. Schiffrin (ed.), *Meaning, Form and Use in Context*, Washington, DC: Georgetown University Press, 11–42.

—— (1989) *A Natural History of Negation*, Chicago: University of Chicago Press.

Huang, C.-T. J. (1983) 'A note on the Binding Theory', *Linguistic Inquiry* 14, 554–61.

Huddleston, R. (1984) *Introduction to the Grammar of English*, Cambridge: Cambridge University Press.

Jackendoff, R.S. (1972) *Semantic Interpretation in Generative Grammar*, Cambridge, MA: The MIT Press.

—— (1977) *X Syntax: A Study of Phrase Structure*, Cambridge, MA: The MIT Press.

Jacobs, J. (1982) *Zur Syntax und Semantik der Negation im Deutschen*, München: Wilhelm Fink Verlag.

—— (1983) *Fokus und Skalen. Zur Syntax und Semantik der Gradpartikeln im Deutschen*, Tübingen: Niemeyer.

—— (1984) 'Funktionale Satzperspektive und Illokutionssemantik', *Linguistische Berichte* 91, 25–58.

—— (1986) 'The syntax of focus and adverbials in German', in W. Abraham and S. de Meij (eds), *Topic, Focus and Configurationality. Papers from the 6th Groningen Grammar Talks, Groningen* (1984), Amsterdam: Benjamins, 103-27.

—— (1988) 'Fokus-Hintergrund-Gliederung und Grammatik', in H. Altmann (ed.), *Intonationsforschungen*, Tübingen: Niemeyer, 89-134.

—— (1996) 'Bemerkungen zur I-Topikalisierung', in I. Rosengren (ed.), *Sprache und Pragmatik* 41, Lund: Lunds Universitet, 1–48.

Jacobs, R. and Rosenbaum, P. (eds) (1970) *Readings in English Transformational Grammar*, Waltham, MA: Ginn and Co.

Jakubowicz, C. (1994) 'On the morphological specification of reflexives: Implications for acquisition', *NELS* 24, 205–19.

Jayaseelan, K.A. (1988) 'Emphatic reflexive X-*self*', *CIEFL Working Papers in Linguistics* 5, Hyderabad (India), 1–20.

Jespersen, O. (1933) *Essentials of English Grammar*, London: Allen and Unwin.

Jo, In-hee (1989) 'A unitary analysis of emphatic *self*-forms as intensifying adverbs', *Journal of English Language and Literature* 30, 255–90.

Joseph, B.D. (1979) 'On the agreement of reflexive forms in English', *Linguistics* 17, 519–23.

Kadmon, N. (1990) 'Uniqueness', *Linguistics and Philosophy* 13, 273–342.

Kameyama, M. (1984) 'Subjective/Logophoric Bound Anaphor *Zibun*', *CLS* 20, 228–38.

Kang, B.M. (1988) 'Unbounded reflexives', *Linguistics and Philosophy* 11, 415–56.

Kay, P. (1990) '*Even*', *Linguistics and Philosophy* 13, 59–111.

Kayne, R.S. (1979) 'Rightward NP movement in French and English', *Linguistic Inquiry* 10, 710–19.

—— (1994) *The Antisymmetry of Syntax*, Cambridge, MA: The MIT Press.

Keenan, E.L. (1971) 'Quantifier structures in English', *Foundations of Language* 8, 255–84.

—— (ed.) (1975) *Formal Semantics of Natural Language*, Cambridge: Cambridge University Press.

—— (1976) 'Towards a universal definition of "subject"', in C.N. Li (ed.), *Subject and Topic*, New York: Academic Press, 303–33.

—— (1987) 'On semantics and the Binding Theory', in J. Hawkins (ed.), *Explaining Language Universals*, Oxford: Blackwell, 105-144.

—— (1988) 'Complex anaphors and bind alpha', *CLS* 24, 216–32.

—— (1993) 'The Historical Development of the English Anaphora System', handout for colloquium, UCLA.

—— (1996) 'Creating Anaphors. An Historical Study of the English Reflexive Pronouns', UCLA, ms.

Kemmer, S. (1995) 'Emphatic and reflexive -*self*. Expectations, viewpoint and subjectivity', in D. Stein and S. Wright (eds), *Subjectivity and Subjectivization in Language*, Cambridge: Cambridge University Press, 55–82.

Kibrik, A. and Bogdanova, E. (1995) '*Sam* kak operator korrektcii ožidanii adresata', *Voprosy Jazykoznanija* 3, 28–47.

Klein, E. (1967) *A Comprehensive Etymological Dictionary of the English Language*, Amsterdam: Elsevier.

Klenin, E. (1980) 'Sentential and discourse prominence: the case of the emphatic pronoun', *Russian Linguistics* 4, 269–80.

Kluge, F. (1957, 1989, 1995) *Etymologisches Wörterbuch der deutschen Sprache*, Berlin: de Gruyter.

König, E. (1981) 'The meaning of scalar particles in German', in H.-J. Eikmeyer and H. Rieser (eds), *Words, Worlds, and Contexts. New Approaches in Word Semantics*, Berlin: de Gruyter, 107–32.

—— (1989) 'On the historical development of focus particles', in H. Weydt (ed.), *Sprechen mit Partikeln*, Berlin: de Gruyter, 318–29.

—— (1991) *The Meaning of Focus Particles: A Comparative Perspective*, London: Routledge.

—— (1993a) 'Focus particles', in J. Jacobs, A. von Stechow, W. Sternefeld and Th. Vennemann (eds), *Syntax. Ein internationales Handbuch zeitgenössischer Forschung*, Berlin: de Gruyter, 978-87.

—— (1993b) 'Contrastive linguistics: language comparison or language pedagogy?', in H.U. Seeber and W. Göbel (eds), *Anglistentag 1992 Stuttgart, Proceedings*, Tübingen: Niemeyer, 289–302.

König, E. and Siemund, P. (1996a) 'Emphatische Reflexiva und Fokusstruktur', in I. Rosengren (ed.), *Sprache und Pragmatik* 40, Lund: Lunds Universitet, 1-42.

—— (1996b) '*Selbst*-Reflektionen', in G. Harras (ed.), *Wenn die Semantik arbeitet. Festschrift für Klaus Baumgärtner*, Tübingen: Niemeyer, 277-302.

—— (1996c) 'On the development of reflexive pronouns in English: a case study in grammaticalization', in U. Böker and H. Sauer (eds), *Anglistentag 1996 Dresden, Proceedings*, Trier: Wissenschaftlicher Verlag.

—— (1998) 'The Development of Complex Reflexives and Intensifiers in English', *ZAS Working Papers*.

—— (1999a) 'Intensifikatoren und Topikalisierung: Kontrastive Beobachtungen zum Deutschen, Englischen und anderen Germanischen Sprachen', in H. Wegener (ed.), *Deutsch kontrastiv: Typologisch-vergleichende Untersuchungen zur deutschen Grammatik*, Tübingen: Narr.

—— (1999b) 'Intensifiers and reflexives: a typological perspective', in Z. Frajzyngier and T.S. Curl (ed.), *Reflexives: Forms and Functions*, Amsterdam: Benjamins.

—— (1999c) 'Intensifiers as targets and sources of semantic change', in P. Koch and A. Blank (eds.) *Historical Semantics and Cognition*, Berlin: Mouton.

—— (1999d) 'Reflexivity, logophoricity and intensification in English', in U. Carls and P. Lucko (eds.) *Form, Function and Variation in English. Studies in Honour of Klaus Hansen*, Frankfurt: Lang.

Koster, J. (1978) *Locality Principles in Syntax*, Dordrecht: Foris.

Koster, J. and Reuland, E. (eds) (1991) *Long-distance Anaphora*. Cambridge: Cambridge University Press.

Kowalski, A. (1992) 'Zur Syntax und Semantik von Gradpartikeln im Deutschen. Syntaktische Bedingungen für die Ausdehnung von Partikelskopus und -fokus', *Magisterarbeit*, Bergische Universität – Gesamthochschule Wuppertal, Fachbereich 4.

Kuno, S. (1972) 'Pronominalisation, reflexivisation and direct discourse', *Linguistic Inquiry* 3, 161–95.

—— (1987) *Functional Syntax: Anaphora, Discourse and Empathy*, Chicago, IL: Chicago University Press.

—— (1993) *Grammar and Discourse Principles: Functional Syntax and GB Theory*, Chicago, IL: Chicago University Press.

Kuno, S. and Kaburaki, E. (1977) 'Empathy and syntax', *Linguistic Inquiry* 8, 627–72.

Larsen, U.B. (1997) 'The element *selv* and the relationship between intensification and reflexivization in Danish', *Screening Paper II*, USC.

Lees, R.B. and Klima, E.S. (1969) 'Rules for English pronominalization', in D.A. Reibel and S.A Schane (eds), *Modern Studies in English. Readings in Transformational Grammar*, Englewood Cliffs, NJ: Prentice-Hall, 145–59.

Leskosky, R.J. (1972) 'Intensive reflexives', *Studies in Linguistic Sciences* 2:1, Urbana, 42–65.

Levin, B. (1993) *English Verb Classes and Alternations*, Chicago, IL and London: Chicago University Press.

Levinson, S.C. (1987) 'Pragmatics and the grammar of anaphora: a partial pragmatic reduction of binding and control phenomena', *Journal of Linguistics* 23, 379–434.

—— (1991) 'Pragmatic reduction of the Binding Conditions revisited', *Journal of Linguistics* 27, 107–61.

Leys, O. (1973) 'Bemerkungen zum Reflexivpronomen', *Sprache der Gegenwart* 24, 152–7.

Löbner, S. (1987) 'Definites', *Journal of Semantics* 4, 279–326.

—— (1995) 'Negation und Prädikation in natürlicher Sprache', Freie Universität Berlin, handout.

Maling, J. (1984) 'Non-clause-bounded reflexives in Modern Icelandic', *Linguistics and Philosophy* 7, 211–41.

McCawley, J.D. (1976) 'Notes on Jackendoff's theory of anaphora', *Linguistic Inquiry* 7, 319-41.

McDaniel, D. and Battistella, E. (1986) 'On the distribution of emphatic reflexives', *CUNY Forum Papers in Linguistics* 12, New York: CUNYF, 133–51.

McKay, T. (1991) '*He himself*: undiscovering an anaphor', *Linguistic Inquiry* 22, 368–73.

Mitchell, B. (1979) 'Old English *SELF*: four syntactical notes', *Neuphilologische Mitteilungen* 80, 39–45.

—— (1985) *Old English Syntax, Volume I*, Oxford: Clarendon Press.

Molnár, V. (1991) *Das Topik im Deutschen und im Ungarischen*, Stockholm: Almqvist & Wiksell International.

Molnár, V. and Rosengren, I. (1996) 'Zu Jacobs' Explikation der I-Topikalisierung', in I. Rosengren (ed.), *Sprache und Pragmatik* 41, Lund: Lunds Universitet, 49-88.

Montague, R. (1974) 'The proper treatment of quantification in ordinary English', in R.H. Thomason (ed.), *Formal Philosophy. Selected Papers of Richard Montague*, New Haven, CT: Yale University Press, 247–70.

Moravcsik, E. (1972) 'Some cross-linguistic generalizations about intensifier constructions', *CLS* 8, 271–7.

Moser, M. (1992) 'The Negation Relation: Semantic and Pragmatic Aspects of a Relational Analysis of Sentential Negation', PhD dissertation, University of Pennsylvania.

—— (1993) 'Focus particles: their definition and relational structure', *CLS* 28, 379–411.

Mourelatos, A.P.D. (1978) 'Events, processes, and states', *Linguistics and Philosophy* 2, 143–60.

Moyne, J.A. (1971) 'Reflexive and emphatic', *Language* 47, 141–63.

Moyne, J.A. and Carden, G. (1974) 'Subject reduplication in Persian', *Linguistic Inquiry* 5, 205–49.

Mustanoja, T. (1960) *A Middle English Syntax*, Helsinki: Société Néophilologique.

OED (1989) *The Oxford English Dictionary*, Oxford: Clarendon Press.

Ogura, M. (1988) 'Him self, him selfe, and him selfa: a reflexive pronoun + uninflected or nominative self', *Studia Neophilologica* 60, 149–157.

—— (1989a) *Verbs with the Reflexive Pronoun and Constructions with Self in Old and Early Middle English*, Cambridge: Brewer.

—— (1989b) 'Simple reflexives, compound reflexives, and compound forms of "refl/non-refl pron + self" in Old and Middle English', *Studies in Medieval English Language and Literature* 4, Tokyo, 49-72.

Parker, F., Riley K. and Meyer, C.F. (1990) 'Untriggered reflexive pronouns in English', *American Speech* 65, 50–69.

Penning, G.E. (1875) 'A History of the Reflective Pronouns in the English Language', inaugural dissertation, University of Leipzig, Bremen: Heinrich Frese.

Pica, P. (1991) 'On the interaction between antecedent-Government and Binding: the case of long-distance reflexivization', in J. Koster and E. Reuland (eds), *Long-Distance Anaphora*, Cambridge: Cambridge University Press, 119–36.

Plank, F. (1979a) 'Zur Affinität von *selbst* und *auch*', in H. Weydt (ed.), *Die Partikeln der deutschen Sprache*, Berlin: de Gruyter, 269–84.

—— (1979b) 'Exklusivierung, Reflexivierung, Identifizierung, relationale Auszeichnung. Variationen zu einem semantisch-pragmatischen Thema', in I. Rosengren (ed.), *Sprache und Pragmatik. Lunder Symposium 1978*, Malmö: Gleerup, 330–54.

Pollard, C. and Sag, I. (1992) 'Anaphors in English and the scope of the binding theory', *Linguistic Analysis* 22, 261–303.

Postal, P.M. (1969) 'On so-called "pronouns" in English', in D.A. Reibel and S.A. Schane (eds), *Modern Studies in English. Readings in Transformational Grammar*, Englewood Cliffs, NJ: Prentice-Hall, 201–24.

Poutsma, H. (1916) *A Grammar of Late Modern English, Part II*, Amsterdam: Benjamins.

Primus, B. (1989) 'Parameter der Herrschaft: Reflexivpronomina im Deutschen', *Zeitschrift für Sprachwissenschaft* 8, 53–88.

—— (1992) '*Selbst* – variants of a scalar adverb in German', in J. Jacobs (ed.), *Informationsstruktur und Grammatik*, Opladen: Westdeutscher Verlag, 54–88.

Pusch, L.F. (1976) 'Zur Syntax und Semantik des Pronomens *dasselbe*', in K. Braunmüller and W. Kürschner (eds), *Grammatik. Akten des 10. Linguistischen Kolloquiums Tübingen 1975. Band 2*, Tübingen: Niemeyer, 253-64.

Quirk, R., Greenbaum, S., Leech, G. and Svartvik, J. (1972) *A Grammar of Contemporary English*, London: Longman.

—— (1985) *A Comprehensive Grammar of the English Language*, London: Longman.

Quirk, R. and Wrenn, C.L. (1955) *An Old English Grammar*, London: Methuen.

Radford, A. (1981) *Transformational Syntax*, Cambridge: Cambridge University Press.

—— (1988) *Transformational Grammar*, Cambridge: Cambridge University Press.

Reinhart, T. (1983a) 'Coreference and bound anaphora: a restatement of the anaphora question', *Linguistics and Philosophy* 6, 47–88.

—— (1983b) *Anaphora and Semantic Interpretation*, London: Croom Helm.

Reinhart, T. and Reuland, E. (1991) 'Anaphors and logophors: an argument structure perspective', in J. Koster and E. Reuland (eds), *Long-distance Anaphora*, Cambridge: Cambridge University Press, 283-321.

—— (1993) 'Reflexivity', *Linguistic Inquiry* 12, 657–720.

Reuland, E. and Reinhart, T. (1995) 'Pronouns, anaphors and case', in H. Haider, S. Olsen and S. Vikner (eds), *Studies in Comparative Germanic Syntax*, Dordrecht: Kluwer, 241-68.

Rigau, G. (1984) 'Connexity established by emphatic pronouns', in M.E. Conte, J.S. Petofi and E. Sozer (eds), *Text and Discourse Connectedness*, Amsterdam: Benjamins, 191-205.

Romoth, S. (1990) *Die Identitätspronomina in der Romania*, Genève: Droz.

Rooth, M. (1985) 'Association with Focus', unpublished PhD dissertation, University of Massachussets, Amherst.

Ross, J.R. (1967) 'Constraints on Variables in Syntax', unpublished PhD dissertation, MIT, Cambridge, MA.

—— (1970) 'On declarative sentences', in R. Jacobs and P. Rosenbaum (eds), *Readings in English Transformational Grammar*, Waltham, MA: Ginn and Co, 222-72.

Russell, B. (1905) 'On denoting', *Mind* 14, 479-93.

Safir, K. (1993) 'Semantic atoms of anaphora: selfish languages and selfless ones', Rutgers University, ms.

Salmon, N. (1992) 'Reflections on reflexivity', *Linguistics and Philosophy* 15, 53–63.

Sánchez, L. (1994) 'On the interpretation of intensified DPs and emphatic pronouns', in L. Mazzola (ed.), *Issues and Theory in Romance Linguistics*, Washington, DC: Georgetown University Press, 479–92.

Saxon, L. (1991) '*On one's own*: the semantics and pragmatics of reflexives', in C. Georgopoulos and R. Ishihara (eds), *Interdisciplinary Approaches to Language: Essays in Honor of S.-Y. Kuroda*, Dordrecht: Kluwer, 501–17.

Schladt, M. (1995) 'Typologie und Grammatikalisierung von Reflexiven', Freie Universität Berlin, handout.

Sells, P. (1987) 'Aspects of logophoricity', *Linguistic Inquiry* 18, 445–79.

Siemund, P. (1998) 'Reflexivität und Intensivierung: Ein deutsch-englischer Vergleich', in W. Börner und K. Vogel (eds.) *Kontrast und Äquivalenz. Beiträge zu Sprachvergleich und Übersetzung*, Tübingen: Narr.

Silverstein, M. (1976) 'Hierarchies of features and ergativity', in R.M.W. Dixon (ed.), *Grammatical Categories in Australian Languages*, Canberra: Australian Institute of Aboriginal Studies, 112-71.

Skeat, W.W. (ed.) (1910) *An Etymological Dictionary of the English Language*, Oxford: Oxford University Press.

Sperber, D. and Wilson, D. (1986) *Relevance: Communication and Cognition*, Cambridge, MA: Harvard University Press.

Sportiche, D. (1986) 'Zibun', *Linguistic Inquiry* 17, 369–74.

Staczek, J.J. (1990) 'Untriggered reflexives in conversational English: variation and change', *XXV International Conference on Contrastive Linguistics and Cross Language Studies*, Rydzyna, handout.

Thráinsson, H. (1991) 'Long-distance reflexives and the typology of NPs', in J.

Koster and E. Reuland (eds), *Long-Distance Anaphora*, Cambridge: Cambridge University Press, 49–76.

Tillyard, E.M.W. (1943) *The Elizabethan World Picture*, London: Chatto & Windus.

Traugott, E. (1972) *The History of English Syntax*, Holt, Rinehart and Winston.

Vendler, Z. (1957) 'Verbs and times', *The Philosophical Review* 66, 143-60.

Verheijen, C.R. (1983) 'Reflexives and Intensifiers in Modern British English', unpublished dissertation, University of Leiden.

—— (1986) 'A phrase structure syntax for emphatic *self*-forms', *Linguistics* 24, 681–95.

Visser, F.T. (1970) *An Historical Syntax of the English Language*, Leiden: Brill.

Voges, F. (1883) 'Der Reflexive Dative im Englischen', *Anglia* 6, 317–74.

Walther, C. (1995) 'Processing reflexives in coordinate NPs: a question of point-of-view', *Journal of Psycholinguistic Research* 24, 39–78.

Watson, G. (1989) 'Clausemate reflexives', *Linguistic Analysis* 19, 99-119.

Weydt, H. (ed.) (1979) *Die Partikeln der deutschen Sprache*, Berlin: de Gruyter.

—— (ed.) (1983) *Partikeln und Interaktion*, Tübingen: Niemeyer.

Williams, E. (1981) 'Argument structure and morphology', *Linguistic Review* 1, 81–114.

Zribi-Hertz, A. (1989) 'Anaphor binding and narrative point of view. English reflexive pronouns in sentence and discourse', *Language* 65, 695–727.

—— (1995) 'Emphatic or reflexive? On the endophoric character of French *lui-même* and similar complex pronouns', *Journal of Linguistics* 31, 333–74.

—— (1996) 'Some wondering remarks on the development of syntactic theories: the case of long-distance reflexives', *Recherches Linguistiques de Vincennes* 25, 141–8.

Sources

Corpora

BNC	The British National Corpus
BROWN	The Brown Corpus
CONV	A Corpus of English Conversation
FC	The Freiburg Corpus
IDP	The Independent 1993
LLC	The Longman/Lancaster Corpus
LOB	The Lancaster-Oslo/Bergen Corpus
TIMES	The Times 1993

Fiction

AFI	*A Fatal Inversion* by Barbara Vine (Ruth Rendell), Penguin 1987.
ASR	*A Splash of Red* by Antonia Fraser, Methuen 1984.
CS	*Colonel Sun. A James Bond Adventure* by Robert Markham (Kingsley Amis), Jonathan Cape 1968.
S&S	*Sense and Sensibility* by Jane Austen, Penguin 1995, first published 1811.

Historical texts

ÆCHom	Thorpe, B. (ed.) (1844) *The Sermons Catholici or Homilies of Aelfric*, London: Aelfric Society.
ÆGram	Zupitza, J. (ed.) (1966) *Aelfrics Grammatik und Glossar*, Berlin: Weidmannsche Verlagsbuchhandlung.
ÆHom	Pope, J.C. (ed.) (1967) *Homilies of Aelfric: A Supplementary Collection*, London: EETS 259.
ÆLet 4	Crawford, S.J. (ed.) (1922) *The Old English Version of the Heptateuch. Aelfric's Treatise on the Old and New Testament and his Preface to Genesis*, London: EETS 160.
ÆLet 3	Fehr, B. (ed.) (1914) *Die Hirtenbriefe Aelfrics in Altenglischer und Lateinischer Fassung*, Hamburg: Verlag von Henry Grand.
Bo	Sedgefield, W.J. (ed.) (1899) *King Alfred's Old English Version of Boethius' De consolatione philosophiae*, Oxford.

Chau   Blake, N.F. (ed.) (1980) *The Canterbury Tales by Geoffrey Chaucer*, London: Edward Arnold.

Chron   Plummer, C. (ed.) (1892) *Two of the Saxon Chronicles Parallel*, Oxford.

CP   Sweet, H. (ed.) (1871) *King Alfred's West Saxon Version of Gregory's Pastoral Care*, London: EETS 45.

GD   Hecht, H. (ed.) (1900) *Bischofs Waerferth von Worcester Übersetzung der Dialoge Gregors des Grossen*, Leipzig: Georg H. Wigands Verlag.

Gen   Crawford, S.J. (ed.) (1922) *The Old English Version of the Heptateuch. Aelfric's Treatise on the Old and New Testament and his Preface to Genesis*, London: EETS 160.

Max   Krapp, G.P. and Dobbie, E.V.K. (eds) (1936) *The Exeter Book. The Anglo-Saxon Poetic Records, III*, New York: Columbia University Press.

Or   Bately, J. (1980) *The Old English Orosius*, Oxford: Oxford University Press.

Index

Abney, S. 41
Abraham, W. 2
action nominalisation 159
additive particles 7, 177, 178, 192
adjectival intensifier, Norwegian 17
adjunction 44, 47; adnominal intensifier 40–1, 44, 47; adverbal intensifier 90, 95, 256
adnominal intensifier: abstract nouns 158; adjunction 40–1, 44, 47; and adverbal intensifier compared 4–5, 17–22, 50, 103, 210–13; adverbial phrase 35; agreement 8, 10–11, 33–4, 52–3; Baker 121, 125, 168; centrality 125; centre/periphery 121, 135, 183; context 179; disambiguation 53–4, 244; dislocation from object position 52–3; extensional readings 161–2; finite verbs 205; focus particle 48, 124, 125, 134–5; focus structure 258–9; German 13, 33–4, 156, 158, 244; identifiability 166–7; imperatives 168; likelihood 127–8; modification 42–4, 45, 61–2; multiple 168–9; non-scalar analyses 130–2; part/whole 149–50; positioning 47, 48–9, 85–6, 95; pronominal modification 61–2; rank 159; referents, human/non-human 179–80, 259; role reversal structures 6, 7, 84–7, 170–5; scalar properties inverted 127–8, 129; semantic analysis 124, 183; stress 103; stylistic effects 149–50; syntax 6, 48–56; topic

marker 52; topicalisation 48–52; transferability 236; untriggered reflexives 80–2, 258; and verb position 89–90; vocatives 168; *see also* noun phrase
adverb groups 97, 98–9; focus adverbs 91, 97, 98, 100; intensifiers 2, 3, 119; manner adverbs 97, 98–100, 231; scalar 129, 213
adverbal intensifier 4–5, 7; adjunction 90, 95, 256; and adnominal intensifier compared 4–5, 17–22, 103, 210–13; as adverb 91, 97–100; agreement 89; aktionsart 184–5, 191; aspectual distinctions 191, 257; co-constituency 94; complex verb phrases 113; disambiguation 12; focus particle 97–8; focus structure 258–9; German 13, 93, 106–9, 110–12, 113, 115; hierarchy 115; identity 218–19; negative sentences 219; noun phrase 100–1, 218; passives 104; polysemy 12, 95–6, 121, 177; positional variation 90, 120; in prepositional adjuncts 115; repeatability 184–94, 205–6; role reversal 85, 86; semantics 18; stress 89, 103; syntactic restrictions 100–3; topicalisation 92–3, 107–9, 257; transferability 194; verb phrase 12, 13, 91–6, 113, 122; verb position 89–90; verbs, intransitive 94; *see also* adverbal intensifier, exclusive; adverbal intensifier, inclusive
adverbal intensifier, exclusive 4–5,

For Product Safety Concerns and Information please contact our EU
representative GPSR@taylorandfrancis.com
Taylor & Francis Verlag GmbH, Kaufingerstraße 24, 80331 München, Germany

9 781138 972919